Obed Macy, William C Macy

The History of Nantucket

Being a compendious account of the first settlement of the island by the English,

together with the rise and progress of the whale fishery; and other historical facts

relative to said island and its inhibitants. In two parts.

Obed Macy, William C Macy

The History of Nantucket
Being a compendious account of the first settlement of the island by the English, together with the rise and progress of the whale fishery; and other historical facts relative to said island and its inhibitants. In two parts.

ISBN/EAN: 9783337325121

Printed in Europe, USA, Canada, Australia, Japan

Cover: Foto ©ninafisch / pixelio.de

More available books at **www.hansebooks.com**

THE HISTORY OF NANTUCKET,

BEING A COMPENDIOUS ACCOUNT OF THE FIRST

SETTLEMENT OF THE ISLAND BY THE ENGLISH,

TOGETHER WITH THE

RISE AND PROGRESS

OF THE

WHALE FISHERY;

AND OTHER HISTORICAL FACTS RELATIVE TO SAID
ISLAND AND ITS INHABITANTS.

IN TWO PARTS.

By OBED MACY.

WITH A CONCISE STATEMENT OF

PROMINENT EVENTS FROM 1835 TO 1880,

By WILLIAM C. MACY.

"We know that all things work together for good, to them that love God."
—ROMANS viii : 28.
"Gather up the fragments that remain, that nothing be lost."—JOHN vi : 12.

SECOND EDITION.

MANSFIELD:
MACY & PRATT.
1880.

Thos. S. Pratt, Printer, Mansfield, Mass.

PREFACE.

It has long been a subject of surprise to the author, that no person has written a history of Nantucket. Such a work, commencing with the settlement of the island by the English, and continued to the present day, could not fail of containing much both of interest and instruction. There are few places of equal magnitude, the annals of which would afford matters for a more valuable volume.

The occasion which drew some of the first families to settle at Nantucket, was that of avoiding the rigors of the law against the people called Quakers. To enjoy the exercise of the rites of hospitality and of religious freedom, they were willing to leave their homes, their friends and connections, to sacrifice their property, and to settle in a place inhabited by some thousands of savages, from whom, in case of assault, no retreat could be made. Driven from civilized society for no crime, but for their virtues rather, they took refuge in a land of *barbarians;* and, without vessels for flight, or arms for defence, they erected their altars and traced their furrows with all that confidence and fearlessness, which is inspired by unwavering trust in the blessing of heaven. They committed themselves to the guidance of divine power, believing that, under His influence, they would succeed in their undertaking. They did succeed; and so rapidly and so peaceably, that, in a few years, they found themselves in possession of the whole island, while neither record nor tradition affords a single instance of hostility between them and their savage neighbors.

The Whale Fishery will be found a leading topic in the following pages, and, it is presumed, one of the most interesting parts of this history. Reflecting at how early a period this business was commenced after the island was settled, the speedy acquisition of knowledge, as to the best mode of carrying it on, and the success in its progress are considerations which must strike the reader with astonishment. The sight of whales playing near the shores led the inhabitants to contemplate the advantages which would arise, could they become possessed of the proper means of taking them. These means were gradually obtained, consisting partly of information derived from Cape Cod, but principally drawn from their own enterprising disposition and indefatigable industry. At first they had neither boats nor craft suitable for the business, and very few mechanics capable of making them. The shore, from which it was most proper to go in pursuit of whales, was on the ocean side of the island, where the surf, constantly breaking, required that they should have good boats and skillful hands to manage them. The whale fishery had its rise amidst these and other difficulties; it succeeded, as will be seen in the following pages, in a surprising manner, and in a few years after its commencement it became the principal business of the place, and the greater part of the people was engaged in its various branches.

A community situated like that of Nantucket, and pursuing a business almost as insulated as their location, must necessarily have some peculiarities. Their manners and customs have often been noticed by travellers, and, it may be, placed in a more striking contrast with those of the continent than comports with strict truth. There is one trait in their character, however, to which they may claim undisputed right; it is a settled, strong, and almost universal opinion, that wars are wrong. This aversion to the spirit of war, by so great a portion of the people, has often proved of material benefit. Their peaceable character has recommended them to the clemency of the common enemy, and in some instances secured to them favors instead of injuries. Situated, in a time of war, beyond the protecting arm of government, they have been exempted from taking an active part in our national contests; surrounded often by the enemy, and always utterly defenceless, they enjoyed a greater immunity from plunder and devastation than fortified seaports or even many inland towns.

Probably the reader, who may be personally acquainted with some of the incidents herein stated, will discover some omissions: these may be accounted for in two ways; first, the author has been studiously careful rather to omit some trifling affairs, than to wound the feelings of individuals by their recital: secondly, although he has taken considerable pains, notwithstanding the work is of so small magnitude, to collect materials from every authentic source, yet, greatly to his mortification, there is very little on record and few documents relating to much of the time embraced within the limits of the History.

To write a history of any country or place must be a pleasing task to a persons possessed with endowments, and qualifications necessary for the right performance of such a work. History may be properly said to contribute to the necessities of our species, inasmuch as the experience of past generations is oftentimes the only criterion by which to judge of the consequences of present acts. To encourage every performance of this kind, is, therefore, the duty of all civilized people. It is not pretended, that the work now presented to the public is free from errors. It is rendered incomplete by want of knowledge on many material points. Having neither the records nor other manuscripts to appeal to for the knowledge necessary to a complete history, the author is aware that some errors may have crept into the work. Tradition, too often replete with errors, has sometimes necessarily been appealed to; but as there is no willful deviation from truth, it is trusted that the reader will be favorable in his censure of the work, and consider it as it is really meant to be,—*A statement of such facts and information as have come to the knowledge of the author; intended for the edification of his family, and such others into whose hands it may chance to fall. With this view, he is willing to trust to the candor of every considerate reader, without further apology.*

INTRODUCTION TO NEW EDITION.

In taking up the pen dropped by my revered grandfather in the year 1835, as he penned the final word in the History of Nantucket, I am inspired to a greater extent with the feeling that he would look with favor on the attempt to reproduce it, with such additions as events of later years may warrant, together with observations on such events as may suggest themselves, than I am with the conscious ability to perform the work simply of those additions, with the accuracy of the author. The original work, like the indefatigable writer, is a plain truth. His was a life of unblemished integrity, accurate, truthful, and remarkably free from any attempt at embellishment. Such was the history he wrote, a plain statement of facts, with only those observations on passing events which seemed necessary. The book has been valuable for this accurate history of the settlement of the island, and subsequent events growing out of it. A great portion of the volume is devoted to the origin and rapid development of the whaling business, as the growth and prosperity of the island depended upon it, making it a subject, and especially so at the time the history was written, of vital importance to the people. The book was written more for the people of the island than from any anticipation of a very extensive demand from abroad, and consequently those matters which more particularly interested that people were largely dwelt on. As years have passed, with new generations rising to the surface, with little idea of the early history of their native place, it is well, in the absence of a more detailed narration of past records of events to give to these generations, as well as many of those who may now be reckoned as of former days, this history, that the young may be taught, and the old refreshed in memory regarding the place of their nativity. In this connection it may be well to quote from an article in the Nantucket *Inquirer*, of August 27th, 1847, showing the appreciation entertained at that time of this work: " Were Mr. Macy's book as generally read here as it deserves to be, what we are about to attemp would be worse than labor wasted, but somehow it has been greatly neglected; why we could never understand, for it is to us a very interesting volume." The article then continues with statistics and information on many points which had been sought for, and could only be obtained by reference to the history in question. For years subsequent to the death of the author the printed sheets were bound in the original style of the book, and disposed of, until it appeared there was not a copy of the original History of Nantucket to be obtained. This state of affairs in connection with this work, has existed for the past seven years, in the meantime the island growing in popularity and extended notice as a watering place, possessing numerous advantages over many others more pretentious. The island now has thousands of summer visitors from all parts of the country, who are anxious to learn the early history of this " Isle of the Sea." They care not so much for the modern, metropolitan appearing Nantucket, as for the story of how it ever came to be, at all. They listen to the uncertain, garbled statements from persons with whom they chance to be thrown, and frequently impressions are received and retained which have not a semblance of truth. It is with a feeling akin to pride, as a descendant of one of the original families, that I have assumed the pleasant labor of again placing before the public this history, if for nothing else than that strangers should obtain correct information in regard to the early days of its settlement, rather than derive it from unreliable sources. In regard to more modern events, which I have supplemented, they have not been enlarged upon as they might have been, from the fact that the ancient records are of more value to a majority of those seeking information than those of modern origin, which more closely resemble the history of a majority of towns in the Commonwealth. I have purposely omitted some events which have transpired since the completion of the original volume, as they may more properly be called annals than historical facts, and would increase the size of the volume without adding to its usefulness. It has been the most difficult portion of the work, in hunting up records of forty years or more, to discriminate between the useful and comparatively trivial, and I am well aware of the criticisms I shall be subject to in this relation. For a period of nearly thirty years the subject of a new history has been agitated, and in looking back through the files of the *Inquirer*, and *Inquirer and Mirror*, I find at least forty communications on the subject, from nearly as many correspondents, all of whom urge upon others the duty of assuming this " labor of love " as it is termed.   These humble efforts to again give to the public some reliable information concerning Nantucket in its early days, together with such events of later years which I have supplemented, are affectionately dedicated to the memory of the author of the original work.

It would have been gratifying to the publishers of this edition of the History of Nantucket, to have elaborated somewhat on the general appearance of the volume; printing it on a finer quality of paper, and binding it in a higher style of art.   This it was thought best to avoid, however, that the book might resemble, as closely as possible, the original edition, which, in its plainness and simplicity, was more in keeping with the taste of the author.

WM. C. MACY.

Foxboro, June 21st, 1880.

CONTENTS.

PART FIRST.

CHAPTER I.

CHAPTER II.

CHAPTER III.

CHAPTER IV.

CHAPTER V.

CHAPTER VI.

CHAPTER VII.

CHAPTER VIII.

CHAPTER IX.

CHAPTER X.

PART SECOND.

PART THIRD.

ERRATA.

On p. 289, 6th line, read Allen for Albee.

On p. 291, 4th line from bottom, read Defrees for Depress.

On p. 293, read returning June 19, 1861, in connection with ship Islander.

HISTORY OF NANTUCKET.

PART I.

CHAPTER I.

THE Island of Nantucket was first discovered in 1602, by Captain Bartholomew Gosnold, an Englisman. He sailed from England in a small bark, with thirty-two persons bound to Virginia, in search of a proper seat for a plantation. Having fallen in with the Cape shore, he pursued his course south till he came up with Sandy Point, the southern extremity of the county of Barnstable, in the state of Massachusetts. It being late in the day, to avoid danger, he stood off to sea, and in the night came in sight of the white cliffs, at the east end of Nantucket, now called Sankota Head, the highest land on that part of the island.

Whence arose the name of the island, we are not certain, but it is generally supposed that *Nauticon*, known by ancient voyagers, and Nantucket, are the same.

We find no other record concerning Nantucket until the year 1641, at which time the whole island was deeded to Thomas Mayhew and his son Thomas by James Forrett, agent to William, Earl of Sterling, or Lord Sterling. This being the first deed, of which we have any knowledge, respecting the purchase of the island, we think it is reasonable to gratify our readers with a copy of it. Though not remarkable in itself. it may be interesting to some, since, among other circumstances, it shows the origin of the ownership of the island, and the consideration for which it was bought. It is as follows:

"THESE PRESENTS DO WITNESS, That I, James Forrett, Gent'n who was Sent over into These parts of America by the Honorable the Lord Sterling, with a Commission for the ordering and Disposal of all ye lands that Ly between Cape Codd and Hudson's River, (and have hitherto Continued my Agency without any contradiction) Do hereby Grant unto Thomas Mayhew of Water Town Merchant & to Thomas Mayhew his Son, free Liberty, and full power to Them and Their Associates, to plant and inhabit upon Nantucket and two other Small Islands adjacent and To Enjoy the Said Islands, To Them, their heirs and assigns for ever, provided that They the Said Thomas Mayhew and Thomas Mayhew his son, or Either of Them, or their associates, Do Render and give yearly unto the Honble the Lord Sterling, his heirs or assigns, Such an acknowledgement as shall be Thought fit by John Winthrop the Eld'r Esq'r or any Two Magistrates in the Massachusetts Bay. being chosen for that End and purpose by the Honble the Lord Sterling, or his deputy, and by the said Thomas Mayhew & Thomas Mayhew his son, or Their Associates. It is agreed That the Government that the Said Thomas Mayhew, and Thomas Mayhew his Son, and Their Associates, Shall Set up There, shall be such as is now Establisht, in the Massachusetts aforesaid; and That the Said Thomas Mayhew and Thomas Mayhew his Son, and Their Associates, shall have as much Privilig, Touching Their Planting, Inhabitants and Enjoying of all and every part of the premises, as by Patent is granted to the Patentees of the Massachusetts aforesaid; and Their Associates.

"In witness hereof, I, the said James Forrett, have hereunto set my hand and Seal, this 13th day of October, 1641.

' JAMES FORRETT.　　[L. S.]

"Signed, sealed, and delivered, in the presence of us,
 ROBERT CORNER,
 NICOLAS DAVISON, and
 RICHARD STILEMAN.

"This is a true copy of the record, as is attested this 14th day of April, 1674, per me,

"MATTHIAS NICOLLS, *Sec'y*."

Although we find, in the body of the deed, that it was made to the Mayhews and their associates, yet it was not conveyed to the associates until the 2d of the fifth month, 1659; the reason of which was, that the Mayhews could not purchase of the natives the Sachem right, until the beforementioned date, and those who intended to join the association were not disposed to engage until that was effected. It may be observed, that the place of record of the foregoing instrument is not mentioned; but, on reference to other documents, it is placed beyond doubt that it was done in New York. At that early period the island was under the jurisdiction of New York; which will be shown more particularly in its proper place.

The following instrument being the principal conveyance by which the owners of the island became legally possessed of it, it is thought expedient to insert it at large:

MR. MAYHEW'S BILL OF SALE.

"Be it known, unto all men, by these presents, that I, Thomas Mayhew, of Marther's Vineyard, merchant, do hereby acknowledge, that I have sold unto Tristram Coffin, Thomas Macy, Christopher Hussey, Richard Swain, Thomas Barnard, Peter Coffin, Stephen Greenleaf, John Swain, and William Pile, all that right and interest that I have in the island of Nantucket by Patent, the right I bought of James Forrett, steward to the Lord Sterling, and Richard Vines, sometimes of Saco, gentleman, steward general to Sir Fardinando George, knight, as by conveyance, under their hands and seals, appeareth, for them, the aforesaid, to enjoy, and their heirs and assigns for ever, with all the privileges thereunto belonging, for and in consideration of the sum of Thirty pounds of current pay, unto whomsoever I, the said Thomas Mayhew, my heirs or

assigns, shall appoint, and also, two Beaver hats. one for myself
and one for my Wife; and further, this is to declare, that I the
said Thomas Mayhew, have reserved to myself that neck upon
Nantucket, called Masquetuck, or that neck of Land called Nash-
ayte, the neck but one northerly of Masquetuck, the aforesaid sale
in any wise notwithstanding; and further I, the said Thomas
Mayhew, am to bear my part of the charges of the said purchases
above named, and to hold one twentieth part of all lands purchased
already, or shall be hereafter purchased, upon the Island, by the
Purchasers aforesaid, to their heirs and assigns forever; because it is
that I really sold all my Patent right to the aforesaid nine men, and
they are to pay me, or whomsoever I shall appoint them, the sum
of Thirty pounds in merchantable pay, in the Massachusetts, under
which Government they now Inhabit, and two Beaver Hats; and I
am to bear one twentieth part of the charges of the purchase; and
to have a twentieth part of all lands and privileges, and to have
which of the necks abovesaid that I will, myself paying for it only,
the Purchasers are to pay what the Sachem is to have for Masquetuck, though I take the other neck.

"And in witness whereof, I have hereunto set my hand and seal,
this second day of july, [which was then the fifth month according
to the style,] 1659.

"Per me, THOMAS MAYHEW.   [L. S.]

Witness, { JOHN SMITH,
           { EDWARD SCALE."

Although there was a verbal agreement made by the
Sachems, to sell Thomas Mayhew a large part of the
island, yet it was not formally concluded until a number
of families had moved and settled there, at which time it
was conveyed by the Sachems to the associates, by the
following instrument, which is the first to be found on the
records of the island :

"THESE PRESENTS WITNESS, May the tenth, sixteen hundred
and sixty, that we, Wanackmamack and Nickanoose, head Sachems
of Nantucket island, do give, grant, bargain, and sell, unto Mr.
Thomas Mayhew of Martin's Vineyard, Tristram Coffin, seniors,
Thomas Macy, Christopher Hussey, Richard Swain, Peter Coffin,

Stephen Greanleaf, Thomas Barnard, John Swain, and William Pile, all the Land, Meadow, Marshes, Timber and Wood, and all appurtenances thereunto belonging, and being and lying from the west end of the island of Nantucket, unto the Pond, called by the Indians, Waqutuquab, and from the head of that Pond, upon a straight line, unto the Pond situated by Monomoy Harbour or Creek, now called Wheeler's Creek, and so from the northeast corner of the said Pond to the Sea, that is to say, all the right that we, the aforesaid Sachems have in the said tract of land, provided that none of the Indian Inhabitants, in or about the wood land, or whatsoever Indians, within the last purchase of land, from the head of the Pond to Monomoy Harbour, shall be removed without full satisfaction.   And we, the aforesaid Sachems, do give, grant, bargain and sell, the one half of the remainder of the Meadows and Marshes upon all other parts of the Islands. And also that the English people shall have what grass they shall need for to mow, out of the remainder of the Meadows and Marshes on the island, so long as the English remain upon the Island, and also free liberty for Timber and Wood upon any part of the island within the jurisdiction. And also, we, the aforesaid Sachems, do fully grant free liberty to the English for the feeding all sorts of Cattle on any part of the island, after Indian harvest is ended until planting time, or until the first day of May, from year to year for ever, for and in consideration of twelve pounds already paid, and fourteen pounds to be paid within three months after the date hereof.

"To have and to hold the aforesaid purchase of land, and other appurtenances, as aforementioned, to them, Mr. Thomas Macy, Tristram Coffin, Thomas Mayhew, and the rest, aforementioned, and their heirs and assigns, for ever.

"In witness whereof, we the said Sachems, have hereunto set our hands and seals, the day and year above written.

The sign of WANACKMAMACK, [S.]
The sign of NICKANOOSE.   [S.]

"Signed, sealed and delivered, in the presence of us,

 PETER FOLGER,
 FELIX KUTTASHAMAQUAT,
 EDWARD STARBUCK.

"I do witness this deed to be a true deed, according to the

interpretation of Felix the interpreter; also, I heard Wanackmamack, but two weeks ago, say that the sale, made by Nickanoose and he, should be good, and that they would do so, whatever comes of it.

"Witness my hand, this 17th of first month, 1664.

PETER FOLGER.

Witness,

MARY STARBUCK,
The mark of JOHN (*I. C.*) COFFIN.

"Wanackmamack and Nickanoose acknowledged the above written to be their act and deed, in the presence of the General Court, this 12th of June, 1677, as attest.

MATTHEW MAYHEW,
Secretary to the Gen. Court."

The island was now fairly purchased of the original patentee, and a greater part of it of the natives. It was owned by an association, most of whom resided at Salisbury, in the county of Essex, in Massachusetts. The purchasers immediately began to make their arrangements to move thither with their families, and to improve the land. Accordingly, in the year 1659, the first family settled in the place, of which family a more particular account will hereafter be given.

The island of Nantucket is situated about 30 miles south of the main or continent; 60 miles S. E. from New Bedford; 100 miles S. S. E. from Boston; and 382 miles E. N. E. from Philadelphia. It lies in north latitude 41°, 15 min., 22 sec.; in west longitude 70°, 7 min., 56 sec. It contains nearly 30,000 acres of land, and is about fourteen miles long, east and west, and 3 1-2 broad, on an average, north and south. The principal harbor is on the north side, in the bottom or bend of an extensive bay, which is formed by two projecting points, one at the N. E. and the other at the N. W. part of the island; both of which extend in a northwesterly direction. The most western of these points is called Smith's Point, the other Sandy or Great Point; on the latter stands a light-house. The harbor is nearly landlocked by two points of beach, about three quarters of a mile apart, one on the east called Coetue, the other on the west, called Brant Point. Within these points, and on the west side, are the wharves and town. Nearly two miles from the shore, to the northward of the harbor, is a bar, which all vessels, coming in or out are under the necessity of passing. Vessels drawing nine feet of water may, with good pilots, pass over this bar and into the harbor. When a vessel comes to the bar drawing too great a draft of water to admit of her passing it with safety, lighters are sent, into which her cargo is discharged till she is sufficiently lightened

The many shoals to the eastward of the island, and the great South Shoal to the southward, render the navigation difficult and compel those not acquainted to keep a safe distance at sea. Although there are no ledges of rocks nor rocky shores, around the island, yet it is not unfrequent, especially in the winter, that vessels lose their way and are wrecked on some part. Such misfortunes, though causing much destruction of property, are not frequently attended with loss of lives.

The channel or sound, between the island and continent, is safe for vessels drawing sixteen feet of water; a greater depth would subject them to danger.

On the north of Smith's point, before mentioned, which projects several miles in a northwesterly direction, is Tuckernuck, an island containing about 1000 acres of land, and inhabited by a few families. This island was once covered with wood, but is now bare except about a hundred acres, from which sheep and cattle have, for a few years been excluded, and which are now occupied by thriving forest trees. There are two other islands a little to the north and west of Tuckernuck, one called Muskecket the other Gravelly Island; both are small and sandy, and without inhabitants.

The Island of Nantucket is generally of a sandy soil, and would not rate above a middling quality, compared with the adjacent continent, although, when first settled by the English, the soil was good and produced equal to any part of the country. In proof of this the following account of the luxuriancy of the soil, though many years after the island was settled, will show, in some degree, the great contrast between that time and the present. Ebenezer Barnard, a man of strict veracity, in the year 1729, tilled five acres in the general cornfield, at that time on the north side of the island, between the Long Pond, so called, and the west end of the town, a tract of land below the medium quality. From these five acres he gathered 250 bushels of good corn, and this quantity was considered rather less than an average for that year's growth. This may be accounted an uncommon growth for any country, still we are inclined to believe in the correctness of the account. The following will show the diminished fertility of the land from that time. In the year 1773, the cornfield was at Madaket and Smith's Point, at the northwesterly part of the island. The land then produced 20 bushels, on an average, to the acre, which was considered a remarkably good crop. Since that time the crops have gradually lessened, and within a few years they would not average more than 10 or 15 bushels to the acre. There are many reasons which might be assigned for this declension: amongst these, the following may be worthy of consideration. At the time of the settlement of the island it was covered with wood, which protected the crops from raw easterly winds, and by a continued supply of falling leaves and other decaying vegetation preserved the richness of the soil. The frequent ploughing of the land, since it was cleared of trees, has exposed the soil to the action of bleak winds, to which the island is very subject, and by which it is blown into the sea. Besides the plentiful production of corn, much wheat was raised. These and other productions sometimes exceeded the wants of the inhabitants, and were carried to Boston and other places to be exchanged for other articles of merchandise.

The land, weakened by the causes above-mentioned, has in many places been overrun by beach grass, which has advanced from the margin of the sea towards the interior, and covered large tracts. This kind of grass grows best in a shady soil; it rises to the hight of about two feet, and is better calculated brooms for than fodder: early in the spring, however, when it begins to grow, it is tender and wholesome food for all kinds of stock. Notwithstanding the many causes which have operated to diminish the natural fertility of the soil, there are many hundreds of acres under good improvement, which produce heavy growths of hay, corn and the common culinary vegetables. There are some excellent farms and fine gardens, in which some of the luxuries, as well as many of the necessaries, of life are annually raised. The cultivation of the grape has, within a few years, attracted the attention of several agriculturists, and it has been proved that both the soil and climate are admirably adapted to the cultivation of this delicious fruit. Hundreds of bushels of the Isabella, and considerable quantities of other kinds, are annually produced.

The wood, that grew here, was of the same kind as that found on adjacent parts of the continent. A great proportion of it was oak, of an uncommonly hard and firm texture. It was used for the frames of houses and other mechanical purposes : some buildings, now standing, framed of this wood, appear to be as sound as ever.

The face of the island is generally level; there are some elevations but no remarkably high hills. There is a considerable number of ponds, some pretty extensive, and well supplied with fish, others small, and serving only as watering places for cattle, or resorts of small shore birds, which are numerous. There are also many swamps, some containing from 100 to 300 acres; those situated near the town have been cleared, and made into valuable meadow land. A considerable quantity of good salt meadow is found bordering on the numerous creeks. But few rocks and not many stony places are to be met with. Among the minerals, found on the island, may be named large beds of blue clay, and also of peat, as abounding. Boulders of granite are common on the hills; specimens of bog iron are found in one location. Fragments of feldspar and porphyry are common. Pebbles of jasper are found on the seashore, and handsome specimens of amber are occasionally picked up there. Fossil shells are often found at considerable depths, when sinking wells.

The inquiry is frequently made by strangers, whether the island increases or decreases in size. On the authority of long and accurate observation it may be stated, that there has been a decrease, and in some places to a considerable extent. On the east and south some hundreds of acres have been washed away, and, if we may credit the accounts of our ancestors, a greater quantity from the north.

If the decrease were in regular proportions from year to year, it might be ascertained, by a simple calculation, at what time the whole island would become extinct. But this cannot be done; for in some years there is even an increase, in others but little loss, in others again, in consequence of hard and repeated storms, such has been the waste, that the final destruction would seem to be the easy work of a very few centuries.

CHAPTER II.

The first emigration of the whites, or English, to the Island being one of the most interesting parts of this account, we shall endeavor to be as explicit on the subject as the nature of the work, and the means possessed, will admit. Our information, however, falls far short of what is necessary to form a complete history.

Thomas Macy being the first settler, it will not be deemed a needless digression, to state what we know of his early biography. In the year 1640, being then a young man, he moved with his family from the town of Chilmark, in Wiltshire, England, and settled in Salisbury, county of Essex, in Massachusetts. He lived here in good repute twenty years, where he acquired a good interest, consisting of a tract of land of 1,000 acres, a good house, and considerable stock. But when this part of the country became more thickly settled by the English, dissensions arose among the people in regard to religion and religious denominations. Notwithstanding the purpose of their emigration from the mother country was that they might enjoy liberty of conscience in religious matters, they themselves commenced the work of persecution, and enacted laws to restrain people from worshipping God according to the dictates of their consciences. Among other restraints, a law was made, that any person, who should entertain one of the people called Quakers, should pay a fine of five pounds for every hour during which he so entertained them. Thomas Macy subjected himself to the rigor of this law by giving shelter to four Quakers, who stopped at his house in a rain storm. This act was soon sounded abroad, for, being influenced by a sense of duty, he had used no means to conceal it. Being cited to answer for the offence, he addressed the following letter to the court, the original of which is preserved in the cabinet of the Nantucket Athenæum :—

"This is to entreat the honoured Court not to be offended because of my non-appearance. It is not from my slighting the authority of the honoured Court, nor fear to answer the case; but have been for some weeks past very ill, and am so at present ; and notwithstanding my illness, yet I, desirous to appear, have done my utmost endeavor to hire a horse, but cannot procure one at present. I, being at present destitute, have endeavored to purchase one, but at present cannot attain it—but I shall relate the truth of the case, as my answer would be to the honoured Court—and more cannot be proved, nor so much. On a rainy morning, there came to my house, Edward Wharton and three men more* ; the said Wharton spoke to me, saying they were travelling eastward, and

---

* Two of these men were William Robinson, merchant, of London, and Marmaduke Stephenson, of Yorkshire, England. They were hanged in Boston, on the 27th of the 20th month, 1659, for supporting the Christian principle, as believed by the people called Quakers.

desired me to direct them in the way to Hampton ; and never saw
any of the men afore except Wharton, neither did I enquire their
names or what they were ; but by their carriage I thought they
might be Quakers, and said I so : and therefore desired I them to
pass on, in their way—saying to them, I might possibly give
offence in entertaining them, and soon as the violence of the rain
ceased (for it rained hard), they went away, and I never saw them
since. The time they staid in the house was about three quarters
of an hour ; they spoke not many words, in the time, neither was
I at leisure to talk with them ; for I came home wet to the skin,
immediately afore they came to the house ; and I found my wife
sick in bed. If this satisfy not the honoured Court, I shall submit
to their sentence. I have not willingly offended—I am ready to
serve and obey you in the Lord.

27 of 8th mo. '59 [1659].   THOMAS MACY."

He could now live no longer in peace, and in the enjoyment of religious freedom, among his own nation ; he
chose therefore to remove his family to a place unsettled
by the whites, to take up his abode among savages, where
he could safely imitate the example and obey the precepts
of our Saviour, and where religious zeal had not yet discovered a crime in hospitality, nor the refinements of civil
law, a punishment for its practice. In the fall of 1659,
he embarked in an open boat, with his family and such
effects as he could conveniently take with him, and, with
the assistance of Edward Starbuck, proceeded along the
shore to the westward. When they came to Boston bay,
they crossed it, passed round Cape Cod, and extended
their course by the shore until they were abreast of the
island to the northward, thence they crossed the sound,
and landed on Nantucket without accident. Thus we
see, that the same persecuting spirit, that drove our forefathers from England, drove Thomas Macy from our
forefathers ; that the same undaunted courage, which
enabled them to breast the storm, and dare the wave, in

search of a free altar and a safe home, prompted him, in search of the same blessings, to meet the same dangers. He sacrificed his property and his home to his religion; he found both in a remote region hitherto hardly known. His religion, we mean not its name, but its spirit, has been transmitted to the present generation, unsullied by the crime of persecution or by the disgrace of inhospitality.

The first care of these strangers was to cultivate a good understanding with the natives, whom they found very numerous, and who flocked around them with seeming amazement, having never before had an opportunity to see English people on the island. The natives were kind and hospitable, and readily lent their aid and assistance whenever they could make themselves useful; being fully satisfied that these new comers had not landed among them with hostile intentions, but in search of a comfortable subsistence. Macy now examined the island adjacent to the place of landing, and finally chose a spot for settlement on the south east side of Madaket harbor, where he found a rich soil and an excellent spring of water. The harbor above-mentioned was undoubtedly thought to be more convenient for navigation, than the one on which the town is now built: but when the island became more peopled, the present situation of the town was preferred to Madaket, and the latter was accordingly abandoned.

It being now late in the fall, the first care was to build a shelter for the family against the inclemency of the approaching season. After this was accomplished, they commenced a particular examination of the character of the place and of the people. They found the island covered with wood, and inhabited by about fifteen hundred Indians, who depended for subsistence on fishing, fowling, and hunting. Game was remarkably plenty, and continued so many years afterward ; and the adjacent shores and waters abounded with many kinds of fish. Here they spent the winter, a single family, confined on an island among native Indians, of whose character and language they were almost entirely ignorant. In the spring following, Edward Starbuck found means to return to Salisbury, where he was met with rejoicings by his friends who, sensible of his hazardous undertaking, had felt doubtful of his safe return. He was now able to give satisfactory information concerning many important things of which before they were entirely ignorant. This information was more interesting, because, as appears by the earliest records, a considerable number of the people of Salisbury had it in in contemplation to remove with their families to the island, about the time when Thomas Macy went there. In 1660, Edward Starbuck returned to the island accompanied by eight or ten families.

It appears on record, that a number of persons at Salisbury associated and purchased a patent-right of the island. A short transcript of this record will explain, in a clearer method than it can otherwise be done, the preliminary means by which the island became settled by white inhabitants.

Salisbury.—"Town order 2d of July, 1659: These persons after mentioned did buy all right and interest of the Island of Nantucket, that did belong to Sir Ferdinando George, and the Lord Sterling; Mr. Richard Vines Steward, Gentleman to Sir Fernando Georges; and Mr. James Forret, Steward to the Lord Stirling; which was by them sold unto Mr. Thomas Mayhew of Martha's Vineyard, these aftermentioned did purchase of Mr. Thomas Mayhew these rights, namely, the Patent-rights belonging to the Gentlemen aforesaid, and also the parcel of land, which Mr.

Mayhew did purchase of the Indians at the west end of the Island of Nantucket, as by their grant or bill of sale will largely appear, with all the privileges and appurtenances thereof."

"The aforesaid purchasers are, Tristram Coffin, senior, Thomas Macy, Richard Swain, Thomas Barnard, Peter Coffin, Christopher Hussey, Stephen Greenleaf, John Swain and William Pile ; and Thomas Mayhew retained one tenth in his own right ; they had the whole and sole interest, disposal, power and privileges of the said Island, and appurtenances thereof. (Thomas Mayhew furthermore retained in his own right, separate from the association, that part of the Island called Masquetuck, or Quaise.")

"The aforesaid ten persons were called the first ten purchasers of the Patent-right of the Island.—For a more particular description the reader is referred to the county records of Nantucket; where may be found many other extracts from the original records at Salisbury, concerning the establishment of the first proprietorship of the Island."

"The aforesaid ten purchasers, finding it necessary to encourage emigration to the island, agreed at a meeting held at Salisbury in the year 1659, which is the same year the first purchase was made, for each owner to take in a partner or associate, which should be left to the choice of each individual to select one. The persons so chosen were John Smith, Nathaniel Starbuck, Robert Pike, Thomas Look, Robert Barnard, James Coffin, Tristram Coffin, junior, Thomas Coleman, Edward Starbuck, and Thomas Mayhew. They agreed at the same meeting, that all purchases made of the Indians by any of the associates at any time hereafter, should be for and on account of the whole proprietorship. This was done to prevent any contrivance in one's taking the advantage over another, which was generally adhered to, until all the Island was purchased of the Indians."

After this they removed with their families, and took possession by agreement of such parts as were best suited to their interest or convenience. Still they found it necessary to add to the number of inhabitants ; and particularly to encourage the emigration of mechanics and other artists. To effect this they offered to such, if they would come and settle among them, certain parts of shares in all the privileges they themselves enjoyed. By this means the number of shares was increased to twenty-seven, which still continues to be the number of shares, under the denomination of the common and undivided land on the island of Nantucket.

These twenty-seven shares include the whole island, except the place called Quaise or Masquetuck, which Thomas Mayhew reserved to himself, when he conveyed the island to the first ten purchasers, as stated in his deed. It is to be understood that the Sachem right was not bought at the time of the aforesaid conveyance, but that it was purchased afterwards, by the English, and at different times until the natives had sold all their right throughout the island. These purchases from the natives were numerous. It was found that they owned the land in small tracts, each one having his own bounds to an exactness that was surprising, considering that the culture of the land was not then an object of importance to them. Although the natives sold their rights in the land, it was always considered good policy to allow them the privilege of tilling as much as they pleased, for through this indulgence they were encouraged to contribute to their own wants by their own industry. It was the usual practice of the Indians in the spring, previous to undertaking voyages in the whaling service, to plow as much land as would be sufficient for their families during the succeeding summer, except some unavoidable occurrence should prevent, in which they were assisted by the English. But notwithstanding this encouragement, it frequently occurred, either through indolence or inebriety, that little or no care was taken to provide for their families. This neglect finally became so troublesome to the English, that in process of time it became necessary to resort to some remedy. The expedient adopted was this : one of the most firm and intelligent of the natives, by the name of Kadooda, was selected and deputized as an auxiliary justice of the peace. It was made his duty to decide on such complaints for trivial offences as might come before him. Neglect of tilling the ground was not one of the least crimes that came under his jurisdiction. In some instances he was authorized, or rather indulged, to inflict corporal punishment. His mode of administering justice was in many cases found of real benefit; yet in some others, the legal justices found their interferance necessary, since Esquire Kadooda was liable to extend his authority beyond the bounds of prudence. It is related, we cannot say with what correctness, that, in some cases brought before him, his first proceeding was to order both parties to be severely whipped. It is further said, that this process had the effect of lessening the number of complaints, and of rendering his duties light; and that otherwise his whole time would have been taken up in his official calling. Whatever may be the truth of this matter one thing is certain, that "Kadooda's laws," have become proverbial; and it is not going too far, we think, to say that their adoption, even in our times, if not strictly legal would, in some instances, be morally just.

The next consideration of moment, was the best method of improvement. It must be borne in mind, that, at this period, there was but a small portion of land cleared and capable of being stocked or tilled to advantage. On this account it was agreed by the proprietors, as we may now style them, that the privilege of stocking to each share, should be limited by the extent of the land cleared; and that each proprietor should stock his own, at his own election, allowing eight sheep to be equal to one neat beast, and two neat beasts to one horse. As the land became more cleared, the privilege of stocking was extended to each share until it amounted to seven hundred and twenty sheep, or other stock in the proportion above stated. Thus the stocking privilege of the proprietors collectively amounts to twenty-seven times seven hundred and twenty or nineteen thousand four hundred and forty sheep,—or two thousand four hundred and thirty neat beasts,—or one thousand two hundred and fifteen horses,—or to a part of each according to the interest or convenience of each proprietor.

At the same time, and from year to year, a certain tract was fenced off from the stock and appropriated to a general corn-field, which was laid out into twenty-seven shares; and the proprietors of each share improved their own privileges according to a subdivision among themselves. The proprietors of these corn-fields rarely manured them; hence they gathered small crops averaging about fifteen, but sometimes not exceeding ten bushels to the acre. This practice continued more than an hundred years in succession; but within a few years, it is said that the land is so worn out, and the soil blown into the sea, that the produce will not pay the expense of cultivation. On this account the field is for the present not laid out.

The island being owned and improved in common, the sheep have not had that attention in the winter, which is the general practice of farmers in the country to give them. They are suffered to run at large throughout the year, exposed in winter to the bleak winds and cold storms, with no place of shelter provided for them. The forest has disappeared, and the greatest part of the island is left a naked plain, where the gale meets with no obstruction and animals find no refuge. It sometimes happens that many sheep are covered in heavy falls of snow, and perish before relief can be afforded, though a large number of men are employed to release them. This mode of keeping sheep may to some appear wrong and even cruel; but it may be observed that the proprietors have always been in that practice, and, by long custom, have become so reconciled to the measure, that the thought of doing wrong has almost become extinct. There are generally from eight to ten thousand sheep owned on the island.

The proprietors, in the early period of the settlement, found it most conducive to their interest and convenience to lay out in severalty certain tracts or parcels of land into twenty-seven shares, in order that each proprietor might enjoy and improve his own share, as suited him best. The following schedule will present at one view all the different tracts laid out, when they were laid out, and the quantity of each:

Date.		Acres.	Rods.
1659.	Quaise, or Masquetuck, which Thomas Mayhew reserved to himself when the island was conveyed by him to the associates.	372	16
"	Special grants at different times,	79	77
"	Held by possession by sundry people,	17	130
1678.	Shimmo and Showkemmo Meadow,	36	94
"	Podpis Meadow,	14	108
"	South Monomoy,	87	150
"	Wesco Acre lots, within the town,	27	—
1717.	Fish lots,	24	158
"	Shimmo,	121	35
1723.	House Lots,	1242	—
"	Ware House Lot, within the town,		64
1723 and 1777.	Swamps,	534	119
1744.	Bochocheco, within the town,	2	61
1732.	Brant Point Meadow,	23	92
1678.	Pookoomo Meadow, salt and fresh,	34	—
1726-7.	West Monomoy, within the town,	73	54

Date.		Acres.	Rods.
1726–7.	South Monomoy,	71	78
1765.	North Beach, 1st division,	4	—
1805.	North Beach, 2d division,	32	110
1765 and 1805.	South Beach, 1st and 2d division,	15	92
1775.	Southeast quarter of the island,	2456	158
1778.	Croskatu,	349	146
1779.	Squam and Pookoomo,	2109	29
1776.	Maddekeet Swamp,	68	—
"	Maddekeet Meadow,	27	17
1813.	Plainfield,	2173	154
1810.	Gibb's Swamp,	380	—
1820.	A tract of land called the Woods, not a tree upon it,	513	—
1820.	Foot of the Plains,	506	—
"	Salt Meadow, at the west end of the island,	70	—
1821.	Middle Pasture,	2106	—
"	North Pasture,	1587	—
"	Trot's Hills,	513	—
"	Great Neck,	304	—
"	Head of the Plains,	567	—
"	Smooth Hummocks,	1566	—
"	Maddekeet,	274	—
		18,387	22
According to a survey of the whole island, made in 1813, it was found that it contained,		29,380	67
1822.	Which leaves of the common land undivided,	10,993	69

It is believed, by many, that nearly all the divisions of common land, made since 1775, have proved detrimental to the interests of the proprietors generally; and it is urged that every instance of division has had a tendency to destroy the system by which the proprietors were governed in their corporate capacity, and so to change the mode of improvement as to render the land less productive. This has had a very material effect to lessen the price of land of that description.

The records of the first proprietors were kept at Salisbury, where, together with the house in which they were kept, they were burnt by accident. This circumstance occasioned some embarrassment, as no part was preserved except a few extracts which had occasionally been made.

It is not our purpose to enter particularly into the proceedings of the proprietors, or to record the rules, orders and regulations, by which they have governed themselves. A volume would be required for this purpose, and it would then be understood by few, and fewer still, perhaps, would be interested in it.

The settlers found themselves among a race of beings, who were peaceable when well used; they were careful, therefore, to keep up a good understanding with them. The natives were willing to labor for them, provided they were in some way compensated; they were also willing to sell their land, which was from time to time purchased of them; the whites never presuming to claim privileges which they had not fairly paid for. Deeds of conveyance were made and recorded whenever there were any purchases, and a right was always granted to the natives, notwithstanding the sale of their lands, to use as much as was necessary for the support of their families.

The first mill, of which we have any record, was one built in 1666, for grinding corn. During the previous year, the town voted to have a mill to grind their grain, which was to go by horse power. This vote, we know not for what reason, was not carried into effect. The one which they erected was carried by water, and was located on Wesco Pond. Peter Folger was agreed with to keep this mill, and his toll was fixed at two quarts for each bushel. This Peter Folger was an-inhabitant of Martha's Vineyard. He was invited to remove with his family to

Nantucket, to officiate as miller, weaver and interpreter of the Indian language; his son Eleazer was to act as shoemaker; and, as a proper encouragement to these several occupations, a grant of one half of a share of land, with all the accommodations thereunto belonging, was made to the father. He accepted the invitation, and, in 1663, removed thither. In 1667 he took charge of the mill. Besides laboring in the callings above-mentioned, he acted as surveyor of land.

The inhabitants did not immediately conclude upon what part of the island to establish a town. Each one, according to his occupation, whether farming or fishing, took up his residence and homestead on the part most suited to his calling, having regard to his ownership. But they generally chose to settle on the north side of the island, finding there the best land and the best springs of water.

The number of inhabitants was now fast increasing. They had amongst them a sufficient number of mechanics and other artisans to perform all the different branches of business necessary for their comfortable subsistence. Rules and regulations were established for their own government; but the records of those times are nearly silent on this subject. Two reasons may be assigned for this; first, the number of inhabitants was yet small, and as each attended to his own business, they did not require much formality in their government; second, they were so illiterate that the little of their writings that have come down to us, is hardly legible or intelligible. The occupation of the people was such as to require little school education. The farmers, the fishermen and mechanics, exchanged their commodities with each other without keeping regular accounts. Their natural dependence and common wants led them to be obliging and accommodating. A piece of chalk and the inside of a door frequently supplied the place of pen and day-book; indeed, many of their business transactions were trusted wholly to memory. If the farmer happened to be out of certain articles, which he expected to reap from his land in proper season of gathering, he would borrow of his neighbor, who would lend without reluctance. These were debts of the highest responsibility, and were always carefully paid.

Although the natives were kind and obliging to the English, yet it was discovered that they had not always lived in harmony among themselves. A little previous to the settlement by the whites, there had been a war between the tribes of the east and those of the west end of the island. The mode in which this controversy was settled is somewhat singular. The king of the west end married the daughter of the king of the east; after this preliminary, they agreed on a division line across the island, running north and south, and covenanted that if the subjects of either party crossed it with hostile intentions, they should be immediately put to death. After this treaty of peace the parties were never again at war with each other.

The whaling business was not commenced till several years after the settlement of the island. In the interval the people were occupied in farming, or in fishing near the shores. Fish were plenty and easily caught. The Indians were instructed in the mode of fishing practiced by the whites, and in return the whites were assisted by the Indians in pursuing the business. Previous to their acquaintance with the English, the natives fished with a rude line of twisted grass, to which they attached a large stone for a sinker, and a clumsy hook of bone. Some of the sinkers just mentioned, remain to this day. They resemble a ship's block in form, and weigh two or three pounds. With this inconvenient apparatus they caught but few fish, compared with the number attained by the better adapted hook and line of the Europeans.

The first whaling expedition was undertaken by some of the original purchasers of the island; the circumstances of which are handed down by tradition, and are as follows :—A whale, of the kind called "scrag," came into the harbor and continued there three days. This excited the curiosity of the people, and led them to devise measures to prevent his return out of the harbor. They accordingly invented, and caused to be wrought for them a harpoon with which they attacked and killed the whale. This first success encouraged them to undertake whaling as a permanent business; whales being at that time numerous in the vicinity of the shores. In furtherance of their design, they made a contract with James Lopar, to settle on the island and engage in the business. The agreement was as follows, copied verbatim from the original record :

" 5th 4th mo. 1672 James Lopar doth Ingage to carry on a design of Whale Citching on the Island of Nantuckket, that is the said James, Ingage to be a third in all respeeks, and som of the Town Ingage Also to Carrey on the other two thirds with him in like manner, the Town doth also Consent, that first one Company shal begin and afterward the rest of the freeholders or any of them, have liberty to set up an other Company Provided that they make a tender to those freeholders that have no share in the first Company and if any refuse, the Rest may go on themselves, and the Town do also Ingage that no other Company shal be allowed hereafter, Also whosoever Kil any whale of the Company or Companys aforesaid they ar to pay to the town for every such Whale five Shillings—and for the Incorragement of the said James Lopar the Town doth grant him Ten Acres of Land in som convenant

place, that he may chuse in, (Wood Land exceped) and also Liberty
for the Commouge. of thre Cows and twenty Sheep and one horse
with necessary Wood and water for his use on Conditions that he
follow the Trade of Whaleing on the Island two years in all the
season thereof, beginning the first of March next insuing. Also
is to build upon his land, and when he leaves Inhabiting upon the
island then he is first to ofer his Land to the Town at a Valluable
price, and if the town do not buy it—then he may Sel it to whome
he please—the commonage is granted only for the time he stays
here."

As it now appeared that there was a prospect of carrying the business of whaling into effect, the town, willing
to give it every encouragement that it required, according
to their knowledge and ability, agreed with John Savage
to remove thither with his family and to serve them in the
occupation of cooper : and to induce his compliance, to give
him ten acres of land, and commonage for three cows
and one horse : nearly on the same conditions as above-
mentioned in relation to Lopar.

How far this plan succeeded, we are in a great measure
unacquainted; the profits of the business were sufficient,
however, to encourage its pursuit.   Finding that the people of Cape Cod had made greater proficiency in the art
of whale catching than themselves, the inhabitants, in
1690, sent thither and employed a man by the name of
Ichabod Paddock, to instruct them in the best manner of
killing whales and extracting their oil.   The pursuit of
whales commenced in boats from the shore, and increased
from year to year, till it became the principal branch of
business with the islanders.   The Indians, ever manifest-
ing a disposition for fishing of every kind, readily joined
with the whites in this new pursuit, and willingly sub-
mitted to any station assigned them.   By their assistance, the whites were enabled to fit out and man a far

greater number of boats than they could have done of themselves. Nearly every boat was manned in part, many almost entirely by natives; some of the most active of them were made steersmen, and some were allowed even to head the boats; thus encouraged, they soon became experienced whalemen, and capable of conducting any part of the business.

The whaling business did not put a stop to the cod fishery, which was the same time carried on from the south and east sides of the island. The habitations of the people were scattered, and mostly remote from the shore; small huts were accordingly erected near the sea-side, for shelter in cold and boisterous weather. In process of time these buildings amounted to a considerable number, and two considerable villages sprung up on the east side, one called Sesacacha, the other Siasconset. The former of these a few years since contained about thirty houses, of which but one is now remaining; the latter consists of about sixty, but they are at present used as places of resort during the heat of summer. '

They sometimes, in pleasant days, during the winter season, ventured off in their boats nearly out of sight of land. It has often been remarked by the aged, that the winters were not so windy and boisterous at that time as at present. though quite as cold; and that it would some-times continue calm a week or even a fortnight.

The process called *saving* the whales after they had been killed and towed ashore, was to use a *crab*, an instrument similar to a capstain, to heave and turn the blubber off as fast as it was cut. The blubber was then put into their carts and carried to their try-houses, which at that early period, were placed near to their dwelling-houses, where the oil was boiled out and fitted for market.

To enable them to discover whales at a considerable distance from the land, a large spar was erected and cleats fixed to it, by which the whalemen could climb to the top, and there keep a good look out for their game. There was no perceptible decrease of the number of whales during the period of the first thirty or forty years from the commencement of the fishery. It appears that in 1726 they were very numerous, for eighty-six were taken in that year, a greater number than were obtained in any one year, either before or since that date. The greatest number ever killed and brought to the shore in one day was eleven. This mode of whaling continued until about the year 1760, when the whales became scarce, and it was by degrees discontinued. Since that date, whales have only occasionally been obtained by boats from the shore.

It is remarkable, that, notwithstanding the people had to learn the business of whaling, and to carry it on under many hazardous circumstances, yet not a single white person was killed or drowned in the pursuit, in the course of seventy years preceding 1760. The whales hitherto caught near the shores were of the Right species.

The first Spermaceti whale, known to the inhabitants, was found dead, and ashore, on the southwest part of the island. It caused considerable excitement, some demanding a part of the prize under one pretence, some under another, and all were anxious to behold so strange an animal. There were so many claimants of the prize, that it was difficult to determine to whom it should belong. The natives claimed the whale because they found it; the whites, to whom the natives made known their discovery, claimed it by a right comprehended, as they affirmed, in the purchase of the island by the original patent. An officer of the crown made his claim, and pretended to seize the fish in the name of his majesty, as being property without any particular owner. After considerable discussion between these contending parties, it was finally settled that the white inhabitants, who first found the whale, should share the prize equally amongst themselves. The teeth, which were considered very valuable, had been extracted by a white man and an Indian, before any others had any knowledge of the whale. All difficulty being now settled, a company was formed who commenced cutting the whale' in pieces convenient for transportation to their try-works. The sperm procured from the head was thought to be of great value for medical purposes. It was used both as an internal and an external application; and such was the credulity of the people, that they considered it a certain cure of all diseases; it was sought with avidity, and for a while, was esteemed to be worth its weight in silver. The whole quantity of oil obtained from this whale is not known. Whales being plenty near the shores people were led to conclude that they should find them still more numerous were they to pursue them with vessels into the "deep." That the pursuit of whales into the ocean was early anticipated, we know by an anecdote, related by one of our' ancestors. In the year 1690, the same in which Ichabod Paddock was sent for from Cape Cod, as before related, some persons were on a high hill, afterwards called Folly House Hill, observing the whales spouting and sporting with each other, when one observed, "*there*," pointing to the sea, "*is a green pasture where our children's grand-children will go for bread.*" It was many years, however, before they began to whale with vessels, but at what precise time it happened we have no means of knowing.

Previous to whaling in vessels, it was necessary to

determine where the harbor should be. It has already
been mentioned that the one at Madaket was at first preferred, but this was afterwardsr elinquished for the present
harbor, which is larger, more land-locked, and in many
other respects better adapted to the purposes of navigation
than the first mentioned. The south side of this harbor
was first selected for the site of the town ; the proprietors
therefore laid out house lots, or homesteads, of one hundred rods in length, and three or four rods in width.
But many inconveniences were afterwards found to attend
this location, and the present situation of the town was
soon after selected. It being now determined where the
town should be, it became necessary to give it a name,
and it was accordingly called SHERBURNE, by order of
Francis Lovelace, Esqr., Governor of the Province of
New York, in his written directions, bearing date, April
18th, 1673.

When the island was first settled by the English, it was
as already mentioned, under the government of the province of New York, which ratified and confirmed the first
purchase of the island from Lord Sterling, and also
allowed the several purchases made of the Mayhews and
the Indians to be valid ; and grants and patents were made
by Governor Lovelace to the people of Nantucket in the
year 1671, and afterwards confirmed by successive Governors of the said province of New York, whereby the
proprietors were allowed many privileges which they
afterwards enjoyed and considered as their standing rules.
Some valuable and exclusive privileges respecting the
fisheries around the island, and in the bays, coves, har-
bors, etc., were granted by the same authority, to the
inhabitants, they paying certain yearly quitrents, which
was carefully attended to by them. This subordination

of Nantucket to the government of New York continued until William and Mary came to the throne of England. They directed, that the lines of the "Province of Massachusetts Bay," in New England, should be ascertained, and, by the request of the inhabitants and proprietors of the Island of Nantucket, the island was included within these lines, and considered to be a part of Massachusetts. This change was confirmed, in May 1693, by the following statute of the province of Massachusetts, and the people of Nantucket were allowed all the privileges, of every kind and nature, which were allowed them by the province of New York.

"*Anno Regni Gulielmi, et Mariæ, Regis et Reginæ, Quinto.*

" Act passed by the Great and General Court or Assembly of the Province of Massachusetts-Bay, in New-England, begun and held at Boston, the thirty-first day of May, 1693.

CHAP. 2.—*An act for Confirmation of Titles within the Islands of Capawok, alias Martha's Vineyard, and Nantuckett.*

" WHEREAS their most gracious Majesties, our sovereign Lord and Lady, *King* WILLIAM and *Queen* MARY, in and by their royal CHARTER or letters Patent, bearing date at WESTMINSTER, the seventh day of OCTOBER in the third Year of their said Majesties Reign; for the uniting, erecting and incorporating of the Colony of the MASSACHUSETT-BAY, and Colony of NEW-PLYMOUTH, the Province of MAIN, the Territory called ACCADA, or NOVA-SCOTIA, and all that Tract of Land lying between the said Territories of Nova Scotia, and the said Province of MAIN, into one real Province, by the Name of the Province of the MASSACHUSETTS-BAY, in New England: Have therein particularly named, comprehended and included the Islands of CAPAWOK and NANTUCKETT as part of the said Province of the MASSACHUSETTS-BAY, and annexed the same thereto: And also all Islands and Islets, lying within ten Leagues, directly opposite to the main Land within the said Bounds.

*　　*　　*　　*　　*　　*　　*　　*

"But for as much as the said Island of CAPAWOK, alias MAR-
THA'S VINEYARD, and the Island of NANTUCKETT, were for
some time under the Rule and Government of the Province of
NEW-YORK, and the Properties and Titles of the Lands upon the
said Islands respectively, &c., &c.

" And the Inhabitants and Proprietors of Lands within the
Island of CAPAWOK, alias MARTHA'S VINEYARD and the Island
of NANTUCKETT, for their better Quiet and Satisfaction, desiring
this Court's Confirmation of the same:—

"*It is therefore declared and enacted by the Governour, Council,
and Representatives, convened in General Assembly, and by the
Authority of the Same*, That all Lands, Tenements, Hereditaments
and other Estates held and enjoyed by any Person or Persons,
Towns or Villages, within the Islands of Capawok, alias Martha's
Vineyard and Nantuckett, and each of them respectively, by or
under any Grant or Estate duly made or granted by any former
Government, or by the successive Governours of *New York* or any
other lawful Right or Title whatsoever; shall be by such Person or
Persons, Towns or Villages, their respective Heirs Successors and
Assigns for ever hereafter held and enjoyed, according to the true
Purport and Intent of such respective Grant, under and subject
nevertheless to the Rents and Services thereby reserved or made
payable. And are hereby ratified and confirmed as fully and
amply to all Intents, Constructions and Purposes, as the Lands in
any other Parts or Places within this Province by Virtue of their
Majesties' Royal Charter."

The first Spermaceti whale taken by the Nantucket
whalers, was killed by Christopher Hussey. He was
cruising near the shore for Right whales, and was blown
off some distance from the land by a strong northerly
wind, where he fell in with a school of that species of
whales, and killed one and brought it home. At what
date this adventure took place is not fully ascertained, but
it is supposed to be not far from 1712. This event gave
new life to business, for they immediately began with
vessels of about thirty tons to whale out in the "deep,"
as it was then called, to distinguish it from shore whaling.

They fitted out for cruises of about six weeks, carried a few hogsheads, enough probably to contain the blubbers of one whale, with which, after obtaining it, they returned home. The owners then took charge of the blubber, and tried out the oil, and immediately sent the vessel out again. At the commencement of this mode of whaling, it was found necessary to erect try-houses near the landing, and a number were built on the beach a little south of the wharves. North from these they erected small buildings, called ware-houses, in which they put their whaling apparatus, and other outfits.

In 1715 the number of vessels engaged in the whaling business was six, all sloops of from thirty to forty tons burthen each, which produced £1100 sterling or $4,888.88·

As the shipping increased, it was found indispensably necessary to have wharves. The first built is that now called Straight Wharf, constructed in 1723. Previous to this there had been places built off, called landing places, which were but temporary, and were often broken up by winter storms.

The island was now in a flourishing condition. The inhabitants were fast increasing in number and wealth; the land was principally purchased of the natives; it was very productive, when improved; the natives very cordially enlisted in the service of the whites; fish and fowls were plenty; the whaling had become a most profitable employment, and promised business for all. What a prospect must this have been to a people like them, remarkable for their industry and prudence, never so well pleased as when they had as much business as they could perform. This being the general character of the inhabitants, they increased in wealth as fast as could be expected. This business, it is true, did not afford great profits, less, perhaps than almost any other ; but the people, being of a frugal disposition, required but little to keep them comfortable, and there were but few among them who aspired after great things.

As the whaling business was found to answer their expectations, they were encouraged to increase the number and size of their vessels. Sloops and schooners of from forty to fifty tons were put into the business. Vessels of this size being supposed to be best adapted to whaling near the coast, no larger ones were employed for many years. At length whales began to be scarce near the shore, and some enterprising persons procured larger vessels and sent them out to the *southward*, as it was called, where they cruised until about the first of the seventh month, when they came in and refitted, and went to the eastward of the Grand Bank, where they continued through the whaling season, unless they completed their lading sooner, which frequently happened. The vessels that went on these voyages were generally sloops, of sixty or seventy tons ; their crews were made up in part of Indians, there being usually from four to eight in each vessel. They were pleased with the business, and always ready to engage in it when called upon.

At the close of the whaling season, the vessels were mostly drawn on shore for the winter, being considered safer and less expensive in that situation, than at the wharves. The boats were placed on the beach, bottom upward and tied together, to prevent disasters in gales of wind ; and all the whaling gear was put into the warehouses.

CHAPTER III.

In order to preserve some connection in our account of the whale fishery, we have traced it forward beyond the date of the general history of the island. We will now return.

It has already been shown that the purpose of the first emigrants to the island was to secure a free exercise of religious faith and worship. Many were at that time deprived of these privileges by law. Nantucket seemed to offer a safe retreat from the spirit of persecution then prevailing, and persons of various denominations removed thither with their families. Differing as they did in religious opinions, they exercised no intolerance towards one another; feeling their own accountability to God, they presumed not to assume His prerogative and arraign their fellow-beings before a human tribunal, to answer for that which concerned only themselves, and pertained only to a future world.

During the first fifty years after the settlement, the people were mostly Baptists; there were some Presbyterians, and a few of the Society of Friends. The little community was kind and courteous to each other, and hospitable to strangers. The prevalence of good feeling was remarked and felt by all who came among them. The nature of their business was such as to expose them but little to the alluring customs and habits of the vicious part of mankind. They were industrious, and therefore virtuous, and consequently happy.

In the moderate part of the year, they were employed in farming, fishing and whaling, and in the winter they prepared materials against the coming season, such as vessels, boats, casks, and whaling gear; at this time they also schooled their children. But little learning was not, in those times, considered a very " dangerous thing." It did not require an extensive education either to prosecute business, or to secure a respectable standing in society. What was necessary was attended to, all beyond was unknown or neglected. Their employment had a tendency to form their customs and manners in many respects. Their dress was moderate and plain, their deportment kind and unassuming. They were satisfied with such habiliments as were comfortable and fitted to the season, disregarding the vain and foppish fashions then prevailing among mankind in general. They were not the less respected for their singularities, as some were pleased to call them, for they had the reputation of being an honest people, and punctual to their promises. They easily obtained credit for such articles as they needed, with no other security than their own promise. It was a remarkable event that one should fail of discharging his debts, or that an estate should be found incompetent to meet all demands against it.

The female part of the community cordially joined and united in these economical principles, always helpful and careful to make all practicable savings in their department. They were industrious neat and cleanly. On the mother devolved almost every family care, both those of the immediate household and those of a more general nature. The husband was a great part of his time at sea, and when on shore his calling was such as to allow him little time for his fire-side. The education or training up of the young was almost exclusively the business of the matron. Great care was used to guard their children against unnecessary expenses arising from costly fashions; and to teach them to be moderate and prudent, it was constantly kept in view, that it was by hard labor that a subsistence could be procured, and that their fathers relinquished home and all its comforts and encountered the danger of the ocean, and its monsters, to procure them bread, and clothing, and home. The nature of their cares, and their common interests gave rise to the most friendly intercourse amongst them; and were the origin of that sociability, that absence of unmeaning ceremony, that cordial good will, and readiness at accommodation, which have ever characterized their descendants. They were a motherhood, ever alive to the calls of duty and of charity. They were always ready, with soothing appliances, to leave their homes to visit the sick, to whom they administered both in the capacity of nurses and physicians. Many were skilled in the use of roots and herbs, the medical properties of which they had learned from the natives. For many years the healing art was practised almost exclusively by females, and more confidence was placed in their skill than in the knowledge of men professionally educated.

The art of surgery, especially that part relating to bone-setting, was little understood by those who practised it professionally, in the early part of our history. Much suffering consequently followed accidents requiring skilful management. In process of time this difficulty was in a great measure removed by Zaccheus Macy, who, though he never studied the science, became, by long experience, assisted by good talents and accurate observation, of very singular service to the public in bone-setting and in various other branches of surgery. He subjected himself to the calls of all who needed his assistance, and, what is most remarkable in his character, as well as commendable, he never received any pecuniary reward for his services. He believed it to be his duty to serve the public without any emolument. During the time of his practice, about fifty years, he set over two thousand dislocations or broken bones, and visited his patients until they were nearly recovered. Notwithstanding his great knowledge, there were some difficult cases, which baffled his skill.

The Indians lived scattered over the island in such parts as best suited themselves. Although the emigrants early purchased their land, they were still allowed to till and improve as much as was necessary for their subsistence. When any were about to go to sea, the whites ploughed as much for them as their squaws and children could cultivate.

The Indians, being with the whites much of their time, they became conversant together, and learned each other's language, which rendered the former very useful in the whaling business, as well as in many other respects; as they were often employed by the whites in various kinds of labor.

King Philip, sachem of Mount Hope, in the year 1665, very soon after the settlement of the island by the whites, came there with a number of canoes in pursuit of an Indian, to punish him for some heinous crime. There being but a small number of English at that time, they had everything to fear. Philip's hostile appearance and preparations made them apprehensive, that he would destroy them, if any measures were taken to arrest his progress in pursuit of the delinquent. On the other hand, if they assisted to search after him, they dreaded the revenge of the island natives. They therefore declined lending their aid in any respect. Philip then went with his party in pursuit of the crimnal, and at length found him on the south-east part of the island. His name was John Gibbs; his crime was the mentioning of the name of Philip's father. Rehearsing the name of the dead, if it should be that of a distinguished person, was decreed by the natives a very high crime, for which nothing but the life of the culprit could atone. Philip, having now the poor criminal in possession, made preparations to execute vengence upon him, when the English spectators, commiserated his condition, and made offers of money to ransom his life. Philip listened to these offers and mentioned a sum which would satisfy him; but so much could not be collected. He was informed of this, but refused to lessen his demand. The whites, however, collected all they could in the short time allowed them, in hopes that he would be satisfied, when assured that more could not be found; but, instead of this, he persisted in his demand with threatening language, pronounced with an emphasis which foreboded no good. This very much provoked the English, so that they concluded among themselves to make no farther offers, but try to frighten him away without giving him any more money. The sum raised, which was all that the inhabitants possessed, was eleven pounds; this had already been paid to him, and could not be required back again. Philip had surrounded and taken possession of one or two houses, to the great terror of the inmates; in this delemnia they concluded to put all to risk;—they told him, that, if he did not immediately leave the island, the would rally the inhabitants, and fall upon him and cut him off to a man. Not knowing their defenceless condition, he happily took the alarm, and left the island as soon as possible. The prisoner was then set at liberty.

The natives early acquired a propensity to strong drink. Some of the whites were wicked enough to furnish them with rum, so long as they could pay for it, although it was done in direct violation of the law, and against the wishes and endeavors of the sober part of the inhabitants. Intemperance prevailed amongst them, and soon reduced them to a station far below what they would otherwise have held, if they had abstained from ardent spirits. By the practice of excessive drinking many were soon reduced to beggary and distress : they were regardless of the cares of their families : and owners of vessels, at the same time that they took the men into their employment, were compelled to furnish their families with the necessaries of life.

Although this was the character of many, it was not of all. Some were sober, steady people, and endeavored to cultivate religious principles among their brethren ; when this disposition was manifest, it was encouraged by the whites. They were assisted by a translation of the New Testament into their language, and encouraged to meet together for divine worship. They at one time had four meeting-houses, one towards the east end of the island, at a place called Okorwaw, near the east end of Gibb's swamp, one at Myercommet, a little south from the town, one other near Podpis, and the fourth in Plainfield, situation not exactly known.*

In these they held their religious meetings, under min-

---

*For some particulars respecting the Indian divisions of the island, &c., we refer our readers to a very interesting article in our second part, written by Zaccheus Macy, the original of which is in our possession.

isters of their own nation. Some of them patterned after the English in many respects; they built neat framed houses, kept cows, horses, and other domestic animals, and lived comfortably. But they did not long enjoy these privileges, for it was the will of Heaven to visit them with an epidemic which cut them off, except a few, and destroyed them as a nation forever. The disease was called by some the yellow fever, and by some the plague. It made its appearance among them on the 16th of the 8th month, 1763. Whether it originated with the natives, has not been ascertained. Some circumstances render it probable that the infection came out of a brig, from Ireland, which was cast ashore on the north side of the island. One of the crew appeared to have the same fever; he was brought on shore, and died at a house whither the Indians frequently resorted. Soon afterwards the disorder broke out among them, and spread to an alarming degree in a short time. The sickness was so general and severe, and the deaths so numerous, that they could not contribute to their necessities. The whites, apprehensive that the disorder would spread amongst themselves, were at first cautious in approaching the sick, but they at length found that the natives only were affected by it, for how much soever they exposed themselves, not one was taken sick. This discovery emboldened the English to go among the Indians, and render such assistance as their distressing situation demanded. They visited them daily, furnished them with provisions and clothing, and assisted in burying their dead. This care was taken by the authority of the town. The kindness of individuals was at the same time liberally extended towards them.

The sickness continued until the 16th of the second month, 1764, at which time it ceased as suddenly as it

commenced; for on the evening preceding the date just
mentioned there was no apparent abatement of the disease, but on the following morning all the sick were con-
valescent throughout their different places of abode. The
following will show the extent of the ravages of this disorder:

34 were sick and recovered.
36 living among the natives did not take the disease.
 8 living by themselves at the west end of the island, escaped.
40 lived among the whites, not one of whom had the sickness.
18 were at sea at the time, and escaped.
222 died with the disorder.
___
358 the whole number belonging to the island before the sickness.

The number of Indians having become so reduced, it is
not worth our while to trace them in a very particular
manner to their final extinction. It will be sufficient to
add, that the few who survived the sickness continued in
their wonted occupation, that of whaling; that, with few
exceptions, they would drink to excess whenever they
could have access to spirituous liquors; that many of them
perished miserably, as is the lot of the intemperate, by
sickness, or exposure, or accident; and that the last of
the race died in the year 1822.

Thus the existence of a tribe of natives terminated, and
thus their land went to strangers. In the simple charity
of nature, they received our fathers. When fugitives
from Christian prosecution, they opened to them their
stores, bestowed on them their lands, treated them with
unfailing kindness, acknowledged their superiority, tasted
their poison, and died. Their only misfortune was their
connection with Christians, and their only crime, the
imitation of their manners.

One occurrence respecting the natives ought not to be omitted. It was frequent for some of them to murmur and find fault with the English, charging them with having unfairly purchased their lands. The English endeavored to satisfy them by appealing to the records, and stating to them of whom the purchases were made; that the sachems had a good right to sell, and that their descendants ought to be satisfied therewith. These reasonings quieted them for a series of years, and always would have sufficed, had they kept clear of rum; for they seldom called this subject into view, unless they were in some degree intoxicated. At length they became so bold as to threaten the English with total extermination, if they refused any longer to listen to their complaints. Whether they intended to carry their threats into execution, and whether they had any settled plan of action to this intent, is uncertain. Intimation was however given to the whites, that the Indians had entered into a conspiracy to rise upon them, on a certain night, and to massacre men, women, and children. At the appointed time, agreeably with the information, the high sheriff, with fifty well armed men, issued out of the town to reconnoitre the settlements of the natives, and ascertain whether they were making any hostile movements. They found all quiet; it was harvest time, and the Indians were merrily husking their corn. Although their fears, for present security, were allayed, prudence dictated that the English should take some measure against future danger. They knew the natives to be quite incapable of acting for themselves in any legal process, and, therefore, lent them their aid to bring the subject before the supreme court, in Boston. This was done by a petition, of which the following is a copy :

" To his Excellency, Joseph Dudley, Esqr., Captain-general and Governor-in-chief, in and over her Majesty's Province of Massachusetts Bay, and to the honourable her Majesty's Council for the said Province.

" The humble Petition of Daniel Spotso, Abel Cain, and Peter Massaquet, all Sachems belonging to the Island of Nantucket, sheweth—

" That whereas your petitioners are very much wronged and oppressed by several of the English inhabitants of the island aforesaid, who did very much overreach your petitioners' forefathers, in the purchase of lands and hedges.—And also, in carrying away all their wood that grew both upon and under ground, to the great grief and damage of your Petitioners, and who will be forced in a short time to leave their habitations, and be utterly ruined, unless some remedy be applied for their relief. And whereas your petitioners are utterly without remedy, and cannot possibly recover their right by law at home, both Judges and Jurors being all parties in the cause, for which reason your petitioners have been feign several times to address the authority of this Province, but as yet without redress.

"Your Petitioners therefore humbly pray, that a special Court of Oyer and Terminer may be constituted and commissioned to set, at the charge of your petitioners, in Boston, with full power to hear and determine all causes that shall be brought before them in behalf of your Petitioners according to Law.

"And your Petitioners shall pray, &c.　　　Signum.

DANIEL SPOOSPOTSWA,
PETER R. MASSAQUIT,
ABEL 1.　　　2 CAIN.

" Copy examined.
　　JOS. ADDINGTON, Sec'y.

" Read in Council and directed that a copy be sent to James Coffin, Esqr., of Nantucket.

JOS. ADDINGTON, Sec'y."

It was not till several years after this, that the petition was attend to. The court at length authorized one of their body to go to Nantucket and make judicial inquiry in the premises, and act thereon, as the necessity of the

case required. Accordingly, in the year 1753, the deputed Judge arrived and convened the parties in the meeting-
house, the court-house not being sufficiently large for the
accommodation of the people. It was a subject of great.
magnitude, and drew together a large concourse of spectators.

The parties, by their deputies, were heard, the records,
and other evidence adduced, and the cause ably argued on
both sides. The trial lasted three or four days, and when
the parties had concluded, the judge addressed them in a
long and ingenious speech, wherein he explained to the
Indians, clearly and explicity, that the English had clearly
and legally purchased their lands ; that they had produced
good and lawful records to prove the same ; that these records appeared without fraud, or intention to wrong them ;
that they were the best records of purchases of land of
natives he had ever met with ; and that it was his judgment that they should be satisfied therewith, and quietly
repair to their homes. On this conclusion the court rose,
the Indians withdrew, and, though not satisfied with the
decision, were never very troublesome about it afterwards.

CHAPTER IV.

As the number of inhabitants increased, the whaling
business was carried on more extensively. Larger vessels
and a greater number were employed, requiring, conse-

quently, a greater number of men. The island did not furnish seamen enough to man the fleet, and recourse was had to various parts of Cape Cod, and thence westward as far as Long Island. From these sources there was at that time a sufficient supply of men, to render that part of the business not difficult.

Notwithstanding the consumption of oil increased in this country, the increase was not in proportion to the quantity obtained. At times the sale was dull, and the price so low, that the prospect appeared discouraging :— these circumstances caused the people to think of a foreign market for their produce. That had, for a series of years, made Boston their chief market, and, probably, would have continued to do so, had the price been adequate to their expectations ; but that not being the case, it led to inquiry what might be done to make the sale better. It was found that Nantucket had in many places become famed for whaling, and particularly so in England, where partial supplies of oil had been received through the medium of the Boston trade. The people, finding that merchants in Boston were making a good profit by first purchasing oil at Nantucket, then ordering it to Boston, and thence shipping it in their own vessels to London, determined to secure the advantages of the trade to themselves, by exporting their oil in their own vessels. They had good prospects of success in this undertaking, yet, it being a new one, they moved with great caution, for they knew that a small disappointment would lead to embarrassments that would, in the end, prove distressing. They, therefore, loaded and sent out one vessel, about the year 1745. The result of this small beginning proved profitable, and encouraged them to increase their shipments by sending out other vessels. They found, in addition to the profits on the sales, that the articles in return were such as their business required, viz. : iron, hardware, hemp, sailcloth, and many other goods, and at a much cheaper rate than they had heretofore been subjected to. This new market for the sale of their oil, and procuring necessaries for the outfits of their vessels, gave new life to the business in general, so that an increase soon manifested itself, in an additional number of vessels, and new adventurers. They continued in this line many years ; some were successful and acquired considerable estate. But, notwithstanding this general prosperity, they frequently experienced a portion of adversity, which was verified in various ways, according to the dispensations of divine providence.

In the year 1755, three whaling sloops and their crews, consisting of thirteen men each, were lost near the Grand Bank. In the year following, three more with their crews, were lost near the same place ; and six were taken and carried to France, where their crews were imprisoned, many of whom never returned. This was, perhaps, the most afflicting stroke the island had ever met with, and was a great discouragement to the business in general. The loss of twelve of their finest vessels in the short space of two years, and, what was far more distressing, the loss of nearly all their crews, either at sea or by imprisonment in France, caused a long season of gloom and mourning. Previous to this, from the beginning of the whaling up to the above date, there had been but four vessels lost with their crews, which events took place at different periods, and were not so severely felt. Notwithstanding these reverses, it was found expedient to continue the business, but in some respects with increased caution. They began now to employ vessels of larger size, some of one hundred tons burthen or more, and a few were square rigged. The whales began to be scarce at the places where they had usually been taken, which rendered it necessary to explore new coasts in search of them. A number of the larger vessels were consequently sent to Davis' Straits, to the Western Islands, and some other places, being furnished with provisions and other necessaries according to the length of the voyages. They were not always successful in these new enterprises; for every new place required experience to teach them how to take advantage of the seasons, the course of the winds and currents, as well as the habits of the whales; so that it was frequent for many vessels to return unsuccessful, though others enriched their owners by making great voyages.

Very little business besides that of whaling was carried on for many years. The attention of the people and their descendants being thus centered in one engrossing subject, they were led to project new improvements, to diminish the expense and to secure conveniences in its prosecution. Time and experience gave them advantages which made it difficult to rival them. Attempts at the business were frequently made in other parts of the country, but generally without success.

The English government, finding that the use of oil increased in England, and that it was less expensive than other light, and better adapted to light streets, gave encouragement to carry on the whaling business from their own ports. They gave so high a bounty as to induce many to engage in it, in that country, and in a few years it became a considerable business at the port of London. Although this measure was sensibly felt at Nantucket, it did not wholly stagnate the business; for the consumption of oil increased in many parts of the world, where it was carried for a market ; the exportation to England was also continued with some advantage.

The whale fishery gradually increased, and, as new countries and coasts were explored, the voyages necessarily became longer. The following schedule will show, as nearly as can be ascertained, the times when the fishery commenced at some places, previous to the revolutionary war, viz :

Davis' Straits, in the year 1746.
The Island of Disco, in the mouth of Baffin's Bay, in the year 1751.
Gulf of St. Lawrence, in the year 1761.
Coast of Guinea, in the year 1763.
Western Islands, in the year 1765.
Eastward of the Banks of Newfoundland, in the year 1765.
Coasts of Brazil, in the year 1774.

The business was also carried on in shorter voyages at the Grand Banks, Cape Verd Islands, various parts of the West Indies, in the Bay of Mexico, the Carribean Sea, and on the coast of the Spanish Main, &c. The following table shows the number of vessels, and the quantity of oil obtained within the period of ten years.

Date.	No. of Vessels.	No. of Barrels.
1762	78	9,440
1763	60	9,238
1764	72	11,983
1765	101	11,512
1766	118	11,969
1767	108	16,561
1768	125	15,439
1769	119	19,140
1770	125	14,331
1771	115	12,754
1772	98	7,825

The price of whale oil in England, was in

1742	£18	13s. per ton.
1743	£14	8s. " "
1744	£10	— " "
1753	£21	— " "

It would seem, by the preceding account, that the people were industrious, and doing well, and that the business was in a flourishing state. No one would suppose that, under these circumstances, any of the inhabitants would feel an inclination to migrate with their families to other places ; yet some, believing that they could improve their condition, removed to Nova Scotia, some to Kennebeck, some to New Garden, in the state of North Carolina, and some to other places, very few of whom benefitted themselves, and some, after a few years' stay, returned.

The inhabitants, generally, were attached to their place of nativity and were seldom desirous of leaving it. They were so closely connected by birth, similarity of pursuits, and habits of intimacy, that in some respects they appeared and conducted as one family. Perhaps there is not another place in the world, of equal magnitude, where the inhabitants were so connected by consanguinity as in this, which added much to the harmony of the people and to their attachment to the place. When strangers came to the island, the longer they stayed, the more they were pleased with the people, their manners and customs: coming with no intention of the kind, they often formed matrimonial engagements, and became inhabitants with their families.

When difficulties arose among the inhabitants, they seldom had recourse to the law for settlement, but chose the short and easy mode of arbitration, the advantages of which are numerous. Instead of one neighbor's subjecting another to many difficulties, such as are generally experienced by those who settle their dispute by the course of law, the parties would come together by appointment in the evening, having invited a sufficient number of their friends to assist, either by counsel or judgment, and without expense or animosity, but in an amicable manner would settle their differences. On the following day, the parties quietly returned to their business. This was the general manner of deciding controverted points: there were, however, some who preferred legal decisions, and who hazarded and suffered the consequences.

The society of Friends, on Nantucket, originated about or after the year 1704, when Thomas Story went there on a religious visit. He remarks, that the people were kind and hospitable, and that many of them appeared to be seeking the right way in religious matters: that he found but two of the denomination of Friends or Quakers at that time, but that the people consisted of various persuasions, and appeared glad of his company and satisfied with his visit; that he had various opportunities with many of them, and advised them to establish a meeting under the auspices and direction of the Society of Friends, since there appeared to him to be a great number who believed in their principles. His advice was attended to, and a meeting established. From this beginning the society increased from time to time. The number of members at one period was about twelve hundred, and nearly as many more attended their meetings, who were not members but fully believed in their principles.

There is much obscurity resting on the early history of the Friend's Society, at Nantucket. In the year 1708, ten persons came to the island to set up a yearly meeting. By some authority the number is stated to have been five, two of them public Friends, and the others acting only in their individual capacity. The first ministers belonging to the island were Mary Starbuck, and her son Nathaniel, Nathaniel Gardner, John Swain, and Priscilla Colman.

In 1698, Thomas Chalkley, a distinguished minister of the Society, visited the island. The following extract from his journal will, doubtless, interest many of our readers :

" The people," he remarks, " did generally acknowledge to the truth, and many of them were tender-hearted. Some of the ancient people said, That it was never known, that so many people were together on the island at once. After the first meeting was over, one asked the minister, (so called) whether we might have a meeting at his house? He said, with a good will, we might. This minister had some discourse with me, and asked, What induced me to come hither, being such a young man? I told him, that I had no other view in coming there, than the good of souls, and that I could say with the apostle, that a necessity was laid upon me, and woe would be to me, if I did not preach the gospel. Then, said he, I wish you would preach at my house in GOD's name. So next day we had a meeting at his house; and, on the first-day, we had the largest meeting that we ever had on the island. It was thought there were above two hundred people. The Lord in his power did make his truth known to the praise of his name. Oh! how was my soul concerned for that people! The Lord Jesus did open my heart to them, and theirs to him. They were also loving and kind to us. The chief magistrate of the island, desired that I would have a meeting at his house, there being no settled meeting of Friends before I came; and after meeting he disputed about religion with me. I thought we were both but poor disputants; and I cannot remember all that passed between us, but that in the close of our dispute, he said, I disputed with your friends in Barbadoes, and they told me, that we must eat the spiritual flesh, and drink the spiritual blood of Christ: And, said the Governor, did ever any one hear of such flesh and blood; for it is a contradiction in nature, that flesh and blood should be spiritual? O surely, said I, the governor has forgot himself; for what flesh and blood was that which Christ said, except ye eat my flesh and drink my blood, ye have no life in you. Why, said he, I do not think they were to gnaw it from his arms and shoulders. I then told him, he had answered himself. Thus our dispute ended. And from that time forward they have continued a meeting, and there is now a meeting-house, and a yearly meeting for worship; it is a growing meeting to this day, and several public friends are raised up amongst them, who preach the gospel of Christ freely."

"At this time a friend was convinced whose name was Starbuck, who became very serviceable, and lived and died ane minent minister of Christ, on that island. Several scores of them came and accompanied us to the water-side; and when we embarked on board our sloop, they desired that I would come and visit them again. So I recommended them to the grace of our Lord Jesus Christ, and we parted in great love and tenderness."

Chalkley visited the island again in 1704, on which occasion, he remarks :

"There were large meetings, people there being mostly Friends, and a sober growing people in the best things; though not of our society, when they first received the truth, yet they received it with gladness; and although divers of the people, called Presbyterians, were very cruel in their expressions, and bitter in their spirits against us, yet there were some who went under that name, who were more open and charitable towards us, and received us gladly with tenderuess; and at some places we had meetings at their houses to our mutual satisfaction."

In 1704, 5th month, Thomas Story visited the island. In his journal, he says :

" I now think proper to give a general relation of the state of the people in the island of Nantucket, with respect to religion, at this time. This small island is inhabited by a mixed people of various nations, and some among them called Christian Indians, but no settled teachers of any kind. There was in this island one Nathaniel Starbuck, whose wife was a wise, discreet woman, well read in Scripture, and not attached unto any sect, but in great reputation throughout the island for her knowledge in matters of religion, and an oracle among them on that account, in so much that they would not do any thing without her advice and consent therein."

"14th. At our landing, we went up to the house of the widow, Mary Gardner; where, after some refreshment, came to us Nathaniel Starbuck, (husband of Mary Starbuck, before mentioned) and his son of the same name; and we proposed to them to have a meeting that day; but there being a court to sit there, by special commission, upon an Indian accused for murdering his wife, we found it improper at that time; and some of our company went home with Nathaniel Starbuck the elder, and others with his son; where we were kindly entertained, though we were strangers, and they at that time not in the profession of truth with us."

"15th. We had a meeting at the house of Nathaniel Starbuck the elder; which was pretty large and open, several of the people being tendered, and generally satisfied with what they heard and felt of the goodness and mercy of God."

"16th. Being first of the week, we had another meeting there, which was not so large as was expected. Many of the inhabitants of this island are convinced of the truth of some points of the doctrine of truth, and some of them have been reached by the Divine virtue and power of it; but some other things they do not yet see, and, if there were no cross, would, in all appearance, come generally under our profession."

"17th. This evening we ascended toward the upper part of the island, to John Swain's (one who came to our meetings, and there was only one more, that is, Stephen Hussey, in all that island under our name,) and there we met with a great company of Indians and other people together, having been raising a timber house for him."

"18th. We had a large, good meeting there among the people; and, that evening returned to Nathaniel Starbuck's the younger, and there lodged."

"19th. We had another large, good meeting, at Nathaniel Starbuck's the elder, his wife, Mary, as before hinted, being the first in that island, who had any regard to the way of truth as among us; but now her three sons and daughters, and sons' wives, are all in a hopeful way to the knowledge of truth, and liberty of the sons of God, with several other tender people at this time, in that small island."

"23rd. 5th month. Being first of the week, we had another large, open meeting at Nathaniel Starbuck's, senior; where several were tendered and comforted; but it was a little bodily exercising and painful to me, for, having a sore throat, and not willing to spare myself, I spit much blood in the time of my ministry."

"One night, before we returned from this island, my sleep was taken from me, under a concern of mind for the settlement of a meeting there, and the chief instrument pointed to in my thoughts, by the truth, for this service, when we should be gone, was Mary Starbuck, before mentioned, to whom I made it known; and in the opening and mind of truth, laid a charge upon her, to endeavor to have a meeting established in their family, once a week, at least, to wait upon the LORD, with all who were convinced of truth in the neighborhood, and in the island, as they had conveniency. This she received with christian gravity, and it affected her much, and became her concern. Having first mentioned it to the friends who were with me, I proposed it likewise to her children, who were all discreet young men and women, most of them married, and hopeful; being all convinced of truth, they were ready to embrace the proposal. Then I advised them to wait sincerely upon the Lord in such meetings, (for they had no instrumental teachers,) and assured them, that I had a firm confidence in the Lord, that he would visit them by his Holy Spirit in them, in his own time, if they were faithful, held on, and did not faint, or look back. And accordingly, some time after we departed the island, they did meet, and the Lord did visit them, and gathered many there unto himself; and they became a large and living meeting in him, and several living and able ministers raised by the Lord in that family, and of others; to the Honor of his own Arm, who is worthy forever."

In the 7th month, 1746, John Griffith, another minister of distinction, of the same society, visited the island, and stayed about six days. He was at their yearly and quarterly meetings, "having good satisfaction therein." He also visited the island in the 6th month, 1766, but did not find the religious condition of the people so satisfactory as before. He says:

" On sixth day the yearly meeting began, and was very large; a becoming plainness appeared in the general; but, alas! the life of religion was very much departed from by numbers in that once truly amiable place, so much noted for a family of love. I went on the island as a stranger to their present state, though I had been there twice before, a witness of better times: much distressing anguish was felt in this meeting, and for some time I expected the current of life would have been wholly obstructed; but at length, through divine mercy, truth arose with gospel authority, setting forth what a great and wonderful manifestation of evangelical light and truth sprung up in the last century, after a dark night of apostacy and error; when the heavenly power being embraced, brought forth the nature and spirit of religion; but endeavors now are too often, to support the same principles in a formal way, by strength and wisdom of man, the Lord, therefore, will not own a people in that state. Many things were delivered on this subject with great dread, and I felt the Lord's power go forth as a fire amongst the briars and thorns; many were struck with sadness and fear, and the everlasting name was exalted: Thomas Gawthorp was there also, and had good service. The meeting ended on second-day, much gospel labor having been bestowed in the several sittings thereof. Notwithstanding the general state of Friends on that island appeared truly deplorable, yet, I believe, a remnant are and will be preserved, fresh and lively in religion. May the number increase."

The people who first settled the Island and their immediate successors, lived to a great age, many to eighty and some over ninety years. But, about the year 1739, the number of old people was greatly lessened; from what cause we shall not presume to surmise. The oldest male inhabitant died that year, aged 73 years; there were probably some females living who exceeded that age, for it has been remarked that they live generally longer than males. Since that time the number of aged people has increased very much. In the year 1810, there were 210 over 70 years of age, more than 60 of whom were over 80, but none exceeded 90. Of the 210, just mentioned,

122 were females, and the proportion of aged women, compared with the aged men, has considerably increased since that time. We have never known any inhabitant of the island to live 100 years, though several have nearly attained that age, and many have exceeded 90 years.

Of the diseases of the island, lung affections may be named as the most fatal, yet it is doubtful whether they are more prevalent here than on the seacoasts generally, in this latitude. Bilious intermittents occasionally occur, in autumn, and scarlet fever has been twice epidemic within forty years.

The small pox has frequently made its appearance on the island, but, through the vigilance of the people, it has never prevailed to a great extent. Whenever any have been attacked with it, they have been immediately removed from the town, and conveyed to some secluded situation. This disease, always alarming, has been rendered peculiarly so to the people of Nantucket, in consequence of their local situation. Whenever it has made its appearance among them, they have justly apprehended, that if it should spread to a considerable extent, its ravages would be the more distressing, by preventing necessary supplies being brought to them from the continent, except at exorbitant prices.

This, and other considerations, caused the people to take more than common precautions against the disease, whenever it was brought to the island. Many of the inhabitants were of the opinion, that, could the inoculation for the disease be established at some place remote from the town, and conducted with care, it would relieve many who were fearful of its contagion, and prove very beneficial to the community at large. An establishment for this purpose was therefore encouraged, and in the year

1771, Dr. Samuel Gelston selected Gravelly Island, which seemed the most suitable situation, for the location of an hospital. Houses were accordingly built, and the business commenced. But it was not long before the people began to murmur, and express their dissatisfaction with the measure; for some who had been there to be inoculated, were so careless as to put the inhabitants in danger of taking the disease on their return. The uneasiness increased so much, that the town, having convened several times on the occasion, at length caused a remonstrance against the inoculation to be sent to the Governor, requesting his aid to suppress it. This put a stop to the business for a time, but it was resumed in 1778, when the town again took measures to put a stop to it, and at length agreed with the doctor, he relinquishing the business, to buy his buildings at cost, which they accordingly did, and paid him the amount of his bills, viz.: £1072 17s. 6d. old tenor.

From the best information that can be obtained, ten persons have been hanged on the island, since it was settled by the English. They were all native Indians, and the crime of each was murder. The first execution, of which we have any particular account, took place in 1704, the last in 1769.*

The putting to death of these persons was, of course, in accordance with the requirements of the law of the land, and cannot be considered as expressing the opinion of the inhabitants on that mode of punishment. We be-

---

* Their names were as follows: Finch, 1704; Sabo, Jo Nobby, 1736; Heppy Comfort, 1739; John Comfort, 1745; Henry Jude, 1750; Tom Ichabod, Joel Elisa, Simon Hews, Nathan Quibby, 1769.

lieve the sentiments of this community are, and always have been, strongly against capital punishments.

Taking the lives of human beings, as an expiation for the most heinous crimes, has so long been practiced throughout the world, that the greater part of mankind have become reconciled to the measure : they seem to have become fully convinced that this punishment is absolutely necessary for the safety of society, and justifiable in the sight of God. Notwithstanding this practice has been long established, and has often been supported by the authority of the Old Testament, we think it not amiss to state our conviction that it is altogether wrong. The subject is one of great importance, and we trust, that a few remarks upon it will not be deemed improper in this place. We are fully sensible, that it is not an easy matter to convince mankind of their error, if it be such, neither is it our expectation to bring about so desirable an object : but we think it is quite time 'for the rulers of the land, particularly those of the denomination of *Christians*, to make a 'pause, for we are persuaded that much depends on them to govern and lead the people aright. It appears by the laws of England, that there were one hundred and sixty offences, not long ago, punishable with death, while in the United States the number does not exceed ten ; how is this difference reconciled, when both nations profess to be led by the same unerring example and precepts of our Saviour.

When a criminal is deprived of life, by the laws of his country, he is either in a good or bad state, as to his never-dying soul. If he has become truly penitent, and received full assurance of forgiveness for his past sins, of which, in some instances there can hardly be a doubt, how awful is it, that his life should be taken from him, by the power of

man, in that state of innocency.   Perhaps, if permitted
to live, he would become a useful member of society, and
contribute to the wants of his family and friends, who,
besides being benefited by his services, would be rescued
from that reproach, which an ignominious death, however
unguilty, entails upon the decendants of the culprit, even
unto the fourth generation.   On the other hand, if he is
deprived of life in a state of wickedness, how much more
awful is the case, taking the truth of the subject into
view, that a soul will thus be hurried to perdition to satisfy
a law, which is not warranted by any part of the New
Testament.   Shall we act counter to that guide, by which
we profess to be governed, and yet say, that we do so under a sense of religious duty.   Let us, for a moment, re-
flect, how much more commendable it would be, in the
sight of Him who rewards us for every good deed, to
restrain the criminal of his liberty, and use our utmost
endeavors to reconcile him to his fellow man, and restore
him to peace with his Maker.   "There is joy in the presence of the angels of God over one sinner that repent-
eth."

Much might be said on this very interesting subject,
but it is not our intention to enlarge this work by discus-
sing matters that may be considered irrelevant to it.   We
leave the subject for more able writers, with strong desire
that a reform may take place, not doubting that it would
prove a blessing to society, and be productive of increased
harmony, to wholly annul the laws by which criminals
are deprived of life.

CHAPTER V.

Between the years 1770 and 1775, the whaling business increased to an extent hitherto unparalleled. In 1770, there were a little more than one hundred vessels engaged; and in 1775, the number exceeded one hundred and fifty, some of them large brigs. The employment of so great and such an increasing capital may lead our readers to suppose, that a corresponding profit was realized, but a careful examination of the circumstances, under which the business was carried on, will show the fallacy of such a conclusion. Many branches of labor were conducted by those who were immediately interested in the voyages. The young men, with few exceptions, were brought up to some trade necessary to the business. The rope-maker, the cooper, the blacksmith, the carpenter, in fine, the workmen, were either the ship owners or of their household; so were often the officers and men who navigated the vessels and killed the whales. Whilst a ship was at sea, the owners at home were busily employed in the manufactory of casks, iron work, cordage, blocks and other articles for the succeeding voyage. Thus the profits of the labor were enjoyed by those interested in the fishery, and voyages were rendered advantageous even when the oil obtained was barely sufficient to pay the outfits, estimating the labor as a part thereof. This mode of conducting the business was universal, and has continued to a very considerable extent to the present day.

Experience taught the people how to take advantage of the different markets for their oil. Their spermaceti oil was mostly sent to England in its unseparated state, the head matter being generally mixed with the body oil; for, in the early part of whaling, it would bring no more when separated than when mixed. The whale oil, which is the kind procured from the species called "right whales," was shipped to Boston or elsewhere in the colonies, and there sold for country consumption, or sent to the West Indies.

The first manufactory of sperm candles in this country was established in Rhode Island, a little previous to 1750, by Benjamin Crab, an Englishman. His candle-house was burnt in 1750 or 1751. In 1753, Obadiah Brown (the father of Moses Brown, a distinguished member of the Society of Friends, now living), erected candle-works at Tockwotten, now India Point, in Providence, and engaged the above-mentioned Benjamin Crab, to conduct the business. After this, in 1754 or 1755, Moses Lopez engaged in the same business, but not extensively, at Newport. Collins & Reveria, Aaron Lopez, John Mausley & Co., Thomas Robinson, and others soon followed. Obadiah Brown, in 1753, manufactured about three hundred barrels, which was nearly all that was in that year saved separate from body oil, and not sent to England. He was disappointed of the information which he expected to receive from Crab, and was obliged to learn the secret of refining by his own experiments. In 1761, there were eight manufactories in New England, and one in Philadelphia.

The candle manufactories gave just enough for head matter to encourage its being separated. Their art was kept secret a considerable time ; they suffered no person to enter their works, but such as were immediately concerned therein. At length, in 1772, one of the most enterprising men belonging to Nantucket found means to obtain the desired knowledge, and established himself in the business. He continued in this line several years, and acquired a large property. Stimulated by his success, others were led to make various experiments, till at length they acquired a knowledge of the art, and gained great profits from it. Thus, by degrees, the manufacture of sperm candles became more and more general, till at length all, who possessed the means of carrying it on, were enabled to share in its advantages.

As the whaling business increased from year to year, and finally gained the pre-eminence over all other branches, the cod fishery in the same ratio dwindled, till it was pursued by a very small number as a permanent business.

The farmers, however, and some of the mechanics, in the spring and autumn, made it their practice to fish at Siasconsett and Sesacacha, on the east side of the island, in boats from the shore. Here they frequently removed their families and resided during the fishing seasons.

The following table, copied from a report to Congress, by Thomas Jefferson, shows the state of the whale fishery in Massachusetts, between the years 1771 and 1775:

STATE OF THE WHALE FISHERY, IN MASSACHUSETTS, FROM 1771 TO 1775.

Ports from which the equipments were made.	Vessels fitted out annually for the northern fish'ry.	Their tonnage.	Vessels fitted out annually for the southern fish'ry.	Their tonnage.	Seamen employed.	Barr'ls of spermaceti oil taken annually.	Barr'ls of whale oil taken annually.
Nantucket, ...	65	4,875	85	10,200	2,025	26,000	4,000
Wellfleet, ...	20	1,600	10	1,000	420	2,250	1,250
Dartmouth, ...	60	4,500	20	2,000	1,040	7,200	1,400
Lynn, ...	1	75	1	120	28	200	100
Martha's Vineyard, . .	12	720	—	—	156	900	300
Barnstable, ...	2	150	—	—	26	240	—
Boston, ...	15	1,300	5	700	260	1,800	600
Falmouth, Barnstable Co.,	4	300	—	—	52	400	—
Swanzey, ...	4	300	—	—	52	400	—
	183	13,820	121	14,020	4,059	39,390	7,650

" The average price in the market, for a few years previous to the war, was about forty pounds sterling per ton, for spermaceti oil; and fifty pounds sterling for head matter.* The average price of whale oil was about seventy dollars, per ton. A whale producing about one hundred and twenty barrels of oil will generally produce about two thousand pounds of bone. A whale producing fifty or sixty barrels of oil, will generally produce nearly ten pounds of bone to the barrel. The bone was chiefly exported to Great Britain, the price about half a dollar per pound."

In 1774, the inhabitants of the island were much troubled by the anticipated war between the colonies and Great Britain. The Americans, believing they had just cause of resentment on account of the usage of the British government from time to time, often manifested a spirit of resistance. This being early discovered by the government, coercive measures were pursued to check the discontent, which, instead of soothing, served rather to irritate the colonists. Massachusetts was considered the leader of the rebellion, as it was then called, and the measures of the government were particularly directed against that province. It appeared to many, that, if the English government had used mild measures to convince the colonies of their error, if it had heard their petitions and carefully investigated the grounds of their complaints, the difficulties then existing might have been removed so far as to prevent a war. Instead of this, force was used to bring about a reconciliation, and acts were passed to restrain the liberties of the people. " The Massachusetts Bay restraining Bill " was passed, intended to restrain the trade and commerce of the provinces of " New England to Great Britain, Ireland and the British islands in the West

---

* The average prices at Nantucket, in the settlement of voyages, from 1769 to 1775, were for spermaceti oil, £35, and for head matter £44.

Indies," and to prohibit their carrying on any fishery on the Banks of Newfoundland and other places mentioned in the bill. The extreme severity of this act caused long and violent debates in Parliament. If carried into effect, it would have been a heavy blow to merchants in London, in the West Indies, and in other parts, who traded in New England: petitions were, therefore, forwarded by them to Parliament, praying that the bill might not be carried into operation. Among other petitions was one presented by the Society of Friends, in England, setting forth, "That a great number of innocent persons, particularly in the island of Nantucket, would, by the prohibitory bill, be reduced to extreme distress. The inhabitants of this island amounted to between five and six thousand in number: the soil of it was so barren, that, though fifteen miles in length, and three in breadth, its produce was scarce sufficient for the maintenance of twenty families. From the only harbor this island contains, without natural products of any sort, the inhabitants, by an astonishing industry, kept an hundred and forty vessels constantly employed. Of these, eight were occupied in the importation of the necessary provisions, and the rest in the whale fishery: which, with invincible courage and perseverance, they had extended from the frozen regions of the North, to the coast of Africa, the Brazils, and even as far South as the Falkland Islands, and some of their fishing voyages continued twelve months." The petition, after expatiating on the innocence, industry, and utility of this colony, the great hazards attending their occupation, and the uncertainty of their gain, showed, that, if the bill passed into a law, they must in a short time be exposed to all the miseries of a famine. The singular situation and circumstances of these people, caused some attention to be paid to them ; and the administration, in all its obstinacy, was abliged to relax a little and afford the relief, which with so much reason had been asked and expected.

The tenor of the above-mentioned petition, and its effects in favor of Nantucket, by causing the obnoxious part of the bill to be struck out, is another proof, among many, that good policy would dictate to the inhabitants of Nantucket, in all cases of national differences, to remain neutral, and manifest that quiet and peaceable disposition, which has ever marked their character among all christian nations.

It appears that the bill, with some modifications, became a law, but its effect was very different from what was expected by the promotors of it : for, as a consequence of it, the British fisheries in Newfoundland, suffered a diminution of near 500,000 pounds sterling.

As many may be interested to know the number of inhabitants on the island, at different periods after its settlement, we shall here exhibit such information on the subject as we have been able to collect, but we cannot vouch for its authenticity in every particular. The records of the town are deficient in information concerning early transactions, and almost silent as respects the census of the island. We introduce the following table now because it will here be convenient to refer to it to see the effect of the revolutionary war on the numbers of the inhabitants :

In the year 1719 there were 721 white inhabitants.
English families, between 1722 and 1724, 170.
In the year 1726 there were 917 inhabitants.
    "   1764   "   3220   "
    "   1774   "   4545   "
    "   1784   "   4269   "
    "   1790   "   4620   "

In the year 1800 there were 5617 inhabitants.
"   1810   "   6807   "
"   1820   "   7266   "
"   1830   "   7202   "

On examining the foregoing schedule, it will be seen, that, during the Revolutionary war, instead of a gradual increase of inhabitants, the number lessened 276. If there had been no war, it is to be presumed that the increase between 1774 and 1784 would have been a little greater than during the ten preceding years. Between 1764 and 1774 the increase was 1325, this number added to 276, the decrease during the war, making 1601, may fairly be taken as the least number that lost their lives during the conflict between the nations, with the exception of about twenty families which removed to other places.

If we could justify any war, it would be that of the Revolution. Repeated injuries were heaped upon the colonists, which, we allow, it was their duty to notice, in a firm and decided manner. Respecting, as we do, and that most sincerely, the rights of man, we have little sympathy with those who supinely submit to unprovoked injuries. In the dignity of Christian charity we bear and forbear, but our endurance then is a defence which even tyranny, will eventually respect. To feel an injury, and to revenge it, are very different things : the highest merit of forbearance consists in the keenest sense of wrong. While then we would bear testimony against all wars, and every species of violence between man and man, we would encourage all to defend their social and individual rights, to cherish self-respect, and maintain their independence ; and we believe that there are ample means for this purpose, without resort to blood, and that wars and fightings are the causes, rather than the remedies of oppression. A course of proceeding which throws two nations into mourning over the harm which they have reciprocally done to each other, seems a strange way of deciding between right and wrong. Let the consequences of war be considered apart from the vain glory, and martial equipments, and mighty enterprises, and great talents, and enthusiastic excitement, which are associated with it; let plunder, and rapine and death; let ghastly wounds, mutilated limbs, loathsome disease, and famine and poverty; let the widow, the childless, the orphan; let the crimes of lawless passion, and the permanent injury to moral and christian virtues, be considered, and who will say that wars are the best means, nay, who will say that they should ever be resorted to, for the purpose of deciding a national dispute? Who is there, that, clothed with the spirit of true christianity, can justify war; when, before it commences, we are sensible of the destruction and misery that must ensue? Alas for man that he is blinded to his best interest!

Previous to entering upon the various scenes occasioned by the approaching war, it may not be amiss to give a statement of the prices of various articles of common consumption, at different dates. Our information on this subject is not extensive, but it is collected from sources which may be depended on as correct; it will serve to show the difference between the value of merchandise or of money, at given dates, and the present time. The prices are given in old tenor, or forty-five shillings to a dollar.

		£	s.	d.
1712	Molasses per gallon,	0	2	6
"	Tobacco per pound,	0	0	6
1713	1 day's mowing,	0	3	0

		£	s.	d.
1713	1 day's carting rocks,	0	3	0
"	1 " threshing,	0	3	6
"	1 ewe sheep,	0	7	0
"	1 pound butter,	0	0	10
"	1 " fresh pork,	0	0	2
"	1 " hay-seed,	0	2	0
1714	1 " beef,	0	0	3¼
"	1 " veal,	0	0	3
"	Weaving cotton and linen, per yard,	0	0	6
1715	" kersey, ell wide,	0	0	8
"	" plain linen,	0	0	8
"	" kersey,	0	0	10
"	" worsted for shirts,	0	0	9
"	1 bushel wheat,	0	6	0
"	1 " barley,	0	2	6
"	1 " corn, till 1730,	0	6	0
"	1 cord wood,	0	14	0
1718	1 quintal fish,	1	6	0
1719	Board for a man, in a private family, per week,	0	6	0
1720	Ploughing, per acre,	0	12	0
1722	Fine wool, per pound,	0	1	6
1723	Yoke of oxen,	14	0	0

The following short schedule will show the prices of a few articles the year preceding the war. The great advance in the value of some articles, found in both statements, may fairly be taken as a criterion for the whole; and will show, with some allowance for the time between 1723 and 1774, the effect of the political aspect of affairs on the value of merchandise generally.

The prices are here, also, given in old tenor currency.

In 1774.

	£	s.	d.
Russia Duck, per piece,	30	0	0
Ravens " "	21	0	0
Sugar, per cwt.,	17	0	0
Coffee, per lb.,	0	9	0

	£	s.	d.
Molasses, per gallon,	0	13	0
Salt, per bushel,	1	2	6
Wood, per cord,	5	12	6
Flour, per cwt.,	7	0	0
Corn, per bushel,	1	2	6
Beef, per barrel,	19	0	0
Wool, per lb.,	0	9	0
Men's shoes, per pair,	2	15	0
Women's shoes, per pair,	2	5	0
Cheese, per lb.,	0	3	6
Butter, "	0	5	$7\frac{1}{4}$
Bohea tea,	2	5	0

The apprehension of war, between this country and England, increased daily. In view of the infant state of the country, this event was dreaded by many, and more particularly by the inhabitants of this island, who had more reasons to deplore a war than the country generally. Their situation was such as to render them exposed to the ravages of an enemy, without the means of making any defence. Being surrounded by the sea, they could be assailed from any quarter, and were liable to be plundered by any petty cruisers which might visit them for that purpose. It was clearly foreseen that the inhabitants could derive no protection from our own country. These considerations filled the minds of the people generally with very serious apprehensions: while others endeavored to be patient, under whatever sufferings might befall them, placing their confidence in that power which it is beyond the reach of man to control. But knowing that nothing could be done to prevent a war, each one hoped for the best, and waited the awful moment with the keenest anxiety that the human mind can conceive. In the mean time prudence dictated that those who had property exposed, which could be secured from the grasp of an enemy, should take care of it in season. Many, by taking this precaution, happily saved what afterwards proved the means of their subsistence.

Towards the close of the year 1774, there were one hundred and fifty sail of vessels, in the whaling service, belonging to the island, and the greater part of them at sea. The owners at this time concluded to strip and haul them up as fast as they arrived, in hopes that the impending storm might blow over without any serious consequences. But, alas! how frail is man, and how blind to future events.

In the early part of 1775, there appeared no doubt that hostilities would soon break out. The country, in the mean time, was making every preparation ·for war of which its defenceless situation would admit. The long expected period at length arrived: even before spring closed, the first blood was spilt in the battle at Lexington. The news of this action spread rapidly to every part of the colonies; in a few days it arrived at Nantucket. The countenances of the people, here, bespoke the anguish of their hearts. All business was immediately at a stand. Discouraged and powerless, they could do little else than meet together and bemoan their fate. Sorrow was depicted on every countenance; every mind was overwhelmed with fearful anticipations, all springing from one general cause—the war. Many were deeply concerned for the welfare of their husbands, children, or brothers, then at sea, on whom they depended for their subsistence and the comforts of life; many were anxious on account of their property, both at home and at sea, on which their dependence was placed. A common distress pervaded all hearts, which was in no way relieved by anticipations of the future. No system of future business could be fixed on;

many believing, that, notwithstanding some blood had been shed, the difficulty would yet be settled, and business be again safely resumed; but others, and the greater part, were of the opinion that the contest would be long and terrible. Time proved the latter to be correct.

The vessels belonging to the island mostly arrived home in safety, for the English government cherished a belief, that, by quelling the difficulties in the province of Massachusetts Bay, the whole country besides would comply with the requisitions demanded of them; they, therefore, did not send out their cruisers in great numbers, until they found their mistake; which gave an opportunity for the whalemen to get home, though many of them were on the coast of Guinea and Brazil, at the commencement of hostilities.

The inhabitants were now driven from their wonted line of business into a state of inactivity, in which many of the laboring poor could not long subsist without a change. Some of these entered into the service of the country by joining the army, others engaged on board of privateers, few of whom ever returned to the island. A few families removed to various parts of the country, chiefly to the provinces of New York and North Carolina. But the bulk of the people concluded to remain in the place of their nativity, and do the best they could, although the prospect was gloomy, let them look which way they would. The property of some was so situated that they could not leave it; others could not remove their families, through want of means.

Whaling having now ceased, the wharves and shores were, for a while, lined with vessels, stripped to their naked masts. The people, however, soon began to turn their attention to fishing on the shoals, and round the shores of the island; and many, to save what property they had acquired, went into the farming business. In one or another of these pursuits all, for a time, found employment. This entire change of business created new thoughts, new ideas, and new conversation, such as would hardly have been understood previous to the commencement of difficulties. Fishing boats, and small fishing vessels, and farming tools, were chiefly called for in the mechanical line, and with these the people went earnestly to work, but with heavy hearts, not knowing how soon they might be deprived of even these means of subsistence by the sacking or burning of the town.

All this was but a specimen of what they were destined to endure. They soon found themselves wholly cut off from all kinds of imported goods. Necessity, however, invented substitutes for many of these, and the same necessity taught that others were not absolutely indispensable. The price of salt was much enhanced, and without it they could derive little advantage from fishing. This encouraged a number of persons to establish salt-works. One company set them up on Brant Point, at the entrance of the harbor; but various causes combined to check their progress, so that very little salt was made. Another company established their works at Podpis, or Polpis, which is up harbor, according to common expression, about five miles east from the town. They made considerable salt, but not enough to compensate for their expenses; so that both companies relinquished their business. Probably the principal reason for their not succeeding was the fog, which prevails around the shores in the summer season, and, keeping the air moist, prevents the water from evaporating as rapidly as the business requires.

West India produce of all kinds, as well as salt, soon became excessively high; and a prospect of profitable business for all was thus presented, too flattering to be disregarded. The harbor was full of vessels of just the right size for the West India trade, many of the owners had oil, candles, fish, lumber, and other articles, in demand, in the West Indies, while an equally good market was promised for such of their return cargoes as should be fortunate enough to escape the enemy. It was a dangerous business, and very few were singly able to fit out a whole vessel, and bear up under a loss, if that should be their fate. A considerable number would, therefore, join and load a vessel in small proportions, which, by experience, was found to be the best way. On this plan a few vessels were soon got away, and, such as returned in safety, made very profitable voyages: for all kinds of American produce sold at great prices, and, in return, West India produce was in great demand. Salt sold from two to four dollars a bushel, and molasses for a dollar a gallon.

This line of business succeeded well, till the British took possession of a number of American seaports, and were thus enabled to send out numerous small privateers. The coast of America was soon so thronged with these, that it was difficult for vessels to arrive in safety. Built, as the latter were, for great burdens, and to be easy and safe at sea, they stood little chance of escape, when pursued by English cruisers. The business, therefore, which commenced so prosperously, soon became exceedingly hazardous. The loss of property by capture was a small evil, compared with the sufferings of those who were made prisoners. As soon as the British took possession of Rhode Island and New York, they established prison-ships, in which thousands of American seamen were pent up, and thousands perished, either through want of the necessaries of life, or by loathsome diseases, engendered by their wretched situation and inhuman treatment.

The Nantucket people now began to feel the misery and distress, which they early anticipated and dreaded. They had had no conception, indeed, of the destructive prison-ship; it was for the refinements of war to invent that capacious instrument of prolonged torture; but they had always been sensible that their situation was such, as to expose them to an uncommon share of suffering, even under the milder aspect of a national conflict.

Although the West India business proved so disastrous on account of the loss of lives, as well as of property, it was still prosecuted, as there appeared no other way of employment. The safe arrival of two or three vessels animated the people greatly, and encouraged them to fit out still more largely.

As the sound was continually infested with cruisers, it was difficult to procure that supply of provisions and fuel, which they otherwise would have received from different places on the continent. This was soon severely felt by the inhabitants, and led them to use every means that invention could devise, or necessity execute, to obtain their necessary supplies. Sometimes strangers, with the prospect of high prices, would venture to the island with such articles as were most needed, and take in exchange fish, salt, oil, &c. A number of the inhabitants ran open sail boats to Connecticut, and elsewhere, with salt and other articles, and brought back provisions and other supplies. They chose those boats, because they could pass Rhode Island in them with greater safety, during the night, than in vessels. And, notwithstanding the danger of navigating such frail barks, they selected the most stormy nights, even in winter, to pass ports in possession of the enemy; for they had rather encounter the hazard of foundering at sea, than of falling into the hands of the British. By these means, and with what breadstuff was raised on the island, the people were prevented, and in many instances barely prevented, from suffering to death.

As long as the vessels lasted, they afforded employment for the poorer class; but their number lessened very fast. The loss of these, however, was not the greatest evil which the people had to sustain. The prison-ship was much more dreaded. Whenever a vessel or boat was seen coming from any quarter, anxiety of mind was depicted on every countenance. All were dependent in some degree on casualties abroad; those, who had property at stake, were desirous of hearing from it; but above all, those who had fathers, husbands, brothers, or other connections, absent from home, were watching, with anxious eyes, every sail that made its appearance, or listening, with intense interest, to catch some tidings from their friends; apprehensive, the while, that the next news would blast forever all their hopes of earthly comfort and happiness. In the middle and latter part of the war, accounts from abroad were rarely received, which did not tell of the death of one or more of the people belonging to the place.

The few, that returned from the prison-ships, gave the most melancholy account of the sufferings of the prisoners. The provisions, which they had to eat, were the most filthy that could be procured, infested with bugs, weavels and maggots; and of even these they were furnished with not half enough to satisfy the cravings of nature. Their scanty pittance of water was offensive to the smell, filthy, and poisonous. A great number of persons were confined within the narrow limits of the sides of the ship; they were overrun with tormenting vermin; on every side the eye rested on the dead, and the ear was assailed with the groans of the dying. These startling and horrid truths wrought so forcibly on the minds of those whose necessities impelled them to follow the sea for a subsistence, and so disquieted the hearts of their wives and children, who must be left in anxious uncertainty both in regard to their future means of subsistence, and the fate of their near relatives, as to bring a gloom over the face of society, too deep and too heartfelt to be described. But untimely deaths and severe sufferings were not confined to prisoners alone; many perished at sea, in consequence of venturing in vessels constructed with a principal view to fast sailing. These vessels were long and sharp, they were built of frail materials, and purposely made weak in order that, by degrees of pliability, they might pass more easily through the water. When pursued by an enemy, they were sometimes subjected to so heavy a press of sail, as to run under and never rise again. The ways were numerous, and the places various, in which the people of Nantucket lost their lives during the war; their sufferings were long felt, deeply deplored, and they will never be forgotten.

Provision, notwithstanding what was raised on the island, or brought from the continent, was at times very scarce and dear; and many suffered by want, having no means to buy and no employment by which to earn any thing. After a few years of the war had expired, those who had property left did not care to risk it abroad, finding that the danger of capture had materially increased; thus a large number were left in a state of inactivity. Many of the middle class, at the commencement of the war, had some hundreds of dollars by them, which they had saved out of their earnings; but they were now under the necessity of disposing of their past savings for the support of their families. Some of this class became exhausted by the middle, others by the latter part of the war.

Corn was frequently three dollars a bushel, and some times more; flour was thirty dollars a barrel, and other bread stuff proportionably dear. This would not have been so severely felt, had there been business adequate thereto; but a total want of employment with the major part of the people rendered it very distressing.

As wood was one of the articles for which the inhabitants were dependent on the continent, it was soon discovered that a new source or substitute must be found; for the coasters, who had usually brought it, turned their attention another way, on account of the risk of capture. Even if a plentiful supply had been brought to the island, few, for the reasons before mentioned, would have been able to buy. The distress, however, was not so great for fuel, as it was for bread. Various substitutes for the former presented themselves, which were readily and thankfully adopted. One was peat, of which an abundance was yearly produced, and which was found to be excellent firing. Some dug up the shrub oaks with their roots, which answered a very good purpose; some, in the winter season, cut brush in the swamps, which burned well, but did not make a durable fire. Others, who had no horses, went "up the harbor" in boats to Coetue, and Coskata, in an easterly direction from the town, from six to ten miles, where, with hard labor, they procured large quantities of pretty good firing, mostly oak, cedar, and juniper, sometimes called savin.

It seems proper to introduce, in this place, a valuation of the ratable property of the island, made in the year 1778, under the authority of the " State of Massachusetts Bay." It is as follows, viz :—

Polls ratable,	970	
"　not ratable,	31	
Dwelling-houses, barns, and other buildings not hereafter specially mentioned, with all yards, gardens and passage-ways to the same belonging,	604	
The just value of the same,		£35,633 5s
Acres or parts of acres of upland, mowing, orcharding and tillage land,	1,566	
The just value of the same,		£14,688
Acres salt and fresh meadow;	270	
The just value of the same,		£4,050
Acres of pasture land,	14,260	
The just value of the same,		£55,840
Acres of woodland and unimproved land,	7,380	
The just value of the same,		£4,338
Wharves of all sorts, and the just value of the same,		£1,708 2s 4d
Still-houses, furnaces, mills of all sorts and iron works,	4	
The just value of the same,		£295
Money at interest and on hand, more than they are indebted,		£11,222 16s 8d
Debts due not on interest, more than they are indebted,		£3,732 10s
The amount of all goods, wares, merchandises and stock in trade,		£8,257 8s
Vessels of all sorts, with their stores, and the true value thereof, whether at home or abroad,		£12,860 8s
Ounces of plate,	1,780	
Horses of all ages,	270	
The just value,		£4,860

Oxen, 4 years old and upwards,	54	
The just value,		£406
Cows, 3 years old and upwards,	540	
The just value,		£3,888
Steers, 3 years old, and all other horned cattle under that age,	155	
Their value,		£620
Sheep and goats of all ages,	9,938	
Their value,		£3,975 4s
Swine of all ages,	299	
Their value,		£430 11s
Grain of all sorts and kinds, and all other produce of the land whatsoever on hand, the just value of the same,		£501
Coaches, chaises, and all carriages of that kind, and all other property whatsoever not before enumerated, except household furniture, wearing apparel, farming utensils, and the tools of mechanics, the just value of the same,		£482
The amount of all the estate, both real and personal, of those persons that shall be doomed by the assessors,		£—
Tons of English hay, one year with another,	243	
Tons of salt and fresh meadow hay, one year with another,	162	
Bushels of corn and grain of all sorts, one year with another,	10,800	
Number of cows the pasture will keep, one year with another,	2,587	
Barrels of cider, one year with another,	——	
Amount of other annual produce,		£324
The annual income arising from any profession, faculty, handicraft, trade or employment, and by trading by sea and on shore, and by means of advantages arising from the war, and the necessities of the community,		£5,134 1s 8d

Although the town was not sacked or burnt during the war, it was often threatened, and the minds of the people thus kept in constant agitation between hope and fear. It was often visited by English cruisers, who would sometimes attempt to put their threats into execution by beginning to plunder and rob, but they never carried their depredations to any considerable length, except in one instance. In 1779, on the 6th of the 4th month, eight sail of small vessels came to the bar, where they all anchored except two, which came into the harbor and were made fast to the wharf. About a hundred armed men then landed, and immediately proceeded to plunder and rob several stores, and to commit some other depredations.[*] The inhabitants, in the mean time, although their feelings were much wounded, remained quiet spectators, and used no means of defence, believing that the plunderers would leave the island, without carrying their ravages to extremes, which they did the next day. It was the opinion of all that these refugees had no authority from the British government to disturb Nantucket. Being confident of this, some of the leading men of the town remonstrated against their conduct in such language as caused them to depart from the island in haste. Many of the inhabitants for a long time had entertained the opinion that the English government had no disposition to distress Nantucket, in any respect; this emboldened the inhabitants, whenever refugees came to the island, to treat them to plain language, and dispute their authority to commit any hostile act; which often had a very good effect.

---

[*] The value of property taken, according to an account of sales by the refugees themselves, was £10,000 13s 4d lawful.

We might fill a volume in enumerating the various vicissitudes and embarrassments, to which the people of this devoted island were subject during the war. Some cases occurred, which called forth the united energy of the community at large in the adoption and execution of measures to ward off impending ruin. The year 1779 was replete with difficulties, one succeeding another, so as to keep the people in continued anxiety. About the sixth month of that year, a committee was appointed by the town to proceed to Newport, and thence to New York, and there represent to the British commanders the difficulties under which the people labored, on account of the war, and particularly on account of the British armed vessels, which had recently come into the harbor and committed depredations on the property of the inhabitants. The committee were furnished with a memorial expressive of the difficulties, and asking to be relieved therefrom. On their return they presented the following report to a meeting of the inhabitants, who assembled on the occasion. As the business was of the greatest importance, the people generally collected. The committee, at the same time, presented a communication from the commander-in-chief of the British forces in America, giving assurance of his good disposition towards the town of Nantucket. These documents are both here inserted. The reader will find, that, if the people of this island had observed a strict neutrality during the war, they could have received at all times, from the British commander-in-chief, that attention which their defenceless situation would seem to demand.

     "NANTUCKET, 7th mo. 5th, 1779.

" To the inhabitants of the town of Sherburne:

" Agreeably to your appointment, we proceeded to Newport and New York, and presented the memorial to the commander-in-chief of the British army and navy, and, after repeated applications, we received their answers (Sir Henry Clinton's was only verbal), assuring us, that he had given orders that no further depredation should be made upon the island, on property belonging to the inhabitants, by persons under the authority of Great Britain; Sir George Collier gave us the same assurance in writing; and for a full knowledge of his disposition, we refer you to the enclosed declaration.

"BENJ. TUPPER,
TIM'Y. FOLGER,
SAMUEL STARBUCK,
WM. ROTCH."

"By Sir George Collier, Commodore and Commander-in-Chief of his Majesty's ships and vessels employed in North America, from the North Cape on the island of Cape Breton, to the Bahama Islands and Florida, inclusive.

"As great numbers of the inhabitants of the island of Nantucket are represented to me to be of the sect called Quakers, and consequently not accustomed to bear arms, and believing the remainder of the inhabitants to be quiet, inoffensive people, who have already suffered severely the calamities of war, I therefore think proper to forbid all privateers, letters of marque, armed vessels, or bodies of armed men, from molesting, ravaging, or plundering, the estates, houses, or persons, of the inhabitants of the said island; and if any shall be found to act inconsistently with these directions, their commissions as privateers, or letters of marque, shall be vacated, and themselves punished for the offence.

"Given on board his Majesty's Ship, the Raisonable, off New York, 23d June, 1779.

"GEORGE COLLIER.

"By command of the Commodore.
JOHN MARR, *Sec'y.*"

Sir Henry Clinton fully united with the foregoing declarations, and gave verbal assurance to the committee that they should be complied with.

The report of the committee, and the communication

accompanying it, were cordially accepted; by which it appeared, that all was done, that could be expected, to preserve the people and the property of the island from the depredations of British armed vessels or armed men.

But, notwithstanding these assurances, it was but a few months, before another difficulty arose, which threatened to be the greatest with which the people had ever met. This evil was averted by the protecting hand of Divine Providence, more conspicuous to the view of the community at large, than common. The event had a tendency to humble the minds of many, and to bring them into a state of dependence, on that Power which preserves from danger without the help of man.

Information was received, from undoubted authority, that a squadron of English armed vessels was preparing to leave New York for Nantucket, for the purpose of sacking and plundering the town, and of burning it, should any resistance be made by the inhabitants. Hitherto there had never been any order, under the authority of the British government, to visit the island in a hostile manner. Those enemies, who had sometimes made their appearance in the harbor, were of that class called refugees, who, not having the authority of the government, did not dare to extend their ravages to a great length, though their menaces were sometimes carried into effect in such a degree as to fill the minds of the people with fear and resentment. But the case now before us was quite otherwise, and caused very different emotions.

These were believed to be government vessels, and authorized by the government, which was a cause of the greater alarm. Their peculiar situation, with no back country whither to flee for shelter, nor any opportunity of leaving the island with safety on account of English cruisers in the Sound, nor even the means of doing so immediately, if this hindrance had not existed ; these circumstances filled the minds of the people with consternation and dismay. They knew not what measure to take, to avoid the impending danger. It was soon known, that the fleet had arrived at the Vineyard, and was waiting a change of wind, which was then to the eastward, to pursue the object of their expedition. As the danger approached, the people became more and more alarmed. The scene now discovered the various dispositions and thoughts of the community. Every person, capable of due reflection, displayed in his countenance a stronger and more powerful language than words could convey. As nothing now appeared to prevent the coming of the enemy, but the continuance of the prevailing east wind, many of the people took this opportunity to secure that part of their valuable property, which was capable of being removed and secreted. Carts, boats, and footmen, were constantly employed, by night and by day, in carrying goods out of the town, or depositing them in scattering houses in the vicinity, where it was supposed they would escape the conflagration. Some buried their goods under the earth, supposing that to be the best means of security. There were yet others, who were not inclined to take any of these precautions for the preservation of their property, but who quietly awaited the event, trusting in that Power which is over all, and to whose will the designs of men are at all times subjected.

A constant look-out was kept every day with the greatest anxiety, and in dread of the moment when the fleet should appear. At length the two commanding officers of the fleet, "Edward Winslow, Esq., captain of a party of troops, and George Leonard, Esq., naval commander of the squadron, and captain of the Restoration twenty-gun-ship," then lying at the Vineyard, wrote to the people of Nantucket, bearing date "16th September, 1779," wherein they made various charges against them. These charges were founded, as was stated, on information received from John Boswell, an officer of marines belonging to a British armed vessel, who had lately been at Nantucket; and were in substance, that the people "wafted a sloop from the harbor, which prevented her capture by the aforesaid British armed vessel; and also that the inhabitants, in violation of their asseverations heretofore made from time to time, had assisted his majesty's enemies; and that, except these charges could be removed, they should consider Nantucket a common enemy, and treat the people accordingly."

As this was one of the most alarming occurrences that took place during the war, it seems proper to insert the communication at large. The reader will perceive, that, in this instance, as in many others, the people of the island were subjected to suffering by false representation.

" By Edward Winslow, Esq., lieutenant-colonel, commandant of a party of troops, and George Leonard, Esq., commander of a fleet of armed vessels in the service of his majesty, George the Third, king of Great Britain, &c.

" To the inhabitants of the island of Nantucket.—Whereas we have this day received information, by John Boswell, officer of marines on board the letter of marque armed schooner Royal Charlotte, that on the 12th instant a certain sloop, in the service of his majesty's enemies, was standing into the habor of Nantucket, and that a number of inhabitants of that place assembled, and by wafts and signals prevented the said sloop from becoming a prize to said schooner Charlotte, and the sloop General Carlton, then at anchor there.

" And whereas the inhabitants of said island have (notwithstanding the generous indulgences to them granted by their excellences, the commanders-in-chief of his majesty's army and navy) discovered in various instances a disposition to aid and assist his majesty's enemies, and to molest and disturb such of his majesty's servants as have in pursuance of their duty put into that place, and by such neglectful and perfidious conduct have justly forfeited all pretensions to that protection, which a continuance in peace would have secured them the enjoyment of;—

" We hereby proclaim and declare to you, the inhabitants of Nantucket, that, unless an immediate and sufficient explanation of your conduct is made to us, relative to these transactions, we shall consider you as the professed enemies of our most gracious sovereign, and shall commence our operations against you as such.

" And having been this day furnished with a true list and description of all the vessels now in your harbor, *we do by these presents* expressly forbid you from suffering any of these vessels to remove from thence without special license first obtained from the commanding officer of the fleet for the time being, in the Vineyard Sound, on penalty of their being forfeited.

" Dated on board the ship Restoration, the 16th day of September, in the nineteenth year of his majesty's reign, Anno Domini 1779.

EDWARD WINSLOW,
GEORGE LEONARD."

This communication, coming directly from the commanding officers of the fleet, added to the alarm which had already taken place in the minds of the people. The inhabitants immediately convened on the occasion, and made the following reply to the charges of the British commanders:

" To Edward Winslow, Esq., lieutenant-colonel, commandant of a party of troops, and George Leonard, Esq., commander of a fleet of armed vessels in the service of his majesty, George the Third, king of Great Britain, &c.

" The town of Sherburne, on the island of Nantucket, have this day received a writing or manifesto signed by you, in which you have made sundry charges against the inhabitants of this place; by information, you say, from an officer of marines by the name of John Boswell.

" The first of which charges is, that a number of inhabitants assembled, and by wafts and signals prevented a certain sloop from falling into the hands of the armed vessels lying in this port, as a prize. Also that said inhabitants have discovered, in various instances, a disposition to aid and assist his majesty's enemies, and to molest and disturb such of his majesty's servants as have put into this place: and for such perfidious conduct we have forfeited all the indulgences heretofore granted us, &c.

" In answer to the first charge, we say, the sloop referred to came over the bar and anchored within one quarter of a mile of the shore, and there lay twelve hours, which we apprehend would not have been the case if they had seen the wafts. But on the town's being informed by the commanders of the armed vessels, that there had been wafts, the principal inhabitants endeavored to find who the persons were that were guilty; after much inquiry, it was found that a number of lads at the sea side were the persons, and upon examination we could not discover that they were sent for that purpose by any person, and the town highly disapproved of any such conduct, and we dare say that nothing of the kind will take place in future; and we must likewise add, that the pilot then on board declares, that neither he nor any other person on board the said sloop (that he knows of) discovered any such wafts, and that they did not omit coming into the harbor on that account, but were informed by a small sloop that British colors were displayed in the harbor, and that the fishing vessels that went in were taken possession of by armed vessels.

" In answer to the second charge, of aiding the king's ememies, we say, that the town of Sherburne, on the return of their committee from New York, immediately assembled themselves in town meeting, and received their report, with the indulgences from the commander-in-chief at New York, which report was accepted by the inhabitants, and a vote passed in a very full meeting, that they would continue altogether peaceable, which the town hath observed, and they know of no instance wherein they have assisted the king's enemies, neither have they molested or disturbed the king's servants that have put into the place, but on the contrary have paid them every respect due to their rank, with as much politeness as we were capable of, and we should have been glad to have had it in our power to say, that all the officers had behaved with that cordiality towards the inhabitants that they had a right to expect from them. After the aforesaid charges you proceed and say, that without our immediate and full explanation of our conduct you shall consider us the professed enemies of your most gracious sovereign, and commence your operations against us as such.

" We think we have given a full explanation of every charge exhibited against us and we hope to your satisfaction, and we further say that this town has done no act inconsistent with the indulgencies, and that we have a right to the continuation of them, until the commander-in-chief in New York sees fit to withdraw them.

" We now beg leave to mention to you the conduct of your armed vessels while in this port. The same day they were piloted into the harbor by the inhabitants, our small fishery fleet arrived, they immediately took possession of them, and kept the fishermen from their families twenty-four hours, and held up every appearance of seizing them as enemies, after which, contrary to the rules of the navy, Captain Duggan let his sailors be on shore in the evening among the peaceable inhabitants, with cutlasses, breaking open shops and plundering the inhabitants, of their property in the most audacious and menacing manner, and himself gave orders to his people (without even consulting the inhabitants) to take their cables, anchors, boats, sails, &c., notwithstanding he had the commander-in-chief's declaration produced to him, forbidding every such act.—We have now taken notice of every matter we think necessary to commit to writing; for a further explanation of matters we beg leave to refer you to the three gentlemen, who are chosen a committee by the town to be the bearers of this answer.

" Signed in behalf of the town,

FREDERICK FOLGER, Town Clerk.

Nantucket, September 18th, 1779."

A committee was then appointed to bear the memorial, and to use their endeavors to give satisfaction ; they accordingly proceeded on their mission, and on the " 23rd of September," made the following report :

" The committee, appointed by the town of Sherberne, to wait on Colonel Edward Winslow, Esq., and George Leonard, Esq., at Martha's Vineyard, beg leave to report :

" That they immediately proceeded there, and repaired on board the ship Restoration, and had a conference with them on the subject of giving signals to a certain sloop, that came over Nantucket Bar.

" Your committee found the gentlemen much dissatisfied, but on a thorough inspection into the matter, and our producing to them the votes of the town of Sherburne, disavowing every such proceeding, they were satisfied, so far as to commence no operations against the town on that account, without the future conduct of the inhabitants should make it necessary.

" The committee further say, that the above gentlemen gave them the fullest assurances, that they had no inclination to distress the inhabitants of Nantucket; but on the contrary would give them every assistance in their power, so long as they adhered to their own votes, and acted consistently with them.

STEPHEN PADDOCK,
TIMOTHY FOLGER,   } Committee.
SAMUEL GELSTON,

Nantucket, ye 23rd Septmr 1779.

During all these transactions the wind continued to the eastward, which prevented them from pursuing the object of their intention ; for the foregoing complaints were considered nothing more than a pretext formed by them to guarantee their conduct in plundering the town, and to screen them from punishment from their own government.

It was pretended that a schooner, which arrived from Rhode Island, brought orders to the commanders of the armament to abandon the enterprise and return to New York, which was promptly obeyed, and they left the Vineyard the next morning.

It finally appeared, however, that their conduct was without the authority of the British commander-in-chief, at New York, and that the plan was instituted and promoted principally by the loyalists.

It is highly probable, that the east wind, which so providentially prevailed during there transactions, alone prevented the immediate execution of the enemy's intentions; and that, during the delay, reflections on the enormity of their meditated act, and the difficulty of rendering an excuse for it to their government, checked any further proceedings. In the view of the people of the island, their deliverance seemed to have been wrought by Him who sets bounds to the wicked. The British government would sooner have contributed to the relief of the inhabitants, than permit one step to be taken to distress them. Past experience of their lenity warrants this declaration; for in every instance of application being made to them for assistance, it was granted, so far as circumstances would allow.

It was always evident to the people, that the town could not be defended against the enemy; it was, therefore, considered wise and prudent to say and do nothing to irritate them, since they at all times had the power of destroying the place, without a risk of being repelled. The American government could not protect the island, and there was a large class of the people, composed of Friends and others of similar tenets respecting war, who did not crave its protection, relying rather on that Power which can never fail, and which is most conspicuous in times of the greatest peril. There were some, however, who always manifested a disposition to make all the defence they could, to secure themselves, and save their property from the possession of the enemy. And they urged this as a duty incumbent upon them. These differences of opinion caused some dissension, which, although never carried to great lengths, added to the trials and anxieties occasioned by the war.

The situation and circumstances of the place, during the existence, and at the close of the war, was known to the general and state government; a heavy tax was, notwithstanding, imposed on the inhabitants. The impropriety of this measure was very evident to the greater part of the people of the island, and to many members of the legislature; but it could not well be avoided. But a small proportion, however, of these taxes was collected, for, after the war closed, the legislature was informed, in a particular manner, of the embarrassed state of the town, by their representative, whose attention to the interests of his constituents, and indefatigable industry, obtained a remission of the greater part of the back taxes, with which the town stood charged. It appeared evident to every rational mind, acquainted with the circumstances, that the inhabitants of Nantucket should be exempted from paying taxes to the government in time of war. There is no place within the limits of the nation more exposed to the ravages of an enemy, and no one more out of the reach of the protection of government than this. With what propriety can a community be taxed for the support of a war, whose only share in it is the entire ruin of their wonted business, and utter exposure of lives and homes to the rapacity of the enemy, or unqualified dependence on their mercy? The inhabitants are fishermen, and by steady industry and enterprising genius they are enabled in times of peace to sustain a respectable standing in the community at large; but whenever their business is obstructed, their every dependence for a livelihood is gone, until the cause is removed: for there is no alternative, no retreat for them. The wide ocean is the source of their livelihood, and they breast its waves and grapple with its monsters in every latitude between the polar ices. The sun never sets on their industry; they labor and worship under the whole dome of the firmament. The objects of their affections are abroad on the deep, or buried for ever beneath its billows; their prayers are wafted on every wind, their tears are mingled with every surge. Insulated in business, as well as in their location, their habits and customs, and in many respects their opinions, partake of the general character of their circumstances. Peaceable in their occupations, they are, with few exceptions, radically opposed to war.

The legislative body, after a full investigation of the situation and circumstances of the place, became fully convinced of the truth of the foregoing facts, in conformity to which the following resolution was passed:

"COMMONWEALTH OF MASSACHUSETTS.

"*In the House of Representatives, June 30th,* 1781.

"On the Petition of the Agents appointed by the Town of Sherberne, on the Island and County of Nantucket:—

"*Resolved,* That the Treasurer of the Commonwealth be and he is hereby directed to suspend issuing his execution against the deficient constables or collectors of the county of Nantucket, until the further order of this court.

"Sent up for concurrence.

"NATHANAEL GORHAM, *Speaker.*

"*In Senate, July 2d,* 1781.   Read and concurred.

"SAMUEL ADAMS, *President.*

"Approved.

"JOHN HANCOCK.

"True copy.   Attest.

"JOHN AVERY, *Secretary.*"

Previous to the war, the place was in a flourishing state, and fully able to contribute its proportion for defraying the public expense in the maintenance of civil government, and it always did so with cheerfulness. But, through the effects of the war, the people were deprived of their property and every means of comfortable subsistence. In this situation they were more nearly in a state of beggary, than in a condition to pay a heavy tax. Notwithstanding these facts, there was a small number of different sentiments, who uniformly urged, that the people of this place were as well able to pay taxes as those of any town within the state.

The fisheries in general, and particularly the whaling business, were of incalculable advantage to the country. The latter not only furnishes the best of light for public and private uses, but also supports a valuable branch of trade to foreign markets. Those who are employed in the whale fishery are a stout, hardy set of men, and are acknowledged to be the best seamen in the world. It has often been remarked, that the small town of Nantucket furnishes a greater number of officers capable of taking charge of ships, than any other seaport in the United States. If this is correct, and we have no reason to doubt it, what a nursery for seamen! From these considerations ought not the whale fishery to enjoy the fostering care of government, especially in time of war?

CHAPTER VI.

Greater suffering was experienced by the inhabitants of Nantucket, in the year 1780, than at any other period during the revolutionary war. During the winter of that year, denominated the *hard winter*, the distress of the people was, on many accounts, very great. The greater part of the people had previously been reduced to a state of penury. The cold weather set in early, and prevented the little supply of wood and provisions which was expected. The autumn had been so uncommonly wet, that but a small quantity of peat could be procured. These circumstances, added to the common calamity of war, produced a state of the most fearful anxiety.

The harbor was closed with ice about the twentieth of the twelth month, 1779, and continued frozen, without intermission, during the winter. The inhabitants soon began to feel the effects of this severity: for the cold increased and the ice was formed on all sides, so that there was no water to be seen from the highest eminences, for the space of several weeks. There were also so much ice and snow on the ground and in the swamps as to almost entirely prevent the obtaining any fuel thence. The shores and creeks were so covered with thick ice, that it was with great difficulty that fish of any kind could be procured.

The cold was so intense, and continued so long, that the ice in the harbor became sufficiently strong to allow loaded calashes to pass over it. An opportunity was thus afforded to those, who were destitute of firing, to procure it at Coskata, far more conveniently and expeditiously than they could have done by the circuitous and very bad road to that spot. By this means the laboring poor, for several weeks, procured all their fuel: it was a hard and laborious task, but, as it was their only resort, even this was thankfully embraced. The distance from town to the place of getting the wood was nine or ten miles, the days were short, and the weather frequently so bois-terous, as to make it hardly safe to expose the human body to its severity. In addition to this, they incurred the danger of breaking through the ice, particularly in places where there was a strong current. Accidents of this kind sometimes happened, to the great detriment of the business; but happily no lives were lost. As the demand for wood increased, the number of persons which had recourse to this mode of procuring it, increased daily, until there might be seen fifty or sixty horses and calashes in a train, pursuing their course homeward with their hard-earned burdens. The wood obtained was princi-pally of two kinds, the oak and juniper. It was hard, and made a durable fire, but very crooked, and none of it large or tall. It had been reserved by the proprietors of the land, as a shelter for their sheep and horses in the winter. But the difficulty of procuring firing was at this time so great, that the owners of the wood were willing to relin-quish their privilege for a very reasonable compensation. Thus by hard toil many of the inhabitants were preserved from freezing.

Still more distress was felt from want of provisions: the poorer class, in particular, suffered exceedingly. The war had made many widows and orphans, who had now to endure the miseries of famine, in addition to the poignant grief occasioned by the loss of their dearest relatives. Of this class many experienced the greatest sufferings, and, although none are known to have frozen or starved, without doubt some were hurried to their graves, through want of the necessaries and comforts of life.

The previous season was uncommonly fruitful, and the farmers had generally raised more grain and vegetables than were needed by their own families; whereby they were enabled to supply, in some measure, the wants of the needy.

Some that were opulent, with a provident benevolence, furnished themselves with considerable quantities of bread stuff before winter set in, and, in this pinching time, sold it out in small quantities to such as had wherewithal to pay; but such as had not were not turned empty away. In addition to these measures, the authorities of the town strove, with the means of which they were possessed to relieve the distresses of the people. Every thing which toil could procure—liberal charity, mutual accommodations and public assistance, rigid economy and patient endurance—all these, though they could not avert, did much to alleviate the asperities of the times.

The suffering for clothing was inconsiderable, both at this period, and throughout the war. For, immediately, on being cut off from the use of English manufactures, the women engaged within their own families in manufacturing cloth of various kinds for domestic use. They thus kept their household decently clad, and the surplus of their labors they sold to such as chose to buy rather than make for themselves. In this way the female part of families, by their industry and strict economy, frequently supported the whole domestic circle; evincing the strength of their attachment and the value of their services to those, on whom they themselves were wont to depend for protection and support.   There being from twelve to sixteen thousand sheep owned on the island, it was easy to procure as much wool as was needed.   A considerable quantity of flax was raised yearly, and some was imported from the continent; so that means were furnished, for all that were inclined to labor, to clothe their families.

In order to relieve, in some measure, the increasing sufferings of the people, the proprietors of the island caused to be laid out and assigned to each owner, a number of large tracts of land of various descriptions, for themselves and their families to improve.   In 1775 a tract of 2456 acres was laid out at the S. E. part of the island.   In 1778 a tract called Croskata was laid out, containing 349 acres; and the following year a large tract called Squam, and Pookoomo, containing 2109 acres.   Croskata was nearly covered with wood of a small growth, which was of great benefit to the people.

For the accommodation of the owners and the people at large, all the swamps to the westward of the town were laid out for the purpose of digging peat.   Also a large swamp, about two miles east from the town, called Tawpawshas swamp; and full liberty was granted by the proprietors to the inhabitants at large, to dig peat from it without allowing the owners any perquisite.   These measures proved of great benefit, for many were thereby furnished with a living, though scanty, which they could not have obtained by any other means at that time.

Whaling being the only business which suited the genius of Nantucket, they constantly kept in view, in order to prosecute it, as soon as a proper opening should present.   But they had become so reduced at this period of the war, and such was the risk of capture, that they could not fit out their vessels in that service.

Repeated intimations from the British commanders in this country led the inhabitants of the island to believe, that, if some regular course could be pursued, some indulgence would be granted to them. The situation of affairs was, however, very critical. The inhabitants were watched as with the eyes of Argus, and threatened that, if any correspondence was carried on with the British, all communication with the continent should be stopped: again, if they risked their property at sea, it was almost sure to become a sacrifice to the British cruisers; and if nothing was done, the only alternative was distress and famine. It was now, however, pretty well ascertained that some of the leading men in the nation were looking with an eye of commisseration on the depressed circumstances of the place.

Under these considerations, Timothy Folger, Esq., was sent to New York, to represent the situation of the people of Nantucket, and to ask permission of the British commander-in-chief to carry on the whaling business, without being subject to capture by the vessels of his government. The following is a copy of the petition, which was presented:

"To their Excellencies, Sir Henry Clinton, Knight of the Bath, and commander-in-chief of his majesty's forces employed in North American, and Marriot Arbuthnot, Esquire, Vice Admiral of the Blue, and commander-in-chief of his majesty's ships and vessels employed and to be employed in North America, and his majesty's commissioners for restoring peace to the revolting colonies, &c.

"The petition of the island of Nantucket humbly shews; that at this time there is five thousand inhabitants on said island, who, through the unhappy dispute that hath taken place between Great Britain and the colonies, are reduced to the most miserable situation imaginable.

" The soil will not produce a subsistence for one third part of the people. Wholly destitute of fire wood, and but a little clothing; such being their situation and circumstances, your petitioners really apprehend, that, without some indulgences from your excellencies, there will many people perish for want, before the end of another winter. Your petitioners hope and flatter themselves that, as they have taken no part whatever in the unhappy war that has brought on these calamities, but have remained these five years in a state of peace, without civil or military officers on the island, or any court of justice, on which account they have been denied more than once of all supplies from the continent, and likewise that more than two thirds parts of the inhabitants are of the people called Quakers, and principled against bearing arms on any occasion,— that your excellencies will take their peculiar situation into your wise consideration, and grant them such relief as will furnish them with a subsistence only.

" Your petitioners do not wish, neither will they presume to ask, any indulgences that will counteract the plans of government. As the inhabitants of said island were heretofore wholly employed in the whale and cod fishery, and at present every other means of subsistence being cut off, they hope your excellencies will permit twenty fishing boats to fish round the island of Nantucket, and four vessels to be employed in the whale fishery, and ten small vessels to supply the inhabitants with wood, and one to go to New York for some little supplies; said vessels being put under such regulations as your excellencies shall see meet. Your petitioners likewise beg of your excellencies, that you will prohibit all armed vessels and armed men from going to Nantucket to take the property of the island from thence.

"And your petitioners as in duty bound shall pray.

TIMOTHY FOLGER,

Agent for the inhabitants of Nantucket."

"New York, 9th July, 1780."

This petition, although it had not that immediate effect which was asked for, proved of much advantage in promoting the much desired object, that of whaling without the risk of capture. The subject was constantly kept in view by the inhabitants, and, as often as opportunity presented, permission was asked of the British for that purpose. In the year 1781 depredations were frequently made by the enemy's cruisers that occasionally came into the harbor. The people were thus kept in constant agitation, not knowing what measures to pursue, except to repeat their petitions and remonstrances to the British commanders. They had frequent occasion to resort to this mode of proceeding, which always appeared to have some good effect, but promised no permanent advantage.

In 1781, notwithstanding the many discouragements presented in renewing petitions to the British commanders-in-chief, yet, no other means appearing likely to prevent the frequent depredations of the enemy on the property of the inhabitants, a memorial was again resorted to, and a committee to bear it was appointed by the town. The committee were instructed to proceed to New York, to Admiral Digby, and to give him a correct statement of the difficulties and embarrassments of the people in many respects, particularly from the conduct of British cruisers as above stated. They were further directed to ask such indulgences as could be consistently granted. On their return, they made the following report to the town:

" To the inhabitants of the town of Sherburne, in town meeting assembled.

" RESPECTED FRIENDS,—Agreeably to the appointment by the town, on the 3d of the 10th month last, we proceeded to New York, and presented your memorial to Admiral Digby, commander-in-chief there. We also represented the peaceable conduct maintained by the inhabitants in general, in the course of the present contest, with the exposed situation of the island, and that recent depredations had been made upon us; upon which an inquiry into the general state and circumstances of the island took place, which determined the Admiral to exercise his authority in our favor, and accordingly gave us his positive order to prevent any further molestation of our persons and property within the bar of the harbor, which we herewith deliver. We are your friends.

" SAMUEL STARBUCK,
WILLIAM ROTCH,
BENJAMIN HUSSEY.

" Sherburne, 12 mo. 19th, 1781."

We regret that a copy of the memorial and also the order alluded to in the committee's report, cannot be found. The town's committee being now in New York, and fully authorized, renewed the petition to whale, and finally succeeded. Towards the latter part of the year a considerable number of permits for that purpose were obtained. The following is a copy of one of them.

" [L. S.]   By Robert Digby, Esquire, Rear Admiral of the Red, and Commander-in-chief, &c., &c.

" Permission is hereby given to the Dolphin brig, burthen sixty tons, Walter Folger owner, navigated by Gilbert Folger as master and the twelve seamen named in the margin, to leave the island of Nantucket and to proceed on a whaling voyage.—To commence the first of January, 1782, and end the last day of————following, provided that they have on board the necessary whaling craft and provisions only, and that the master of said brig is possessed of a certificate from the selectmen of the said island, setting forth that she is bona fide the property of the inhabitants of the island, with the names of the master and seamen of her; and that she she shall not be found proceeding with her cargo to any other port than Nantucket or New York.

The twelve seamen named in the margin:

James Chase,
Obadiah Folger,
George Coleman,
Silvanus Swain,
Charles Russell,
Peter Pollard,
Andrew Coleman,
Obed Barnard,
Jonathan Briggs,

" Dated at New York, the first day of December, 1781.
                              ROBERT DIGBY.

" To the commissioners of his majesty's ships and vessels of war,
    as well as of all privateers and letters of marque.
              " By command of the Admiral.
                          THOMAS M. PALMER."

This privilege seemed to give new life to the people.
It produced a considerable movement in business, but the
resources of the island had so diminished, that but a small
number of vessels could take the benefit of these permits.
Those who had vessels, and were possessed of the means,
fitted them out on short voyages, and, had there been no
hindrance, it is probable that they would have done well;
for the whales, having been unmolested for several years,
had become numerous, and were pretty easily caught.

To carry on the whale fishery under permission of the
government of Great Britain, was a proceeding somewhat
novel, and could not pass unnoticed. Although it was
not publicly known, yet it was generally believed, that
some kind of indulgence had been shown by the enemy
to the people of Nantucket. This caused some clamor
on the continent; but our government well knew the situation of the place, and its large participation in the
calamities of war, and was, consequently, rather inclined
to favor than to condemn the acceptance of favors from
the English. Although the government could not grant
an exclusive privilege to any particular part of the union,
yet such encouragement was given by the leading men of
. the nation, in their individual capacity, as to warrant the
proceeding. Several vessels, whaling under these permits, were taken by American privateers, and carried into
port, but in every instance they were soon liberated.
Whenever it was found that the permits were used for

no other purpose than that for which they were granted, and that the vessels using them had not been engaged in illicit trade, there was no hesitation in releasing them.

In the early part of the war, notes or bills were issued by the state legislature, and also by congress, called money. This paper medium was freely taken by the people of Nantucket, and served in lieu of specie in the line of trade; but it was not long before it began to depreciate in its nominal value. Still as there was little real money in circulation, this paper, having been made a lawful tender, the people continued to take it; indeed it was difficult to avoid doing so, and yet carry on business. This paper currency continued to be the circulating medium during the war, but it gradually depreciated from year to year, until it became valueless. Many people suffered from this cause; some, who sold their oil in the early part of the war, took the money in payment, and laid it by until the war closed, at which time it was worth nothing. Those who held it were flattered for years afterwards, that government would redeem it, but this was never done.

In 1782 there began to be joyful anticipations of peace. The English government this year acknowledged the independence of America. Favorable omens animated the minds of the people. The prospect continued to brighten, though each one was cautious not to place too great confidence in appearances, through fear of disappointment. The year 1783 commenced with renewed encouragements that peace would soon be established, which was verified by General Washington's resignation of his commission to congress in the twelfth month. Joy pervaded all parts of the country, and was no where more heartfelt than at Nantucket; for, perhaps, no place had suffered more. In the early part of the year 1784 peace was ratified between the United States and Great Britain.

In 1775 the tonnage owned at Nantucket, as nearly as we can ascertain, was 14,867 tons. During the war 15 vessels were lost at sea, and 134 were captured; total loss in tonnage, 12,467 tons, of which more than 10,000 tons fell into the hands of the enemy. It would be difficult, at this period, to make an estimate of the value of these vessels; many of them had on board valuable cargoes. They were navigated by the youth and manhood of the island. Of the crews, some perished miserably in prison-ships, others lingered years in confinement; some entered the service of the country, others returned home destitute to destitute families. To these considerations, if we add losses by plunderers, the almost total stoppage of all business during the war, the insufficiency of the soil to produce food for the inhabitants, the almost constant blockading of the harbor by the English or the Refugees, it will not be doubted that Nantucket paid as dearly for the independence of our country as any place in the union.

CHAPTER VII.

The joyful sound of PEACE now echoed through the land, in which the people of Nantucket thankfully participated. Although the greater part were miserably poor, yet they were not insensible of the manifold favors shown them during the continuance of the war. They were at all times more exposed to the enemy than the people of many places which had been plundered and burnt. They had been favored beyond their expectation, at times when nothing appeared but imminent danger. English armed vessels often visited their harbor, but except in a few instances, already mentioned, there had been little loss of property on that account. It was evident, at many times, that an overruling Power had watched over them, and assisted them through many difficulties which would otherwise have proved distressing. The seafaring people, whose necessities exposed them to the casualties of war, suffered very much. Many were cut off, in the prime of life, by the prison-ship, by disasters at sea, in battle, or by other causes produced by war. Many mourning families were thus driven to beg their bread. Many bereaved and aged parents were left to mourn over their offspring, snatched from them by violence or disease in distant parts and under distressing circumstances. But peace was now restored, and all were glad to exchange severe sufferings and sad forebodings for active business and pleasing anticipations. It was, however, with feeble efforts, that they at first attempted to resume their wonted occupations. At the commencement of the war, there were more than an hundred and fifty vessels belonging to the place; at its close there remained only two or three old hulks. The town exhibited the appearance of a deserted village rather than of a flourishing seaport containing upwards of four thousand inhabitants. The buildings had received no paint and scarce any repairs during the war, and a considerable number of the oldest houses were in a rapid course of dilapidation.

The following extract from the valuation taken in 1784, will show, in some measure, the situation of the place at that time:

Families	767
Inhabitants	4,268
Houses	551
Widows	202
Orphan children	342
Indians	35
Horses	267
Cows and oxen	693
Sheep	3,000
Tons of shipping, the greater part of which was purchased since the close of the war	2,400
Tons of shipping lost and taken since 1775	11,131

Such is the picture of the situation and circumstances of the place at that period. Although it wore a gloomy aspect, the minds of the people were animated, and they manifested a lively disposition for business.

About this time many young men came home from different parts, where they had been confined as prisoners. Some of them had been absent so long, without being heard from, that their connections had relinquished all hope of ever seeing them again.

Those persons, who had capital left, resumed the whaling with a small number of vessels. The whales, having been but little disturbed during the war, were very numerous on the coasts where they were sought, so that the few vessels engaged in the business generally made prosperous voyages. The oil sold immediately for a good price, which encouraged new adventurers to embark in the business, whose limited means compelled them to take small risks at the commencement.

The peace produced as great a revolution in business as the war had done. The currency of paper, as a substitute for money, which had caused such confusion in the prices of articles, having now ceased, and the paper itself having become valueless except as a representative of loss and ruin, trade began to assume a regular course. The following table will show the prices of a few articles, the first year or two after peace took place :

						dolls.	cts.
Spermaceti oil .	.	.	.	.	.	144	67
Head matter .	.	.	.	.	.	213	33
Molasses, per gallon .	.	.	.	.	—	67
Sperm candles, per pound	.	.	.	.	—	41
Corn, per bushel	.	.	.	.	.	—	67
Fish, per quintal	.	.	.	.	.	3	00
Wood, per cord	.	.	.	.	.	2	61
Sugar, per cwt.	.	.	.	.	.	8	00
Flour, per barrel	.	.	.	.	.	5	50
Common labor, per day	.	.	.	.	—	67

The foregoing prices continued without much variation for several years, and they may be taken as a criterion for the value of other property, except oil, which lessened in price very much, causing thereby considerable discouragement to the whaling business.

The price of most kinds of real estate was very low for

many years after the peace, which was occasioned by the great want of money, to enter into business with. The price of cows' commons varied from ten to twelve pounds. Other real estate, such as houses and settlements in various parts of the town, that sold for five hundred dollars, would, ten years before, have sold for three or four times that amount. One cause for the depreciation of real estate, was, that those who carried on farming, during the war, now abandoned that employment and turned their attention to whaling or fishing, or some branches of business connected therewith. The farming was thus left in a declining condition, there being but few other than aged men, and young lads to conduct it.

The long projecting point at the north-east part of the island, called Great Point, had long been considered a suitable situation for a light-house, but the late war prevented the building of one. In 1784 a light-house was erected there by the state, which stood until 11th month, 1816, at which time it was destroyed by fire. Soon after another was built of stone. The first was considered one of the best in the United States. The light, when kept in good order, shone more brilliantly, it was said, than any other on the coast. The point, on which it stood, projected far into the sea, which renders the light very beneficial to vessels passing through the sound. The site was ceded to the United States in 1790.

The first light-house on Brant Point, at the entrance of the harbor, burnt down in 1759; the fire was supposed to have been communicated from the lamps. The second was blown down in 1774. A third was burnt in the fall of 1783; in this instance, also, the fire was thought to have communicated from the lamps. The next was a wooden lantern, with glass windows, which was hoisted between two spars with grooves to steady the lantern.

This was a dim light, hence it received the name of "bug light." The fifth was a frame, with the top fitted for the lights; this blew down. The light-houses on Brant Point, above-mentioned, and the expense of keeping them, were at the charge of the town. When the general government was about to furnish the sea coast with light-houses, it was thought expedient, by the inhabitants, that a new one should be erected, which was done on application to that effect; and the land on which it stood was accordingly ceded to the United States. This last, being old, was a few years since taken down and another erected in its stead, with a dwelling-house for the keeper attached. The government has placed buoys on the shoals and bar, near the entrance to the harbor, to guide vessels passing in and out. They are taken away in the winter to prevent their being carried off by the ice.

At the close of the revolutionary war, there was a considerable number of men too far advanced in life to resume the whaling business, in which they had previously been engaged. " Having lost nine years of their life to no profit," to use their own expression, it became necessary to resort to other business for a subsistence.. The cod fishery at that time appeared likely to become a permanent business of the place. It was therefore adopted by this class. The encouragement to prosecute this branch appeared very promising to a number of commercial men, who embarked therein with their property. The fish, on the great fishing banks, were found exceedingly plenty, by the people of Marblehead, and Cape Cod, &c., and the price was such as yielded a good profit. With these prospects, a number of vessels were put into the service, some of which went to the Grand Bank, Newfoundland, Cape Sable, and other places eastward, and others of small burthen went out upon the shoals to the eastward of the island. They generally obtained good voyages, and the fish sold well for the first two or three years. The business, however, dwindled by degrees; at length it was clearly proved, that it was not suited to the genius and inclinations of the people. The vessels, except a few that continued to fish in the vicinity of the island, were put into other employment.

It may be asked, why could not the people of Nantucket carry on the cod fishing to as much advantage and profit as the people of Marblehead and Cape Cod? The reasons are obvious. First; the middle-aged, as before mentioned, who were too far advanced in life to return to their former business, were the only class to be met with that would engage in the fishing : and of these there was not a sufficient number to prosecute the business, with the energy and to the extent which the nature of it required, in order to render it profitable. In the second place, the people were unaccustomed to the business, and unwilling to engage in it, for their attention and study were constantly fixed on that of whaling. They could not be brought to believe, that the cod fishing would answer on any principle upon which it was conducted. It was, therefore, impossible to obtain men of the first abilities to go in the vessels. The owners had recourse to the Cape to man their vessels, where they had to encounter similar difficulties ; for the most capable and active part of the population there engaged in this employment, could always have all the encouragement which the business afforded, without leaving their homes.

Under these considerations, the cod fishing was abandoned, as before stated.

In 1785, the whale fishery gave promise of much profit: provisions and other articles used in outfits were soon reduced to moderate prices, while that of oil was high. This continued, however for but a short duration, for in the latter part of the following year, sperm oil, in its crude state, sold for £24 and head matter for £45 per ton; which caused much discouragement in the minds of the people, and led them to think of other and more profitable business. The people in general had flattered themselves that all difficulties and embarrassments in their line of business, would cease with the war; and that they might, with every prospect of advantage, pursue the whale fishery with quietness. Many embarked all their property; but what was their disappointment, after obtaining a good fare of oil, to find that it would not defray the expense of the voyage! This was not only discouraging, but alarming, to the principal commercial men. Many ways were devised to remedy these difficulties. It was urged that, if the island could be placed in a state of neutrality it would be beneficial to the whole community; that it would increase the trade to various parts of the world, which, together with the little whaling that would be carried on, would be likely to remove every complaint: and that the country at large would derive many benefits from the measure. As nothing could be done without legislative assistance, several town meetings were held to deliberate on the subject, and at length a large committee was appointed to draft a memorial to the general court, representing the situation of the town, and asking such relief as might appear adequate to the emergency. The committee was also instructed to take the subject of the

neutrality of the place under consideration, on which they
made the following report :—

" The committee appointed by the town to draft a memorial to
present to the general court, in behalf of the inhabitants of the
island, have attended to that business, and have reported the same to
the satisfaction of the town, and as the same committee were directed to form a plan for the town to proceed upon, such as they
apprehended would answer the best purposes, and be most for the
interest of the whole, crave leave to report, that, it is the unanimous
opinion of the committee, that the whale fishery cannot be preserved
to this place, nor any part of that business can be carried on by the
inhabitants of the island, without great loss attending it, which
will of course reduce the inhabitants to a state of poverty and distress; and it is their opinion that the only possible remedy is, in
placing the island and its inhabitants in a state of neutrality, which
if obtained may perhaps put it in the power of the inhabitants, to
preserve so much of the whale fishery as may procure them a subsistence.

" But as the memorial says nothing respecting a state of neutrality, but only requests the government to point out some method
for us to secure some part of the whale fishery, which, if they
should do, and it should appear to the agents of the town on this
business, that it will effectually answer the meaning and intention
of the memorial, in that case a state of neutrality may not be
moved for, but the committee are fully of the opinion, that a matter of so much consequence must, in a great measure, be left to the
wisdom, prudence, and integrity of your agent, or agents, that may
have the conducting of this business with the government.

" The above report was signed by the committee, consisting of
nine persons.

" Nantucket, 5th mo. 2d, 1785."

The memorial, mentioned in the above report, was forwarded to the general court by a committee who were
instructed to use their endeavors to have the whole carried into effect, the subject of neutrality, as well as that
pertaining to the whale fishery.

But the subject of neutrality did not meet with that

cordial reception, which was anticipated. It was deemed inconsistent by the legislature, to grant an indulgence to one section of the commonwealth, by which all could not be benefited, and by which the general interests of commerce might be injured.

The depression in the whaling business was, however, too evident to need proof; and the legislature seemed disposed to render their aid and assistance as far as it would be consistent with the interests of the commonwealth. In conformity with this purpose it was thought necessary to encourage the whale fishery throughout the state, by putting a bounty on the different kinds of whale oil. A resolve passed the legislature, in 1785, of which the following is a copy :—

" Whereas this court, having a due sense of the high worth and importance of the whale fishery, are desirous of its preservation, not only to this state, but to the United States in general; therefore, resolved, that there be paid, out of the treasury of this commonwealth, the following bounties upon whale oil, of the different qualities hereafter mentioned, viz.:

For every ton of white spermaceti oil, five pounds.

For every ton of brown or yellow spermaceti oil, sixty shillings.

" For every ton of whale oil, (so called,) forty shillings, that may be taken or caught by any vessel or vessels, that are or may be owned and manned wholly by the inhabitants of this commonwealth, and landed within the same, from and after the first day of January next, until the further order of the general court.

" And be it further resolved, that the selectmen of each town, within this commonwealth, where said fishery is carried on, be, and they hereby are empowered and directed to appoint an inspector or inspectors, who, (first making oath for the due performance of his or their duty,) shall inspect all such oil, so landed, with an iron oil-searcher, and with a marking-iron, mark on the head of each cask so inspected, the initial letters of his name describing the quality of the oil by the letters W. B. Y. W. O. annexed, and make certificate thereof to the selectmen of such town, as aforesaid, under oath; such inspector or inspectors to be paid by the owner or owners of such oil, so inspected, on certificate being produced as aforesaid.

" And it is futher resolved that, in order to entitle the owner or owners of the oil, so taken, landed, inspected, and marked, as aforesaid, to the bounty or bounties aforesaid, the owner or owners of the vessel or vessels, that took and landed the same, shall produce to the governor and council, a certificate, from under the hands of the selectmen of the town, where the said oil was landed and inspected, as aforesaid; which certificate shall be in the following words, mutatis mutandis:

" N——, ss. 178-. This certifies that the —— A. B. master, owned by E. F. of ———, in the county aforesaid, arrived at this port from a whaling voyage, on the —— instant, (or as the case may be,) and had on board the following quantities of oil, hereafter named, viz. :—

—— Tons of white spermaceti oil.
—— Tons of brown or yellow spermaceti oil.
—— Tons of whale oil.

The whole of which was landed at said port of ———, and there inspected according to law, and a certificate thereof, under the hand of A. B., sworn inspector of the port aforesaid, to us produced.

} Selectmen of ——.

" And it is further resolved, that the said owner, or owners, together with the master, mentioned in the said certificate, shall each of them subscribe the same; and the said owner or owners, together with the said master, shall make oath before some justice of the peace, for the same county, in the form following, to wit.:—

" You, A. B. and C. D., do solemnly swear, (or affirm,) that you were the sole owners of the ——, A. B. master, mentioned in the certificate, during the whole time she was employed in the whale voyage, herein mentioned, and that the quantity of oil, aforesaid, was taken or caught by the persons employed on board said vessel, during said voyage, which vessel was navigated and manned wholly by the inhabitants of this state, and that no foreigner, directly or indirectly, hath, or had, any share, part or interest therein, and that the whole of said oil was taken or caught after the first day of December, A. D. 1785.

"So help you God.

"And it is further resolved, that upon such certificate being produced to the governor and council, the governor, by and with the consent of the council, be and he is hereby empowered to grant a warrant on the treasury of this commonwealth, for the payment of the bounties in the manner aforesaid.

"And it is further resolved, that the secretary be and he is hereby directed to publish the foregoing resolve in Adams and Nourse's, the Essex, Falmouth, and Plymouth newspapers."

This resolve was carried into operation, and in some measure afforded relief, but it was attended, at the same time, with embarrassments which were not anticipated, and could not be obviated. The duration of the bounty was not limited by the resolve, and it did not continue long in operation; ways and means opened beyond reasonable expectation, which gave encouragement to the whale fishery, and the bounty was withdrawn.

The bounty was at first a pleasing thing and what many had been laboring for a long time. It extended to all who had any share in the oil. The desired relief, thus afforded, animated the people to renewed activity, but the effect was directly opposite to what was anticipated. The bounty, being granted to the inhabitants of the state generally, held out such flattering prospects, as to induce people in many places to enter into the whaling business. Thus the result was injurious rather than advantageous to the interests of Nantucket.

The principal cause to be assigned for this was, that the consumption was not sufficiently extensive in this country to command a sale, except at reduced prices; for there had been a suspension of the use of oil for many preceding years, and the people generally, throughout the country, used tallow candles. Little oil was used at that time either for lighthouses or towns. In England that whaling business was already so established, and carried on so extensively, that it would not produce much profit to ship oil there, subjected as it was to duty after the revolutionary war. Some oil was, however, sent thither, whilst the price was very low here, which, together with the rapid increase of its use in this country, created a good demand for it, at a good price. It was found, on trial, to be better than tallow and to give a much more brilliant light.

The prospect was now changed, and the inhabitants began to make new advances, with the pleasing hope that the principal obstacles to their business were removed. But another difficulty soon arose, which lessened the demand for oil, as it reduced the price in England so that it would not bear shipping there from this country, and considerably clogged the whaling business for a time. The English government had ever found it for their interest to encourage the whale fishery within their own dominions. Besides the many advantages derived from procuring their own oil, they valued it as one of the best nurseries for seamen. No opportunity was, therefore, neglected to promote its interests. In order to encourage the business in America, they fixed upon Halifax as the most eligible place for that purpose. Here was an excellent harbor, in or out of which vessels of any burthen could pass, either in winter or summer. It was probable that a good market would be found for oil imported there, as soon as it was landed. The government held out such alluring prospects to such of the people of Nantucket as should remove thither and pursue the whaling business, that a considerable number were induced to try the experiment.

In 1786 and 1787 they settled on the shore opposite to the town of Halifax, and there built dwelling-houses, wharves, spermaceti candle-works, stores, &c., calling the name of the place Dartmouth. There they carried on the business several years, and reaped the benefit of every advantage which the government was willing to allow them. They appeared likely to succeed in their undertaking, and the place seemed destined to become of great importance. But their prosperity was not of long duration: for, in a few years, some of the principal promoters of the removal grew uneasy, having a prospect of greater advantage held out to them by the government, to remove to Milford Haven, in the west of England, there to establish and prosecute the whale fishery. This being greatly to the detriment of many of the settlers at Dartmouth, it was opposed by them, but to no purpose. In a short time, therefore, the flourishing little settlement was nearly broken up. A number of families removed to England, carrying their property with them; which proved so injurious to the interests of the remainder, that they began immediately to abandon the enterprise and the place, disappointed in the hope which they had a few years before entertained, that they had gained a settlement which would prove to their lasting comfort and advantage. They could not leave the place without making great sacrifices in the sale of such property as could not be carried away with them. The place became nearly depopulated in a short time, for it was not a situation inviting to other business than that of whaling.

Those who removed to Milford Haven carried on the business extensively during many years. The privileges allowed them by government were such, as to give every encouragement that could reasonably be desired.

By the removal to Halifax, Nantucket was deprived of much capital and of many of the most active whalemen. The loss was severely felt, and operated as a discouragement to the whaling business. But the market for oil grew better, and it was not long before this seeming difficulty was removed. The business became prosperous, many new adventurers engaged in it, and the number of vessels considerably increased. Sloops and schooners, and a few brigs had heretofore been employed, which were mostly sent to the West Indies, the coast of Guinea, and to different ports on the coast of North America. The whales having become scarce at these places, it was necessary to explore new coasts in search of them. Larger vessels were accordingly introduced into the business, some of them ships, which were sent to the coast of Brazil, where the right whales were very numerous. They frequently obtained considerable quantities of sperm oil on these voyages, which brought a much greater price than whale oil. The ships generally returned with full cargoes.

In 1787 some difficulties arose in the state of Massachusetts, which claimed the attention of the legislature; and in their deliberations the necessity was urged of causing all persons holding any or either of the principal municipal offices in the commonwealth, to take and subscribe the oath of allegiance prescribed by the constitution. This was carried into effect by the following resolve :—

" In the House of Representatives, March 10th, 1787.

"*Resolved,*—That the several persons that have been or may hereafter be chosen for the present year as selectmen, assessors town clerk, town treasurer, constables, and collectors in the several towns, districts, and plantations of this commonwealth, be and they hereby are required, before the town clerk, or before some justice of the peace, to take and subscribe the oath of allegiance as prescribed in the constitution of this commonwealth, and the same certificate shall be made, if taken before a justice of the peace, as is already provided by law for the oaths of town, district or plantation officers; and the town clerk is directed to record the same in the book in which he is directed by law to record the several oaths to be taken by the said officers respectively, to qualify them so perform the duties thereof; and no act of either of the officers aforesaid shall, after one month from the passing of this resolve, be esteemed valid in law, until they have taken and subscribed the oath aforesaid; any law, usage or custom to the contrary notwithstanding.

"*And be it further resolved,* That in case any person, chosen to either of the offices aforesaid, shall neglect or refuse, within one month from the passing this resolve, and hereafter, annually, within seven days from the time of his election, the town to which such person or persons belong, at a legal meeting appointed for that purpose, shall proceed to make choice of some other person or persons, to serve in the office or offices to which the person or persons so neglecting or refusing had been elected; and the person or persons so refusing or neglecting to take the oath as aforesaid, shall be liable to the same penalties as is by law provided in case of refusal to serve in the office to which he or they have been elected.

" And that the secretary be and he is hereby directed to publish these resolves in the several newspapers, three weeks at least, successively, and to transmit a copy of the same to the clerk of each town, district, or plantation in this commonwealth."

The above resolve was very obnoxious to the people of Nantucket, there being in the town a large number of the society of Friends, and many others who could not conscientiously take the formal oath on any occasion. When it was found that so large a portion of the inhabitants were deprived of the common privileges of citizenship, and the town of their services as annual officers, it became necessary to take some measures to obviate the evil. The town convened on the occasion, and preferred a petition to the legislature, asking relief, which was not at that time granted to the satisfaction of the town. The petition was renewed at the next session of the general court, and a committee appointed to present the same. By this means the case was more fully understood, and satisfactory relief was consequently afforded. The following is a copy of the petition :

" *To the General Court of the Commonwealth of Massachusetts.*

" The petition of William Rotch, in behalf of the inhabitants of the town of Sherberne, on the island of Nantucket, respectfully showeth,

" That the inhabitants of Nantucket are much embarrassed in the prosecution of the internal affairs of that island, on account of a resolve passed in the general court, dated March 10th, 1787, requiring a test of certain town officers therein expressed, by which, from the very small number that can submit to such a declaration, a great part of the inhabitants are deprived of the privilege of that free choice of such persons as they apprehend the most suitable to conduct the affairs of the town; the inhabitants addressed the general court last year by petition on the subject, and stated their grievance, which was taken into consideration; and the senate and house of representatives respectively made an essay for their relief, adequate to the object desired, but they not uniting in the mode, the matter was dropped, and the inhabitants left without that redress they had reason to expect, and that the court had endeavored to extend.

" Your petitioner, therefore, prays your consideration on the subject, and that you would be pleased to grant us such relief from the operation of said resolve, as you in your wisdom may think fit.

" WILLIAM ROTCH.
" In behalf of the Inhabitants of Nantucket.

" Boston, 11th mo. 4th, 1787."

Previous to the late war, it was found that the manufacturing of sperm candles was a lucurative branch of business. Several new factories were now established for that purpose. The proprietors purchased the crude oil as it came from sea, from which they separated the sperm. The candles were mostly sent to the different seaports on the continent, and thence large quantities of them were shipped to the West Indies, and other parts of the world. The oil, separated from the sperm, was almost wholly consumed in the United States. Oil, in its unmanufactured state, was sometimes sent to England, but the duties there were so high as to allow but little profit to the exporters.

The light-houses within the states began to augment in number, about this time, which increased the consumption of sperm oil, and added to its price. Whale oil was obtained in greater quantities than sperm oil, and being afforded at about one half the price of the latter, it gave an opportunity for a more general use to be made of it. Although it does not give so brilliant a light as sperm oil, it will last nearly twice as long, so that on the whole it is very much cheaper, and will answer tolerably well for common lights. It is also serviceable in machinery and for sundry other uses, which renders it a valuable commodity. At the time we speak of, it commanded a ready sale in most of the larger seaports on the continent, from which it was shipped to various parts of the world, particularly to the West Indies. It generally constituted a part of the cargoes of most of the West India traders. Sometimes one barrel of it would bring two of flour from Baltimore or Philadelphia, clear of expense.

The obtaining of so great a number of right-whales produced more bone than could find a ready market, so that the price was reduced very low. Previous to the war, it frequently sold for one dollar a pound, it was now sold at ten cents, and sometimes even lower. The number of vessels increasing very fast, rendered it sometimes difficult to procure, on the island, enough men to navigate them. None of the natives were left, capable of going to sea. It therefore became necessary to resort to the continent for a considerable portion of each crew, whence there were brought some Indians and a great number of negroes. Many of the latter took up their residence here, and became the heads of families. They built a cluster of houses near the south part of the town, which is called New Guinea. Their inebriety and want of economy, generally kept them poor, although they made great voyages.

Blest with the enjoyment of peace, all were glad to turn their attention from the distressing scenes of the late conflict to the pursuits of peaceful life. But the effects of the war on the manners and customs of the inhabitants yet remained. Coming from various parts of the world, where they had been detained as prisoners, or whither they had wandered as exiles from their native home, many had brought with them the fashions and the morals of other nations. The change was observable in their dress and mode of living: it added materially to their expenses, and sometimes led to permanent injury. The great success in whaling, though it pretty generally overbalanced the increased expenses in living, had no tendency to lessen the immoralities which were unhappily introduced into society.

The whaling business gradually increased from year to year, though it occasionally met with depressions which checked its progress and created considerable uneasiness. In 1792 the people of New Bedford turned their attention to it more particularly than heretofore. A number of vessels were put into the service there, and some from Boston and Long Island. The quantity of oil thus imported exceeded the consumption, and kept the price below the cost to importers.

A few years previous to the revolution in France, in 1792, a new market opened for whale oil in that country, which gave encouragement that it would eventually be the best place for the sale of the article that could be found. Its use received every encouragement from some of the first characters of that nation, under a conviction that it was better adapted to common purposes than oil from seeds. Some shipments were made, which met with a profitable sale. Sperm oil was also introduced into France by way of trial, and lamps were sent there from England by private individuals to encourage its use. There appeared every prospect of success, and it is probable that France would soon have become a great mart for oil, if the revolution had not taken place. The confusion which followed that event put an end to all favorable prospects from that quarter. The shipments which were made there afterwards did not meet with prices sufficient to pay costs.

It is probable, that the business of killing whales may appear, to those entirely unacquainted with it, to be a very dangerous employment; as the people engaged therein are under the necessity of approaching the leviathan within the reach of a harpoon. Experience has taught them the best method to execute their business with the least danger. It is not common for any person to lose his life while thus engaged. The business is found to be as healthy as any on land or at sea. It has been remarked, that every man, belonging to a fleet of about thirty sail of whaling vessels, returned in good health, from a voyage of nearly a year's duration, from the coast of Brazil. Experience indeed has shown, what might at first view seem incredible, that fewer men die in the whaling service than in any other branch of navigation.*

During several years previous to 1790 many profitable sealing voyages were made from England and other places. This induced the people of Nantucket to turn their attention to that business, with a view to prosecute it, if it presented a good prospect of advantage. Sealing was in many respects, nearly allied with whaling. Seals and whales were generally met with on the same coast; it required as large vessels and as many men to engage in taking the former as the latter; the outfits were nearly the same, and the voyages were of like duration. In 1790 one vessel was fitted out for the coast of Africa, on a sealing expedition, but the original plan of the voyage was not adhered to, and the cruise was unsuccessful. But it had some good effect; for some useful knowledge was acquired respecting the different parts of the business, which was afterwards prosecuted to a considerable profit.

In 1791 vessels first went from Nantucket into the Pacific Ocean, in pursuit of whales. Some successful cruises had been made on the western coast of South America by vessels from England, previous to this time, which encouraged the people of Nantucket to engage in similar voyages. Although the prospect of success was very promising, it was with diffidence that they engaged therein, knowing that these voyages must necessarily be longer

---

* For some further particulars as to the mode of conducting whaling voyages, &c., we refer our readers to Second Part.

than they had been used to, and that they must suffer much inconvenience, if not embarassment, from laying out of their property so long a time. The ships first sent out returned loaded with oil, and reported that whales were plenty, the coast agreeable to cruise on, and the climate healthy. This was sufficient encouragement, notwithstanding the length of the voyages, for a considerable part of the whaling interest to be directed that way. An additional number of vessels was then fitted out, which together made a considerable fleet.

The space which we have allotted to ourselves will not allow us to frequently enter into minute details. But the following brief description of the outfits, &c., of the first ship that doubled Cape Horn, from Nantucket, is too interesting to be omitted. We are indebted for it to Capt. Worth, who commanded the ship. A comparison of the tonnage, cost, outfits, and duration of the voyage of the Ship Beaver with those of ships now engaged in the service, will, we think, show an onward progress in the whale fishery, to which we shall hardly find a parallel in any other business.

" Captain Paul Worth, in a new ship of 240 tons burthen, called the Beaver, sailed from Nantucket, on a whaling voyage, in the Pacific ocean, in the year 1791.

" The whole cost of said ship, fitted for the voyage, together with the cargo, amounted to $10,212.

" She carried 17 men, and manned 3 boats of 5 men each, which left 2 men, called ship-keepers, on board the ship when the boats were out in pursuit of whales.

" The principal part of her cargo, when fitted for sea, consisted of 400 bbls. iron hooped casks, (the remainder, about 1,400 bbls. were wooden hooped,) 40 bbls. salt provision, 3½ tons of bread, 30 bushels of beans and peas, 1,000 lbs. rice, 40 gallons molasses, 24 bbls. flour.

"All the additional provisions during the voyage were 200 lbs. bread.

" The ship was out 17 months, and was the first belonging to the island, that returned from the Pacific ocean.

" Her returned cargo was 650 bbls. sperm oil, worth £30 per ton, 370 bbls. head matter, worth £60 per ton, and 250 bbls. whale oil, worth £15 per ton.

" The ship was not coppered. There were four other ships, belonging to Nantucket, whaling on the same coast, that season."

The different branches of business appertaining to whaling were now carried on briskly; there was employment for all who were disposed to labor, the vessels generally arrived with good voyages, the markets were tolerably good for the sale of oil and candles, a cheerful smile was seen on every countenance. This might justly be termed the golden age of Nantucket. It was a season of prosperity which ought to be remembered with gratitude to the Giver of all good.

About this time a number of new ships, and other vessels, were added to the fleet, and many houses, candle-factories, and other buildings, were erected. Considering the shortness of the time since the close of the war, and comparing the appearance which the town, and every thing pertaining thereto, and the people themselves made, at that time, with the present circumstances of the place, the contrast was, beyond description, pleasing and encouraging. The people, at times, almost forgot the state of humility, which they had once experienced.

It has often been remarked that seasons of adversity follow close upon the heels of prosperity, and frequently at times when least expected. It has already been mentioned, that the French revolution in 1792 disappointed the expectations, entertained by oil-dealers, that France would become a good market for oil. The effect of this stoppage in the sale of oil was not anticipated in season to prevent serious losses. All the foreign markets were glutted with oil, when the price suddenly fell below what it could be obtained for at Nantucket; which was very discouraging, and caused the business to go on heavily, although the vessels generally obtained full cargoes of oil.

The people had been so long engaged in whaling, that they could not put their shipping into other business without loss. Another circumstance, and not the least, operated much against the interests of Nantucket. This was the increased price of provisions and every other article necessary for the outfits of vessels engaged in the service. The owners of the shipping found that they should suffer a great loss by keeping their vessels at home; they therefore concluded to send them out, with these gloomy prospects, hoping that time would bring about a change to their advantage; but they were disappointed, for the business continued to grow worse, and new difficulties presented themselves.

It was hard for this country to keep within the limits of strict neutrality, in the war between France and England. Many, for the sake of good profit, violated the law, which created a suspicion with the belligerents of Europe, that the Americans were furnishing each other's enemies unwarrantably. These circumstances caused the rate of insurance to be increased, which, combined with what has before been mentioned, produced a stagnation in the whaling business. Many sold their vessels for what they would bring, while others, hoping better things, laid theirs up and unrigged them. Some who had prospered better than their neighbors, and made a little profit in the business, were confident of final success, notwithstanding these accumulated embarrassments; they continued, therefore, to fit out their vessels.   Of these some did well, but others suffered losses, and were under the necessity of re-linquishing the business.

Notwithstanding the various vicissitudes of fortune, and the discouraging prospects which often presented to view, yet the wealth of the inhabitants was rather increasing, which led the enterprising genius to contemplate projects to acquire an increase of property; one of which, and not the least, was to establish a bank.   This subject had long been in contemplation with a small number of commercial characters; but, being a novel undertaking for the people of Nantucket, many revolted at the idea, from an apprehension that there would not be business to warrant the undertaking.   Others, who were advocates for the scheme, urged the public utility which would probably result from its establishment; that it would increase the business of the place, and enable those of small capitals to execute their business with more despatch and a greater profit. It was many months that the subject was in contemplation, before an attempt was made to carry it into effect,   However, in the year 1795, the people having become pretty well reconciled, a charter was obtained, and the business of the bank commenced, with perhaps as great a degree of cheerfulness as is common in similar cases.   But how was the scene changed, in a very short time after its commence-ment in business, when it was announced to the public that the bank had been robbed of twenty thousand dollars. What could be more sudden, or what event could happen that would give a greater shock to the community in so trifling a loss.   The people were not in the least suspi-cious of the act, consequently they were not prepared to receive the information.   The event could not but excite the greatest anxiety on the public mind that could be imagined; it caused them to leave their business, and throng the streets for many days.

The loss of the money was not a consideration, compared with the vindictive spirit which the robbery afterwards occasioned. The effects on the community at large were solemn. Many, who were not immediately concerned, had to deplore the unhappy state in which their friends and neighbors were involved, and out of the reach of a mediator.

To give a minute account of the transactions growing out of this affair, is not our intention or wish. The inhabitants of Nantucket, and all others acquainted with the circumstances, will appreciate our reasons for passing it over thus briefly.

This year, 1795, the name of the town was changed. It had hitherto been called *Sherburne*, agreeably with the patent of Francis Lovelace, governor of New York, in 1673. This name, being attended with some inconvenience, was now changed to that of *Nantucket*.

It is generally conceded, that the people of Nantucket possess as great share of enterprising genius as those of any other place in the union; but the business they follow, and principally depend upon for a subsistence, requires their steady and persevering application. They have often experienced, that a small deviation therefrom has resulted in loss, and sometimes in serious embarrassments. Although it may appear to strangers who visit them, that the business they follow is very lucrative, from a consideration of the number of ships in port and the bustle of fitting them out, still the voyages yield but small profits; for very few persons, even of the most fortunate, have obtained any considerable fortunes by the whale fishery. Industry, and steady habits, and frugality, rather

than great gains, have made the place what it is.   All are
remotely or immediately interested in the success of the
business; and there are few, whose income is not increased
or diminished just in proportion to the high or low price
of oil.   In times of peace the property of the island has
on the whole gradually increased.   But in war all business is at a stand; the circle of dependencies is broken,
the merchant, the sailor, the mechanic, are each thrown on
his own resources, and driven often to seek his living in
occupations, for which he is qualified neither by education
nor inclination.   We have but faintly delineated the embarrassments and sufferings of the inhabitants during the
revolutionary struggle; but the picture, though imperfectly
drawn, exhibits their situation clearly enough to convince
the reader, that, under the most favorable aspects, war is
to them the most terrible event that can occur.   If imprisonment and its attendant pestilence, to which in war
many of her sailors must be exposed; if want, in all itr
forms, in which most of her residents must be involved;
if dependence on the mercies of an assailing enemy, from
which none can be exempt,—if these do not give force to
her voice when she solicits peace, then may Nantucket
indeed despair of success, and her sons hold in light
esteem a government, which they have done so much to
enrich; and its independence purchased at a price, which
millions cannot repay.   Others may discover advantages
in war, and necessity for it; but we can see nothing but
madness in an act, which, to avoid one evil, deliberately
and knowingly incurs another a thousand fold greater.

In 1796, the business of the place was at a low ebb.
Many expedients were resorted to, aside from whaling,
some of which were advantageous to those who engaged
in them.   But, in general, those who departed from the

beaten tracks of their ancestors encountered great difficulties. Many of the most able seamen sailed from other places in the merchant service, some of whom did well, and acquired handsome estates; while others met with hard fortune and got along but indifferently.

One ship was sent out on a voyage to the East Indies, the owners of which, not being acquainted with the advantages to be taken in that trade, did not succeed to their wishes. The cargo consisted of whale oil, sperm candles, Madeira wine, hard soap, and Spanish dollars. If that part of the cargo, which was the produce of the business of Nantucket, had been exchanged for commodities more suited for that market, or converted into specie, it is probable, that the voyage would have resulted in a good profit. This voyage, however, was not without its advantages, for it was a means of obtaining knowledge highly necessary for that trade, which was afterwards acted on by some of these same owners with considerable advantage.

The year 1797 was ushered in by a natural phenomenon rendered very terrific by some circumstances with which it was attended. The evening preceding the 1st of the 1st month was uncommonly pleasant. There was not a cloud to be seen. Not long after midnight, the inhabitants were instantly aroused from sleep by one of the heaviest peals of thunder ever heard, attended with vivid lightning and an uncommon shower of hail. The whole town was immediately lighted up, as if by a general conflagration. Some thought, that the town was in flames, even the very houses they were in; others thought, that the dissolution of all things had commenced. But the consternation subsided when, it was discovered, that the fire proceeded from two barns in the outskirts of the town.

The people immediately repaired to the fire, but too late to save the cattle or any other contents of the buildings; they could only remain spectators of the devouring element.

In 1798, in addition to the discouragements in business heretofore stated, there was great apprehension of war between the United States and France. War was, at this time, particularly dreaded, for the shipping was mostly out on long voyages, some of which were not expected to terminate in less time than twelve or eighteen months. Many of the adventurers had their whole property afloat. Accounts were received almost daily of spoilations on American vessels, and the government was on the point of commencing hostilities. But it is not our purpose to enter into the merits of the controversy between the two nations. The commotions naturally attending the incidents above recited brought their evils to the people of Nantucket. The price of provisions was raised, and the rates of insurance increased in a short time to twenty per cent.; which must have subjected ship-owners to loss, according to the price of oil at that time, even if their ships had arrived with full cargoes. Four Nantucket ships were captured during the existence of these difficulties. This was sufficient to fill the minds of the people with dismay, for they were almost ready to conclude, that a war had already taken place, without a declaration to that effect. There were, however, no other ships captured belonging to the place, and the people again resumed their business of fitting out, although it was with very dull prospects. Some of the ship-owners being quite discouraged, sold their shipping, and turned their attention to other objects for a subsistence, which, though perhaps less lucrative, yielded a greater share of satisfaction. The discouragements continued in a greater or less degree for a number of years, which necessarily caused many of our best seamen to leave the island in pursuit of business from other seaports. Many talked of removing into the country, and some did so.

In 1799, the people were somewhat alarmed for the safety of their ships round Cape Horn. They had long been apprehensive, that the Spaniard did not feel friendly to the whale ships in the south seas, and were now confirmed in their fears by the detention of several ships at St. Marys. Later accounts, however, gave information of their liberation in a few days without damage.

In 1800, on the tenth of the fourth month, a number of whales were seen on the north side of the island, from one to three leagues distant from the land. Several boats were immediately sent in pursuit of them, and, on coming up with them, commenced an attack with that spirit and activity which is ever drawn out on such occasions. A great number of spectators on shore were pointing their glasses towards the scene of action, to view the operations of their townsmen, who were now engaged in the conflict. At length they had the gratification of seeing two of the monsters of the deep yield to the dexterity of their pursuers. In the course of the day, the whales which had been killed were towed into the harbor and brought to the wharf. The people were familiar with every circumstance relative to whaling, but many had never beheld the animal of whose prodigious size they had heard so much. To exhibit one of the whales to the best advantage, it was drawn upon the wharf, where thousands of people during the day had an opportunity of beholding what had hitherto been to them only the theme of their songs or of their fireside, and which is so beautifully

though simply described by one of their own poets, who
had himself wielded the harpoon and lance.

> " Thou didst, O Lord, create the mighty whale,
>   That woudrous monster of a mighty length;
>   Vast is his head and body, vast his tail,
>   Beyond conception his unmeasured strength.
>
>   When he the surface of the sea hath broke,
>   Arising from the dark abyss below,
>   His breath appears a lofty stream of smoke,
>   The circling waves, like glittering banks of snow."

The larger of the above-mentioned whales produced
thirty-one, and the other, sixteen barrels. Only nine
days afterwards, another whale was brought into the
harbor, which produced thirty barrels of oil. We find
no instances of the kind in any former period of our
history.

An academy was incorporated in 1800, and a building
erected for the school, on what is called Academy Hill.
The same year a bell, weighing one thousand pounds, was
placed in the steeple of the north congregational meeting-
house.

The number of inhabitants on the island at this time,
was 5617.

Some of the difficulties, heretofore stated, as attending
the whaling business, had now, in some degree, been removed, still it was attended with some embarrassments.
The high price of provisions, which is one of the principal articles in the outfits of the ships, and the advanced
prices of most things necessary to their equipment, prevented any increase of the shipping at present.

CHAPTER VIII.

We have already stated, that a bar extends across the mouth of Nantucket harbor. This bar has ever been a great hindrance to the passing of large vessels in and out. Much expense yearly accrues from the necessity of employing lighters for all vessels drawing a considerable draft of water, and in some instances losses and even shipwrecks have occurred in attempts to pass the bar with vessels, after all precautions have been used to make them as light as possible. It has been the opinion of some, that the employment given to the large number of men, necessarily engaged in getting large vessels in and out of the harbor, more than counterbalances the disadvantages above stated. This consideration, however, has not deterred the most enterprising citizens from devising various methods, from time to time, of deepening the channel across this bar. But no plan had ever been devised, which seemed sufficiently practicable to warrant public action upon it, till the year 1803. A proposition was then made at a town meeting, to petition congress to assist Nantucket, in any way which might be deemed expedient, in digging a channel from Brant Point to the outer part of the outer bar. The subject underwent a long discussion : many were opposed to it, from an apprehension that government would not grant the request; but a committee was at length appointed to bear a petition to congress, and to use their endeavors to carry it into effect. The committee, on their return, reported that congress had so far attended to the request, as to authorize the appointment of suitable persons to survey the harbor and bar, at the expense of the government, and to estimate the probable expense of the undertaking. This report was very flattering and satisfactory to the people in general, and a committee of five was chosen to wait on the surveyors, when they should arrive at the island, and to act as necessity should require in carrying the whole subject into effect. A larger committee was also chosen to assist by advice or otherwise in forwarding the important work.

Many were now so elated with the prospect of effecting the desirable object, that their views extended from digging a channel to building stone piers from the points of Coetue and Brant Point in a northerly direction to the outer bar, or as far as should be found expedient to accomplish the end in view. This plan, differing so much from the one first proposed, met with great opposition. The subject became the common topic of conversation. The people, generally, opposed every plan but the original one, that of digging a channel, from the conviction that piers would be the means of obstructing the navigation, by causing new shoals, and that, being built of stone, they would endanger passing vessels, especially in the night.

In the summer of the same year, the surveyors arrived and very diligently attended to the business of their appointment. The committee of the town faithfully waited on them till the survey was completed. They had been led by observation, to believe that stone piers would be injurious to the harbor, but they proposed that piles should be driven down, eight or ten feet apart, and the spaces filled with plank, by which means they supposed that the velocity of the tides would be increased, and the channel by that means deepened without much digging.

The town was again convened for the purpose of hearing the report of the committee, who stated that the surveyors were of the opinion that it would be expedient to build wooden piers: one extending from the north-west point of Coetue to the south-west corner of the black flats; the other to begin about one-third of the distance from the end of Brant Point to the cliff, and to extend to the north-east corner of Cliff Shoal; both upon straight lines. A long debate then ensued, when it appeared that the general voice was against having piers of any kind, from the apprehension that they would cause new shoals, and thus obstruct the entrance of large vessels into the harbor. No objection, however, was urged against digging a channel, and a committee was appointed with instructions to use their best endeavors to have the original plan of deepening the water by digging carried into effect. But when congress next met, the proposition was rejected, and thus the whole matter ended.

The price of oil of late had considerably increased, which animated the people and gave new life to the whaling business. This rise was principally occasioned by the following causes. First: many ships had been sold out of the service, or hauled up by reason of the depression of the times, as heretofore stated; which reduced the importations of oil below the demands of the market. Secondly: the consumption of oil and sperm candles was fast increasing in this country, for experience had plainly shown that they were, on many accounts, far preferable to tallow. People needed only to use sperm candles, and sperm oil, to be convinced that they are less expensive than tallow, and that they give a better light. The first cost of sperm candles is indeed greater than that of tallow, but the difference in the price of the two kinds is more than counterbalanced by the quantity of light produced from the former. Sperm candles are clean, they emit no disagreeable smell, and, very little smoke. As these circumstances became more and more known, the demand for oil and sperm candles increased at every seaport on the continent. Fresh encouragement was consequently given to the whaling business and new adventurers engaged in it. Notwithstanding the high price of provisions, the number of ships increased, and the voyages were generally advantageous to the owners.

The reader will probably have noticed, in the course of this history, that small depressions in the times have had a material effect on the minds of the people of Nantucket: that from causes apparently temporary and unimportant, they have been discouraged and almost ready to leave the island, supposing that the whaling business " is done," an expression sometimes used on these occasions. This may be accounted for by the. consideration, that the business in general affords small profits, and that a small change to its disadvantage is in consequence immediately and keenly felt. On the other hand, a few years of good fortune animates the people, and encourages them to take increased risks. This was the case at the time of which we were last speaking. The ships have generally, for the last few years, brought in good voyages. Oil met with a ready sale at prices, which kept every branch of the business in active operation.

In the year 1804, the Pacific Bank and two insurance offices were established.

In 1805, a new jail was built.

Forty-eight ships at this time belonged to Nantucket, not one of which was in port; a similar instance never before occurred.

Some fears have long been entertained, that the Spaniards of South America would commit depredations on the whale ships. Threats to this effect had frequently been made, and some ships had actually been detained in Spanish ports to the great detriment of their voyages. A war was much talked of, and expected by many, between our government and that of Spain. The detention of the ships, added to the difficulties apprehended between the two nation, enhanced the rates of insurance, by which the profits of the business were proportionably lessened. Soon after this, however, some arrivals dissipated the fears of the inhabitants in some degree, since no very serious difficulty with the Spaniards had occurred.

Although the independence of the United States had long been acknowledged by Great Britan, still, a restless, overbearing disposition had almost uniformly been manifested towards this country by the British government, ever since the revolutionary war. The depredations on our commerce, the impressment of our seamen, and their forcible detention in the British service, form a part of our national history too familiar to our readers to need a repetition by us. It is sufficient to say, that the embarrassed affairs of the nation, and uncertain duration of peace, had a serious effect on the people of Nantucket.

The price of provisions, and, indeed, of every article of necessity, was kept very high; the rate of insurance was also considerably enhanced. Fortunately, not a single whaling ship, belonging to Nantucket, was taken and arried into port.

The quantity of oil imported into the country in 1806, and during the previous year, was considerably greater than the consumption. The price was at times merely nominal, and large quantities remained on hand for a long time. This period of our history may be considered a time of plenty. Many buildings were erected within a few past years, among which was a banking-house for the Nantucket Bank. Every branch of business was conducted with propriety, and produced a good profit: every class of people appeared satisfied with their lot, from the common laborer who could earn one dollar and twenty-five cents a day, to the most wealthy merchant.

Although during a number of past years the business at Nantucket frequently assumed a gloomy aspect, in consequence of the commotions of the belligerents in Europe, yet, at this time, a tide of success had lulled the people into a state of security; so that arrangements were now made to engage more extensively in the whale fishery. But, alas! how short-sighted is man! How liable to disappointment, even amid the best prospects of success. On the 22d of the 6th month 1807, the British ship of war Leopard fired into the United States ship Chesapeake. The annunciation of this event, which seemed but a precursor of approaching war, cast a gloom over the prospects of Nantucket deeper and more heartfelt than had been caused by any occurrence since the revolutionary war. The embargo, which soon followed, had the effect of keeping down the price of oil and candles, by preventing the exportation of these articles from the country. But as the act did not embrace whaling and fishing vessels, a considerable number of owners concluded to send out their ships, although the probability of success was not equal to the risk incurred. The vessels were lying at the wharves, fitted or fitting for sea; and many articles of outfits, some of them perishable, were ou hand. There was good reason to suppose, that but a small fleet would be put to sea under existing political affairs, and that the few vessels which might venture out would make profitable returns, if they should be so fortunate as to escape capture. It was, however, found that no insurance could be made either on the island or abroad; and the owners, unwilling to incur the hazard of total loss, abandoned their enterprise, stripped their ships and hauled them up. Employment for laboring men nearly ceased, and mariners belonging to Nantucket, who had been sailing from other ports, were returning home destitute of business. In the year 1809 the prospect seemed more flattering than heretofore, that the storm which had so long raged in Europe would subside; and owners were prompted to send out their ships, trusting to their return before the jarring elements of war should disturb our own country. This year many families, wearied with the vicissitudes almost daily experienced, removed to different parts of the country. The streets of the town were thronged with laboring poor, already so reduced as to be quite at a loss to know whence articles of the first necessity were to be obtained; some were quite destitute of the means of subsistence.

The anxiety, constantly manifested by the people for the welfare of the absent ships, increased towards the close of the year. Our government was preparing for either event, of war or peace. In this state of suspense, although a large part of the business capital of the island was at sea, six or eight ships were, in 1810, fitted out for the Pacific Ocean. None ever sailed under more discouraging circumstances. In the tenth month of this year, every ship belonging to the port was at sea, some in pursuit of right whales, but the greater part in the Pacific Ocean.

In the year 1810, when the enumeration of the inhabitants was taken, the whole number was 6807, among whom were 210 over 70 years of age. The number of widows was 379, of fatherless children 474. There were found about 4000 who had not received either the small or kine-pock; it was also at the same time found that there were about 1322 families and 2055 ratable polls; dwelling-houses 937, all other buildings 872; horses 332, oxen 15, cows 505, swine 355, sheep about 10,000.

In 1811, the probability of war increased. The events of the revolution were familiar to the recollections of many of the inhabitants. The loss of a large number of the young men of the island during that struggle, either in the service of the country, by accidents at sea, or by suffering on board prison-ships, and in other places of confinement, was yet deeply felt. Every new omen of war seemed to threaten a [renewal of similar sufferings and distress. Owners, however, continued to fit out their ships, and men were willing to go in them, for no other business presented. Commerce, generally, was so embarrassed, that the young men could find no employment in other places; they therefore preferred meeting the chances of war in the whaling service to remaining idle at home. The ships were sent out with nearly the same freedom as if no war was anticipated, but with very different prospects. Insurance offices, in the early part of the year, refused to take any risks; but before its close, owing to some little change in the aspect of affairs, they offered to insure at twenty per cent. Even at this rate they declined taking large amounts. So great a premium was considered by owners disproportionate to the risk, and but little was insured. The rate of insurance soon after fell to fifteen per cent., and insurance was effected on large amounts.

Many of the inhabitants now began to turn their thoughts towards the country. Some families had already removed, and many others were making preparations to follow them. It was anticipated, that, if war should take place, the value of real estate would be immediately reduced, particularly houses. Before the year closed, sixty dwelling-houses were offered for sale, the owners of which intended to go into the country. The thoughts of those who proposed to move were, in general, turned towards Ohio, attracted by the flattering accounts received from that state of the salubrity of its climate and the luxuriance of its soil.

In 1812, the infringements of the English on our rights still continued, and our government appeared to be making preparations for war. Although it was generally believed that, without an alteration on the part of Great Britain, war would ensue, yet the people of Nantucket cherished the belief that the Orders in Council, which had so long constituted the greater part of the contention between the two governments, would be revoked. Under this impression, many fitted out their ships. About the 4th month, our government laid an embargo, to be of three months continuance. This measure was an almost sure presage of war, being designed to give an opportunity for the shipping to arrive before that event, and to prevent vessels in port from venturing out, and thereby falling into the hands of the enemy. Had the first embargo act extended to whaling vessels, much of the property of the island would have been saved. But now few of the owners of the ships belonging to Nantucket could avail themselves of any advantage of the warning of our government, for their property was mostly on the ocean, with prospects that little would return in less time than two years.

As the political affairs of the nation drew nearer to a crisis, the scenes of the revolution became more vivid in the recollections of the people; and caused them to deplore the situation of the inhabitants and their property. A town meeting was held for the purpose of taking into consideration the expediency of sending a memorial to Congress, giving a true statement of their situation and circumstances. That the reader may fully conceive the feelings which then prevailed, we insert the memorial at large.

" To the Honorable Senate and House of Representatives of the United States of America, in Congress assembled, the memorial of the inhabitants of Nantucket respectfully showeth:

" That from a conviction of their rights to assemble and deliberate in a peaceful manner, they have this day convened in legal town meeting, to consider the serious and alarming situation, in which the politics of the nation seem to be placed. They are aware of the legal and exalted situation in which you are placed by the people, and believe you are constantly disposed to alleviate every section of the Union. It is under that impression that they now address you; as they are persuaded their situation is not fully known to many of you, they take the liberty of a retrospective view.

" In the year 1775, they were in possession of 150 sail of vessels, which were employed in the whale fishery; they had also several more employed as coasters, and in the merchant service. When the revolutionary war commenced, the greater part of the seamen were compelled to leave their heretofore peaceful occupations, and engage in a kind of employ not suited to their former habits, in consequence of which a great number of valuable and enterprising men were brought to an untimely end, and hundreds of widows,

with many fatherless children, were left with only a precarious de-
dendence on surviving friends.

" Your memoralists would also further observe, that, in addition
to the common calamities of maritime war, their harbor was frequently visited by ravaging enemies, whose insatiable thirst for
plunder and devastation left but little for the subsistence of the
inhabitants, and eventually the once flourishing town of Nantucket
was left resembling an abandoned village.

" After the blessings of peace were restored, the spirit of enterprise again displayed its feeble but pleasing countenance, and the
progressing industry and perseverance of the citizens has in a degree
surmounted the evils of war, as a general state of comfort is prevailing, while some are above necessity and others are opulent.
Therefore after viewing things as they actually are, and considering
that Nantucket is an island that may be invaded at any point, and
its situation without, or beyond, a protecting distance from the continent, your memorialists cannot, under these gloomy circumstances,
fail to deplore the necessity of commencing a foreign war; and
are probably influenced in their feelings from knowing the miseries of those, that are so unfortunate as to fall within the vrotex
occasioned by the conflicting powers of Europe.

" It is further observable, that seven eighths of the mercantile
capital is now at sea, three fourths of which is not expected to return
within twelve months from the present date.

To conclude: while your memorialists feel that confident assurance, which ought to possess the minds of the people towards the
their rulers, they have no desire to control, yet they have no hesitation
respectfully to declare their belief, that the declaration of a foreign
war would be desolating to the inhabitants of this island. And it
will be the constant prayer of your memorialists, that the necessity
of such a declaration may be averted.

" ISAAC COFFIN, Moderator.
" JAMES COFFIN, Town Clerk.

" Nantucket, 9th, 5th mo. 1812."

This memorial was read three times, and claimed the
serious attention of the people ; solemnity pervaded the
whole meeting in a striking manner. After some perti-
nent remarks, it was unanimously voted to accept it, and

the selectmen were made a committee to forward it to congress.

The apprehension of a war had now become so general, that it began to have a material effect on the business of the place. Many of the inhabitants still continued to talk of removing into the country; but their property could not be sold without a sacrifice, which caused some to relinquish their intention, while others carried it into effect, and settled in various places. Most kinds of business had become so unsettled, that very little was done. All were daily expecting to hear of something decisive from the government, that would fix the fate of Nantucket as to peace or war. The rumors, which were continually circulated, helped to increase the general anxiety. This state of suspense continued until the 24th of the 6th month, when official accounts were received of a declaration of war by our government against Great Britain, on the 18th of the same month.

This information, though it had been for some time expected, produced inexpressible inquietude of mind. It proved the fallacy of the opinion, or rather hope, which many of the inhabitants had fondly cherished, that the English government would rescind the Orders in Council, and thus remove what was considered the principal cause of the difference between the two nations.

There seemed no alternative left for the people, but to submit to the calamities which this event would probably bring upon them. The reflection on the situation and circumstances of the place was appalling. Nearly the whole amount of the trading capital was in the Pacific Ocean, the greater part of which was not likely to return in less than one year, and some perhaps not in two. This consideration, added to that of the exposed situation of the place, led many to devise measures to ward off impending ruin.

The fleet of ships at sea more immediately claimed the attention of the public, for the welfare of the community depended on the whaling interest. Some of the principal ship-owners convened for the purpose of taking into consideration the gloomy aspect that pervaded the commercial concerns of the place, and to devise, if possible, some plan whereby the property at sea might be saved from capture. After a general discussion of the subject, it was concluded to consult with the other ship-owners and commercial men on the expediency of adopting some measure, through the influence of the British minister, Foster, then at Washington, to save the place from the calamities of war, and more especially, the ships at sea from capture; by representing, that the people of this place were determined to take no active part in the war, but to observe a strict neutrality, so far as would be consistent with the circumstances of the place. The plan proposed was, to request the British minister to use his influence with his government to rescue from capture the whale ships belonging to Nantucket, then in the Pacific, and to secure to the inhabitants the privilege of whaling, under certain stipulations, during the continuance of the war. After some deliberation, the opinion prevailed, that the prospect of success was too faint to warrant the attempt, and the plan was abandoned. It was the opinion of many at that time, and subsequent events have strengthened the opinion, that had the town united in the attempt, and done all in its power for the promotion of the object, very great advantages would have resulted. The fleet at sea might, perhaps, have been saved, and the liberty secured to carry on the whale fishing without molestation.

In support of this opinion we refer to the report of the
town's committee in a succeeding page. That committee
was sent to Admiral Cochrane on the subject of importing
provisions and fuel from the continent. They found the
Admiral very friendly toward the people of Nantucket,
and when the subject of whaling was mentioned to him, he
told the committee, that if they would state in writing the
wishes of their constituents, the document should be forwarded to his government the next day by dispatch vessel,
where, he had no doubt, it would meet with a favorable
reception. The kind treatment of this committee by Admiral Cochrane, and his granting their request to bring
provisions, &c., from the continent, particularly the liber-
ality of his views in relation to whaling, lead us to believe
that every reasonable indulgence would have been granted,
had it been asked, in a proper manner, at the commencement of the war.

Many were apprehensive that the island would soon be
visited by the British in a hostile manner. Those who had
property exposed, which admitted of being removed, immediately took measures to secure it, by shipping it with all
possible despatch to some seaport on the continent. Many
families, whose removal into the country had heretofore
been prevented by the difficulty of disposing of their property, now concluded to leave it unsold; some went to the
state of Ohio, others to other places.

The apprehension of an invasion by the enemy was
strengthened by a groundless report, that an armament
was preparing in Halifax for that purpose, which added
to the confusion and terror already too prevalent. A
considerable number of the poorer class were obliged to
leave the island to seek employment. From the time of
the first embargo to the present, the business of the place

had been in so depressed a state, that those, who depended for subsistence on their daily labor, were reduced, through want of employment, to great distress. Some could not subsist without the assistance of their friends. This class first felt the pressure of the times. Many of them removed to places, where there appeared a prospect of obtaining bread, a large part of whom returned, at the close of the war, to the place of their fondest associations and strongest attachments, from which nothing but the most pressing necessity could have compelled them to remove.

The immediate effects of the war were experienced, in the 7th month of this year, 1812, in the capture and burning of a whaling schooner, to the northward of the Gulf Stream, together with the oil which she had obtained. The crew were made prisoners of war. This was the first capture of a Nantucket vessel after the commencement of hostilities. There were, at this time, belonging to the island, 43 ships, 47 sloops, 7 brigs, 19 schooners; total, 116 vessels, whose tonnage amounted to nearly 11,000 tons.

It is not our purpose to enter into a detail of all the embarrassments and sufferings occasioned by the war; but to endeavor to state such particulars as may be useful or interesting to the reader. In a few months after the war commenced, many of the inhabitants were reduced to great distress. Want of employment, as has already been stated, had before reduced large numbers of the laboring class to want; loss of property, and other circumstances was now daily bringing others to poverty. It was difficult to procure flour and corn. British cruisers were so numerous on the coast, as to render it very hazardous for those coasters to pass, which had usually supplied the market with bread-stuffs. Late in the fall no bread-stuff could be bought, and little was expected to be brought to the island; and there was less wood than had been known for many years. Hundreds of the laboring poor might daily be seen in the streets, destitute of the means of subsistence, because destitute of employment.

The scarcity of provisions, the approaching inclement season, and the danger of venturing out with vessels, claimed the serious attention of every class of the community. At length a number of vessels were sent to different places westward to bring flour, corn, and other necessaries. Some of the freighters were not induced to this measure by pecuniary considerations. Their object was to secure the inhabitants from suffering during the winter, when it would be impossible to have any communication with the continent.

In the 11th month a load of corn arrived, which was much needed. The corn sold for one dollar and twenty-five cents a bushel, and the flour for thirteen dollars and fifty cents a barrel. Although the price was high, the whole cargo was sold very fast: higher prices would have been obtained, if demanded. It was truly melancholy to see the people thronging and pressing to take their turns to be served with articles of food, while many came on board the vessel, equally in want, but destitute of the means to buy. Such a picture of distress had not been displayed since the revolutionary war. Previous to the war, not a beggar was to be seen in the streets; at this time many received their daily pittance from the hand of charity.

In this season of distress the banks did not feel themselves safe. The apprehension of a fleet from Halifax induced the directors to secure what specie could be spared from immediate use, by placing it in some safe keeping on the continent. The public, discovering their fears, immediately called out their deposits in specie, and also thronged the doors of the banks with their paper. The pressure however was sustained, and all demands promptly and satisfactorily answered.

In addition to the numerous difficulties already experienced, the easterly part of the town was, in the 12th month, attacked by fire. The fire was first discovered in one of the lower buildings on the old south wharf. It was a favorable circumstance that the wind blew briskly from the northward, for there were no buildings to leeward. But, notwithstanding this, and the most active exertions of the inhabitants, eight buildings were consumed. The loss was estimated at $6000.

The winter did not commence with that gloom which had been anticipated. The means of procuring provisions had so far succeeded, as to remove the danger of famine. The poverty, and the number of the poorer class, however, rapidly increased.

Some of the homeward-bound whale ships were captured by the enemy, yet a few arrived safely, which materially benefited a large number of every class of citizens. For the nature of the business is such, that the loss of a single ship injures many, and many are benefited by the safe arrival of one.

A number of the citizens, feeling the distress of war increasing upon them, and considering that they had a right to address the chief magistrate of the nation in a respectful manner, in their individual capacity, addressed the following petition to the president, representing some of the embarrassments with which they were surrounded:

"NANTUCKET, NOVEMBER 21st, 1812.

"*James Madison, Esq. President of the United States.*

" Sir,—The republican citizens of Nantucket are conscious, that, when the government find it expedient for the support of our national sovereignty and independence to declare war, the people mus^t expect to submit to burdens and privations they are not accustomed to in time of peace; but the peculiar situation of Nantucket has induced us to address you.

" The island in its detatched situation, being beyond the reach of protection from the continent, is exposed to the ravages of an enemy.

" The island contains a population of nearly seven thousand inhabitants, many of whom were employed in the various mechanic arts, and other employments, peculiarly applicable to the whale fishery, who, since the declaration of war, have been without employ, and thereby reduced to indigent circumstances.

" Experience has taught that the whale fishery, for which this place has ever been famed, cannot be prosecuted while it is exposed to the ravages of war; and should it continue, we fear it will in a great degree, be lost; it has been considered of such national consequence as to induce both England and France to offer great encouragements to the citizens of this place to remove and establish it within their dominions.

" We are aware that the constitution of the United States expressly provides, that no preference shall be given to one state over the others; at the same time we are fully sensible, that, when a resort to arms is considered unavoidable, our government will afford that consistent relief to such parts of the community as are deprived of the means of subsistence by a continuation of the war. Such appears to be the situation we are approaching, as most of the trading capital of the island is now in the Southern Ocean, some of which will not be on its return within one year from the present date; and if the war continues, we fully believe the greater part, if not the whole, will fall an easy prey to the enemy.

" As we are thus situated, and deprived by nature from obtaining a subsistence on the island, it seems we have no choice, but that of respectfully soliciting your attention and that of our government, to our alarming condition; requesting also liberty to ask, if in your wisdom any means can be devised to save our fleet of whale ships now in the Southern Ocean, and if any method can be adopted, whereby we may prosecute the cod and whale fisheries without the risk of capture by the enemy.

"We also beg leave to ask, if any stipulation can consistently be effected with Great Britain, whereby the cod and whale fisheries of both nations may be exempted from the ravages of war.

"In behalf of the republican citizens of Nantucket, we have the honor to be with the greatest respect, sir, your obedient servants.

"Signed by a committee and forwarded."

In 1813 the American coast became so infested with British ships of war and privateers, that it was dangerous to go to any port on the continent. The supply of provisions and fuel was thus rendered very precarious. The distress of the people still increased: driven from their usual avocations, they were compelled to seek employment of any kind that would administer to their daily wants. Some engaged in fishing round the island; a greater number turned their attention to farming. The prospects of this latter class were not very encouraging: many of them owned neither land nor implements. They were obliged to take leases of land for two years, and give the owner a certain proportion of the produce. There was little left to them, after paying the rent and other expenses incident to the business. They labored hard for a poor living, with no encouraging prospect, but that of a speedy peace. Others of a younger class followed the sea from other ports. Removals from the island still continued, some to avoid present distress, others with a view to permanency.

CHAPTER IX.

The subject of inoculating for the kine-pock early engaged the attention of the people of Nantucket. In the year 1810, it was ascertained, by request of the health committee, that about four thousand had not been inoculated for either the small or kine-pock. At that time it was contemplated to have a general vaccination, but the measure was not very spiritedly taken up, and finally failed of being carried into effect. In 1813 Benjamin Hussey, a native of Nantucket, arrived from Europe. He had been absent from the island about twenty-six years, the last ten of which he resided principally in France, where he introduced vaccine inoculation. He inoculated, in the city of Dunkirk and parts adjacent, upwards of seven thousand, for which services he received no pecuniary remuneration. His benevolence, however, gained for him high encomiums from the French government. The experience which he had acquired in the art, and the success which had attended his practice, encouraged a few individuals to request him to undertake a general inoculation at Nantucket, on the condition of receiving a reasonable compensation from the town for his services. After some deliberation he assented to the proposition, and named the sum of three hundred dollars as the amount which would satisfy him for his labor. A town-meeting was immediately held for the purpose of taking the subject into consideration, at which the advantages of the proposition were set forth, and some documents read, to show the propriety of the services offered, on the terms proposed. A large number, however, opposed the measure; and a majority finally decided not to improve this opportunity to introduce a general inoculation. Notwithstanding this unexpected result, he proceeded to the vaccination of all who called on him for that purpose; and before he left the island nearly a thousand had availed themselves of his services, for which he received no compensation, except in small presents from a few individuals.

The disastrous effects of the war now daily increased. By almost every arrival, accounts were brought of the capture of some vessels belonging to Nantucket. Many of the whale ships were already taken, and it appeared very probable that a greater part of the remainder would fall into the hands of the enemy. The coast was so infested with British cruisers, that it had become hazardous to go out of the harbor. Some of the small craft which were bringing provisions, fuel, and other supplies, were captured. Among the vessels taken in the Sound was the beautiful packet sloop which transported the mail between Nantucket and Falmouth. The captors plundered and pillaged as many of the letters, &c., as they chose; the rest, with the passengers, were landed at Falmouth, and the vessel sent to New London, where a squadron of the British lay.

The fishing and whaling vessels on the shoals, to the eastward of the island, had hitherto been preserved. Humpbacks (a species of the right-whale,) and cod fish were plenty, which gave encouragement to many, who would otherwise have been idle, to engage in the pursuit of them. But unfortunately a privateer came among the fleet and took several vessels, one of which belonged to Nantucket. Others were fired on, but made their escape. The vessel taken belonging to Nantucket was sent to St. Johns, but it was supposed that she foundered at sea, for she was never heard of afterwards.

A great proportion of the people had now become so reduced, that small disappointments caused dismay. The seamen who had been taken, were coming home destitute of property. Many of them had families looking to them for support. On the approach of winter, many were destitute of the necessaries of life, and of the means of earning any thing. Although some had removed with their families to seek business elsewhere, there were still a great number remaining, in indigent circumstances. The greater part of those, who have heretofore hired their labor done, were obliged to retrench their expenses, and to do their own work. In these discouraging circumstances, the town was noticed by government that a direct tax of $5000 would be levied upon them. Although the sum was not large, and would not have been injuriously felt, if the island had been in a flourishing condition, yet at this time when the people were suffering under accumulating evils, the call brought a gloom over the whole community. Taxes are generally proportioned to the means of paying them. But in this case those whose only property consisted in a poor tenement, were subjected to pay, while those who were opulent and yet possessed no real estate, were exempted. It was, besides, a source of much, and perhaps just complaint, that Nantucket, situated beyond the protecting power of government, should still be subjected to contribute towards the general expense. These considerations claimed the serious attention of the inhabitants, and various expedients were suggested to obviate

the pending embarrassments. At length the expediency
was suggested of petitioning congress to mitigate the tax,
suspend its collection, or otherwise to grant some relief
to the present distress. A town-meeting was accordingly
held on the 26th of the 11th month, at which it was
unanimously voted to send a petition, and a person was
appointed to bear it. The following is a copy of the
petition :

"To the Honorable the Senate and House of Representatives of
the United States in Congress assembled, the Petition of the
Town and County of Nantucket respectfully showeth:—

" That the unavoidable fate of the war, in which the nation is involved, has so reduced them in circumstances, as seemingly to
leave no choice whereby relief can be obtained, other than by the
interferance of Congress, not only as respects their present condition, but from distressing appearances, the reality of which, they
have reason to believe, will eventually meet them.

" They have already realized losses by war in a very extensive
degree; a number of valuable ships with full cargoes of oil have
been captured and totally lost, and, what is truly lamentable, several of the owners, that were heretofore in opulent circumstances,
are now reduced to indigence.

" And they have further to anticipate a very considerable, if not
a total loss of fifteen valuable ships, now absent in the whale
fishery.

" Many vessels employed as coasters, and some in the merchant
service, have also been captured and lost, to a great amount in
value.

" The whale fishery, which has constantly been considered the
staple of Nantucket, must inevitably decline under the present
state of things. In truth the partial failure, already realized, appears to threaten a total extinction of the means by which that valuable branch has been so successfully prosecuted.

" The present stagnation of the mercantile, and also of most other concerns, has induced, or, rather, compelled hundreds of people
to remove to the continent, in search of the common necessaries of
life, which could neither be afforded nor procured here, as the

small remaining capital of our island is fast exhausting, without a present prospect of replenishing.

"It is neither the intention nor wish of your petitioners to present an exaggerated account, but merely a statement of facts, while they feel impelled seriously to request, that (if consistent) some provision may be made, whereby the fisheries may be prosecuted, without being subject to losses by war.

"Your petitioners are aware that the time for collecting the direct tax and internal duties is fast approaching, respecting which they beg leave to observe, that it appears to have been contemplated for the defence of the country. Their detached situation from the continent prevents almost every benefit that can arise from its appropriation, their exposed and defenceless condition, considered with the natural situation of the island, which renders it impossible for adequate defence to be afforded, are circumstances which they believe are but partially known to congress.

"The ruinous losses already realized, and those that are anticipated, and seemingly inevitable, added to a general suspension of the means of subsistence, are circumstances which, when duly considered, your petitioners are persuaded, will entitle them not only to countenance and commiseration, but to such consistent relief as seems indispensable for their continued existence.

"Isaac Coffin, Moderator.
"James Coffin, Town Clerk.

"Nantucket, 26th, 11th mo. 1813."

By accounts from the Pacific Ocean, it appeared that a number of whale ships had been detained by the Spaniards, and materially obstructed in the pursuit of their voyages, and that Commodore Porter had captured the greater part of the English whalers and caused the American ships to be released. The latter, being at liberty, mostly put away to come home. Much anxiety was felt for their safe arrival. There was a constant lookout for them both at Nantucket and at the Vineyard, and large pecuniary rewards were offered to those who should pilot them in, or give information to the owners which should be the means of securing their safe arrival. The arrival of several was hailed with great joy, and enabled those, whose property was still at risk, to effect insurance, though at the high rate of fifty per cent. Indeed the coast was so thronged with cruisers, that owners were willing to give almost any premium : and their apprehensions in the end proved to be well founded, for few ships arrived afterwards.

In the 12th month an embargo was laid on the vessels of the United States, with the design of preventing the enemy's being supplied by the people of this country. " This act was an effectual seal upon the commerce of the United States both foreign and domestic. No vessel was allowed to depart from any port in the Union, to any other even in the same state, except in certain specified cases. The effects of this measure were felt very severely in many sections of the Union, particularly in the eastern states." The conditions of the act were such as nearly to cut off all communication between Nantucket and the continent. Without some modification, a great number of the inhabitants must have moved off; for it was evident that they could not subsist without supplies of provision and fuel from abroad.

On the return of the person appointed by the town to bear the petition mentioned in a preceding page, he reported, that the President and Heads of Departments commiserated the condition of the inhabitants, and expressed their readiness to render all the assistance in their power, consistent with the interests of the nation ; and that they had promoted the passage of an act, mitigating the restrictions of the embargo ; and vesting full power in the Executive to grant such relief to the island, in allowing provisions and other necessaries to be brought from the continent, as its situation required.

The embargo act did not have the desired effect, and it was repealed in the 4th month of 1814. An opportunity was thus given to all to resume their commercial business. But he people of Nantucket, having lost the greater part of their trading capital, could not derive any material benefit from the measure.

The difficulty of procuring bread stuff, and other necessaries from the continent, now increased and produced great alarm. Some of the British vessels were constantly at Tarpauline Cove. Whilst engaged there in procuring water and other supplies, they sent their boats, from time to time, up and down the Sound, which captured all the coasters they met with ; they plundered some, and others they destroyed or exacted a ransom for them in money, pretty much on their own terms. These circumstances reduced the town to such a condition that famine seemed inevitable, unless a change should soon be brought about. There was not a bushel of corn to be bought.

The whaling business, as we have already shown, is the source of almost all the employment of every class of citizens on the island. There is hardly an individual, who does not, directly or indirectly, receive a share of the profits or participate in the losses of each voyage. No chain of dependencies can be more perfect than that which exists between what are called the lower and the higher orders of society. This chain was now broken. A great proportion of the property at sea had fallen into the hands of the enemy. The mechanics, hitherto constantly employed in preparing the materials for voyages, were without business. The sound of the axe and hammer was no longer heard. The seamen were daily coming home from places of confinement among the English, many of whom found a cheerless welcome, for poverty and distress met

them at the doors of their friends and connections. Amidst
the gloom which prevaded all classes of the community,
there was no object, on which the eye could rest, that
gave promise of better things ; nothing to revive the droop-
ing spirits, but the whisperings of that kind angel, Hope,
which

——"lingers still, nor quits us when we die."

In the 6th month, 1814, some boats arrived with corn,
which, although dear, afforded a timely relief to the inhabitants.

A Chebacco boat, said to be a tender, belonging to the
British frigate Nymph, had been for some time cruising
between Tuckernuck Shoal and Great Point, stopping
every passing vessel, and either plundering their prizes
of all the articles of value on board, or exacting ransom-
money from the unfortunate sufferers. This practice was
carried to so great a length, and became so distressing to
the citizens, that they grew impatient. On one occasion
an officer was sent on shore to receive ransom-money,
which added to the agitation already heightened by repeated losses. The streets were immediately thronged
with a large concourse of people, who, feeling themselves
so injured by so insignificant a force as a small Chebacco
boat with only ten men, could no longer restrain their
feelings, and publicly uttered treats of hostility. The persons foremost in this proceeding were principally strangers,
who had been plundered of provisions and fuel, which
they were bringing to the island. It was deemed advisable to persuade them to be quiet, and consider that the
use of force by the people of the island would only invite
a greater force in return, and one which nothing but madness could prompt them to resist. Under these consider-

ations the selectmen and others interfered and were successful in their attempts to quiet the crowd. The officer was permitted to depart with his booty. The affair, however, occasioned increased distress to the inhabitants, for many of the coasters determined not to come again to the island, until there should appear a fairer prospect of avoiding the grasp of the enemy.

It would be impossible, and perhaps not very interesting, to detail all the difficulties and embarrassments occasioned by the war. A people, situated as those on the island of Nantucket, must necessarily have felt the pressure to an unlimited degree beyond those of many other places. It is their very pursuits in times of peace, that render them most exposed in times of war. With always a vast amount of property invested in ships, abroad on the ocean, navigated by hundreds of their own friends and relatives, engaged in voyages of three years' duration, war must necessarily involve great numbers in misery and ruin. Their location and their religious character forbid their participating in national quarrels.

If nations must, or rather if they will, persist in war, why should they countenance indiscriminate depredations on the property of individuals? In other words, why legalize plunder, and encourage the worst passions of the worst men, by giving them commissions to commit acts, which, but for those commissions, would render them odious to the whole world and criminals by the letter and spirit of every code of laws? Why train up a band of pirates by making them first privateersmen; and thus prepare subjects for the halter by putting a premium upon crime? We believe that nothing would be more effectual towards putting an end to all wars, than to allow trade and commerce to continue, under certain restrictions, during national conflicts. It would prevent, in a great degree, that personal rancor which individuals of belligerent nations are constantly imbibing against each other, by witnessing or feeling the effects of individual rapacity.

The distress and difficulties occasioned by the war to the people of this devoted island were now daily increasing. British cruisers thronged the sound and blocked up the harbor, which wholly prevented a supply of provisions and fuel. Necessity required that some uncommon exertion should be made to obtain relief. Not the poorer class only was interested, but those more particularly on whom the poor and indigent were making their daily dependence. It was therefore deemed expedient, that the inhabitants should convene together for the purpose of adopting such measures as might appear necessary to remove the present calamity. A meeting was accordingly held, and the subject was introduced by statements concerning the affairs of the town, made by the selectmen, overseers of the poor, and others. After much debate, it was voted, that the selectmen, and overseers of the poor, should be authorized to import provisions from the continent for the support of the poor under their immediate charge, in any way or manner they might deem expedient, not exceeding the value of five hundred bushels of corn at one risk. This gave an opportunity to send for a small supply by every vessel that ventured out.

On the 23rd of 6th month there was a violent gale of wind from the N. W. and the weather, at the same time, so cold that aged people, in passing about, wore mittens. The inhabitants in general made fires in their houses. The season had before been dry, which caused the wind to have such an effect on the fields of corn as to injure much of it in some places where it was most exposed;

but afterwards it pretty generally recovered its growth and yielded a tolerably good crop.

The Chebacco boat, before mentioned, still continued on her station between Nantucket and the Vineyard, chasing all passing vessels, and plundering all that could be caught. None, who fell into the hands of this cruiser, escaped without loss; for, however small their craft and poor their lading, there was still something to lose. There was great apprehension that the crew of this cruiser would land in the night, and commence their plunder and robbery, while the inhabitants were asleep. To guard against this, a night-watch was established, to patrol the streets, with direction to sound an alarm in case they landed. This measure had the desired effect so far, that the people could take their rest quietly.

The continuance of this craft at and near the bar of the harbor was attended with so much embarrassment in obtaining supplies from the continent, as to cause much alarm. At length the selectmen, by the advice of many of the inhabitants, deputed two of their number to repair on board and remonstrate with the captain against staying any longer. They attended to their appointment, and endeavored to persuade him to leave, by stating the difficulties under which the town already labored by want of a free communication with the continent. They urged, that common humanity was sufficient to prevent his adding to the distress of a people feeling already the want of the necessaries of life. At first, instead of listening to their arguments, he made high demands of vessels and other things, but he at length said he would go away. After several days he departed. He carried away some thousands of dollars in specie, and sundry articles of goods.

A number of boats and small vessels now arrived with provisions and wood, which supplied the market, to the great relief of the people, although the prices were high : flour fourteen dollars per barrel, corn one dollar and forty cents per bushel, and wood seven dollars per cord.

A tender from the Nymph frigate soon afterwards made its appearance between the point and bar, watching every passing vessel and boat, in order to make a prey of the defenceless. Several vessels coming from the main with supplies were taken, from all of which they exacted something in ransom ; they permitted some light vessels to pass out of the harbor unmolested. This cruiser was a sloop commanded by Charles Goulett, the person that commanded the Chebacco boat before mentioned. Some indiscreet persons had furnished him with a New York paper, wherein was an article, purporting to have been written at Nantucket, and tending, as he said, to vilify his character. He took umbrage at this, and addressed a letter to the chairman of the selectmen, threatening, in strong language, to pursue measures injurious to the island. The people were not in any degree intimidated ; some would have chosen to have him attempt the execution of his threats. The major part of the inhabitants, however, wisely considered that it was more advisable to appease, if possible, than irritate him. A paper was drawn up and signed by a large number, setting forth that the publication was not authorized by the town, and that they did not know who was its author. This was sent off to him, and after some altercation and explanation, he seemed satisfied with it. The committee which carried the communication, then pressed him to leave his present station. He promised to do so, but said that he should probably be back in a short time. He did leave, and in a few days returned again. The people, having become familiar with his mode of depredations, were careful to keep out of his reach. He, however, found ample opportunity to convey his threats to the inhabitants, that he should enter the harbor and set fire to some of the houses. This was neither expected nor dreaded.

British cruisers were so numerous along our seacoast, that our government considered it expedient to discontinue the public lights, wherever it was probable that the enemy would be benefited by them. The collector of Nantucket, who had the care of the lights there, discontinued them from time to time, as circumstances required. The buoys on the corners of the shoals and at the bars were taken up for the same reason.

The harbor had now been a long time blocked up by the British. There was no wood provided for winter, and the stock of provisions was considerably reduced. All agreed that it was necessary to take some measures to avoid distress; but it was difficult to agree as to what those measures should be. The selectmen were at length requested to call a town-meeting to deliberate on the subject. The meeting was held on the 23d of the 7th month, 1814, at which, after some discussion, the following vote was passed: " That we appoint the present selectmen of this town a committee, with full powers to make use of such means as may appear to them most eligible for this town to pursue, which the constitution and laws of this country do not forbid, for the inhabitants to bring wood, provisions and other necessaries, from the continent of the United States, for the consumption of the inhabitants of Nantucket."

The selectmen, feeling themselves authorized by the additional powers now vested in them by the town, and being fully sensible of the necessity of taking some measures to obtain relief, fitted the sloop Hawk, David Starbuck, master, and qualified her as a flag of truce; and appointed Silvanus Macy and Isaac Coffin, Esquires, as commissioners, and qualified them accordingly; giving them written instructions to proceed to the British naval commanding officer on the North American station, and to represent to him, in an impartial manner, the situation of the people of Nantucket. The commissioners were directed to ask permission to import wood, provisions, &c., and liberty to whale and fish about the coast. The following are copies of instructions to the commissioners and to Captain Starbuck:

"By this present instrument you are hereby appointed and legally qualified, by the selectmen of Nantucket, as commissioners, to embark in the sloop Hawk, Captain David Starbuck, who has received instructions to carry you without delay to the British naval commander-in-chief on the North American station.

"When you may meet the commander-in-chief, you will carefully and faithfully represent to him the present state and condition of the inhabitants of this town, adding, also, that they are seriously apprehensive of the over-whelming effects of famine, which it seems can neither be evaded or eluded, except permission can be obtained of the commander-in-chief to import the necessary provisions and fuel from the continent to the island; but as you are acquainted with every particular, it is considered needless to add any thing more on this subject, than to mention our confidence that you will give it all the attention which its importance may seem to demand.

"You are also so well acquainted with the exhausted state of our finances, and the necessity of ways and means to replenish them, and that the fishery has heretofore been our constant dependence for that purpose, but little need be said on the occasion; we would, however, recommend that you mention the facts of things to the commander-in-chief, and, if possible, to obtain permission to prosecute it as heretofore.

"It is presumed we need not add any thing more, than to call your pointed attention to the several particulars herein contained.

"[Signed by the Selectmen.]

" Nantucket, July 27, 1814."

" To Capt. David Starbuck:

" It having been determined by the selectmen of the town of Nantucket to despatch the sloop Hawk, now under your command, to Chesapeake Bay, or elsewhere, as a *flag of truce*,—you will, with all possible convenience, prepare your vessel for that undertaking, and, after being equipped for the voyage, you will embrace the first favorable opportunity, and proceed to the place of your destination, subject, however, to the following instructions, viz.:

" You are to display the white flag at your topmast head, and continue it abroad (as occasion may require) during the time you are considered as a cartel.

"As Silvanus Macy and Isaac Coffin, Esquires, will embark with you, as commissioners, to negotiate or transact the business of the town, under direction of the selectmen, you will, in every case, be subject to their control, and attentive to their orders, keeping constantly in view that one important point of your duty will be to convey them to the British naval commander on the North American station, with the least possible delay.

" You will not admit any passenger or article of merchandise whatever, at any time during your voyage, to be taken on board your vessel, except it be by the express direction of the above-mentioned commissioners.

" [Signed by the selectmen.

" Nantucket, July 27, 1814."

The commissioners sailed on their mission the day following the date of their instructions.

A private vessel was also sent at the same time, with a committee, and, as was said, for similar purposes, but, as this was a measure taken by individuals, and not by authority of the town, we shall say but little about it; not being in full knowledge of their commission, or of the effects thereof.

A great number of the inhabitants were now busily employed in procuring peat from the swamps. They gladly took the benefit of this substitute for wood. It was indeed considered a great blessing, and it saved, at that time, several thousands of dollars.

About the 22d of this month, the British armed brig Nimrod came to the bar and anchored, and, sent a boat ashore, bearing a flag of truce., The selectmen immediately convened, and sent a message to the officer, informing him that they were in session, and ready to receive any communication he might be pleased to make to them. He informed them, that the captain of the brig had a communication from commodore .Hotham, which would be delivered to a committee who should be authorized by the town to receive it on board the brig. The selectmen appointed a committee out of their number, and authorized them to go on board, which they attended to the following morning, and were politely received by captain Newton and his officers. After the usual ceremonies, the captain informed them, that his business was to propose a stipulation of neutrality, to be observed by the people of Nantucket. He then read to them a communication signed by commodore Hotham, the purport of which was, that, if Nantucket would observe strict neutrality during the war, he would permit a certain number of vessels to import wood, provisions, and other supplies. The time and place was not suited to a full consultation on the subject, and its importance was such that the committee did not feel authorized to act upon it. They therefore left the brig and came on shore, with an expectation of being furnished with the original communication, or a copy of it. The brig's barge also came on shore at the same time. The selectmen immediately met in order to receive a copy of the communication, as had been promised.

Notwithstanding the officer of the boat was now ashore, no communication was received by the selectmen in less time than two hours. A delay of this nature, at so critical a time, was attended with disagreeable sensations. When the communication was at length received, it was found necessary to call the town together, which was done the same afternoon at 6 o'clock. During the time of these transactions, the people of the town were in great commotion, for the subject had not been so fully opened to the public, as tb allow of their comprehending its nature and importance. There was a very general apprehension, that the British had secret intentions of a hostile charac-ter; that the present fair appearance was only designed to lull the people into a state of security; and that the design was then to add to the distress already felt. The streets were crowded with the inhabitants, who appeared in much anxiety for the event.

A town-meeting was held at the time appointed There was a general attendance, for the subject wa novel as well as interesting, and drew the attention o nearly every male inhabitant. The meeting was held ii the street near the Friend's south meeting-house. Th communication from the British commander was thei read, the substance of which was:

" That the people of Nantucket shall observe a strict neutralit between the two contending powers during the existence of th present war; shall refrain from taking up arms against the sul jects of Great Britain; shall surrender up all public arms, gun; ammunition, and all other public property of every kind and natur

" That, in case of a compliance, they would permit a limited bi small number of vessels to import wood, provisions, and othe necessaries, to the island, and if a surplusage should appear, a British vessels coming to Nantucket should have liberty to pu; chase refreshments, provided it did not distress the inhabitant;

and that a deputation from the town should meet the commodore
at Gardner's Bay to conclude the treaty."

Some short remarks were made at the meeting, chiefly
purporting, that nothing unreasonable was required in the
communication, and that if the conditions were complied
with so far as was consistent, the much-needed relief
would be obtained.   It was generally believed, that
neither our government, nor any reasonable man, would
criminate the town for embracing this opportunity to obtain the privilege of importing the necessaries of life from
the continent.   In accordance with these views the following votes were taken.

" That this town will not take up arms against Great Britain during the present war between Great Britain and the United States
of America, collectively or severally.
" That this town will surrender up all such public arms, amuni-
tion, and other public property that shall be found in said town.
" That this town will not take up arms to defend any public
property.   .
" That this town will make no opposition against any British vessel coming into this harbor to refresh.
" That this town will choose a committee to wait on Commodore
Hotham, at Gardner's Bay, or elsewhere, agreeably to his request."

A committee was then chosen, after which it was voted,

"That the committee inform Captain Newton, commander of the
brig Nimrod, of the proceedings of this meeting, and that they are
appointed to wait on Commodore Hotham in Gardner's Bay, or
elsewhere.
" Nantucket, August 24th, 1814."

The forementioned communication from Commodore
Hotham appeared, from its tenor and other circumstances,
to have originated from certificates given by the select-

men and magistrates of Nantucket, to qualify a vessel to go and meet the British commander-in-chief, and from him to endeavor to obtain permission to bring a load of bread stuff from Virginia for the sole consumption of the inhabitants, stating the distressed situation of the island at that time.   Admiral Cochrane, on receiving this information, directed Commodore Hotham to send a vessel to Nantucket, and make the foregoing provisions of neutrality.

The day following the meeting, the Nimrod left the bar, accompanied by the sloop Experiment, both intended for Gardner's Bay, to meet Commodore Hotham.   The Experiment carried the town's committee.

On the 30th, the committee returned, having performed the business of their appointment agreeably with the foregoing plan.   They reported, that they were received on board the ship Superb, then lying in Gardner's Bay, and treated in a polite manner.   That they there made a general statement of the situation and circumstances of the inhabitants of Nantucket; and that there were no arms, artillery, ammunition, warlike stores, or government property of any kind on the island, except the two light-houses and a scanty supply of oil for the season, which they requested might remain unmolested.   General satisfaction being given, the commodore signed a stipulation of neutrality, a copy of which follows.

" By the Honorable HENRY HOTHAM, Commodore, commanding his majesty's ships and vessels employed on the coast of North America, between Nantucket and the Delaware.

" The island of Nantucket having been this day declared neutral by a deputation appointed at a legal town meeting, held on the 23d instant, to wait on me to stipulate for the relief of the inhabitants, who engage they shall take no part whatever in the war between

Great Britain and the United States of America, and that such refreshments as it can afford, without distressing themselves, shall be as free for the use of his majesty's ships as at other friendly places; and having, by the direction of Vice Admiral, the Honorable Alexander Cochrane, K. B. commander-in-chief, &c. &c. &c., in consideration thereof, granted them permission to import provisions, live stock, fuel, and other necessaries of life, from the continent of the United States, and furnished certain vessels with passports to perform such voyages, unmolested by the ships and vessels of his majesty, and by the private armed vessels of his subjects;—

" These are to request and direct, that no hostilities nor depredations be committed by those which may arrive at or communicate with that island.

" Given under my hand and seal on board his majesty's ship Superb, off New London, the 28th of August, 1814.

" HENRY HOTHAM.

"To the commanders of his majesty's ships and vessels, and of the private armed vessels of his subjects.

" By command of the commodore,

JOHN IRVING."

In accordance with the foregoing agreement, the commodore granted three passports to go to the Delaware, and three to go to New York, to bring provisions, and other necessaries; and fifteen vessels to bring wood.

The following is a copy of one of the passports to bring provisions.

" [Seal]   By the Honorable HENRY HOTHAM, Commodore, commanding his majesty's ships and vessels employed between Nantucket and the Delaware.

" Having, by the direction of the vice-admiral, the Honorable Sir Alexander Cochrane, K. B. commander-in-chief, &c. &c. &c., stipulated with the magistrates and selectmen of the island of Nantucket for the neutrality of that island, and, in consideration thereof, granted permission to the inhabitants to import provision, live stock, fuel, and other necessaries of life for their use, from the United States of America;—

" These are to require and direct the commanders of his majesty's ships and vessels, and of the private armed vessels, not to molest or interrupt the sloop********of about fifty-five tons burthen, navigated by inhabitants of Nantucket, carrying no guns or other arms of any kind, in the employment of conveying the above described articles from the Delaware to Nantucket; or sperm candles or oil from that island, provided she be not-found carrying on any other trade, or commerce, with his majesty's enemies, nor fishing in the open sea; in either of which cases, she will be committing an infraction of the agreement made this day by the aforementioned parties respectively, and will be liable to capture.

"Given under my hand and seal on board his majesty's ship Superb, off New London, 28th August, 1814.

"HENRY HOTHAM.

"To the commanders of his majesty's ships and vessels and of the private armed vessels of his subjects.

"By command of the commodore.

"JOHN IRVING."

The dates and tenor of the other passports were similar, except such variations as the circumstances required.

Notwithstanding the trouble and expense to which the town had been subjected, in obtaining permission to import provisions and fuel, the people were not satisfied. The privileges were so limited that they could not fish nor whale without the risk of capture, nor carry fish to market; and no passengers were allowed to go in the privileged vessels. The passports being specially granted to certain vessels therein named, no others could be benefited by such limited restrictions. This created a considerable degree of dissatisfaction among them, who had vessels lying at the wharves, and others, who had large boats fitted for the New York trade. Besides, the number of licensed vessels was so small, that they were not sufficient to furnish all the required supplies.

One other circumstance had considerable weight with many; notwithstanding the necessity of the case, which might reasonably be pleaded in extenuation of the measures of the town, if some person, with malicious intent, should have made complaint to the government, it would at least embarrass, and might bring the town into additional difficulties, and, instead of proving a benefit to the community, end in distress.

These reflections became so forcible on the minds of many, that in the 9th month a committee was deputed to wait on Elbridge Gerry, the vice-president, previous to his leaving his home to attend to the duties of his office at Washington. They reported, on their return, that, after giving him a full statement of the transactions of the town with the British, he had said, that he could not condemn the proceedings, and that he knew of no other way in which they could have done so well. He further promised to represent the subject to the government, and to use his endeavors to secure its approbation of their conduct. He also recommended their giving a statement of the case to congress.

The commissioners, who were appointed by the authority of the town, on the 27th of the 7th month, to go to Admiral Cochrane, now returned and reported in substance as follows:—Believing that the admiral was at Bermudas, they had pursued their course thither, but to their mortification they found, that he had sailed thence, two or three days previous to their arrival, for the Chesapeake. Their vessel needing some repairs, and they were necessarily detained a few days, in which time they visited the governor of Bermudas, who received them courteously, and seemed to lament with them the lost opportunity of meeting with the admiral there.

They made him acquainted with the nature of their mission. He was a man of high respectability, and ever ready to manifest his benevolence, when it could be consistently exercised. In this case he could do little more than to advise them to pursue their mission to the admiral, in whom, he stated, they would find a man of feeling, who, he believed, would do every thing in his power for the relief of Nantucket. He asked them, whether they did not believe, that the people of that island would be benefited by being placed under the jurisdiction of Great Britain. And he stated, that if direct applications should be made to Admiral Cochrane for that purpose, and if the admiral could be well assured, that it would benefit the inhabitants, he did not doubt that a small force would be sent to accomplish the business, and protect the place.

The committee informed him, that they did not believe that such a change in the government of the island would be beneficial; but that it would, on the contrary, add to the troubles already experienced.

He said, that it appeared, that the application had been made by the authority of the town, and he supposed that they had come to act in the premises. They replied, that it did not come from the authority of the town, and that the town did not want it done. He then informed them, that a letter, signed by the chairman of the selectmen had been received by the admiral, making the request. They stated, that it was a forgery,* committed by some malicious persons, to answer some sinister ends; for there had never been any movements made by the town, by any ways or means whatever, to come under the British government, and that most of the inhabitants

---

* One of the commissioners was the chairman of the selectmen alluded to in the forged letter.

would abhor the idea of changing their government for any other on earth.

After completing their business at Bermudas, they left, in company with the Madagascar frigate, and arrived at the Patuxent river, in the Chesapeake, where they found Admiral Cochrane. He received them on board his ship in a very friendly manner, and after finding who they were, the business they came upon, and that they were properly authorized by the town as a flag of truce, he treated them cordially, and said that he believed the statement, which they made, to be correct; and that he would do all he could, consistently with his duties, for the relief of Nantucket. He made many inquiries, respecting the situation of the island, and seemed to take a deep interest in its condition. He told them, that he had been informed, in some degree, of the sufferings of the people, and that he had made arrangements with Commodore Hotham, at Gardner's Bay, for their relief.

Finding so much freedom in his carriage, the committee proposed to him an extension of the privileges already granted, so as to allow whaling to be carried on without the risk of capture. The admiral stated, that this could not be granted without the consent of his government; but he said, that, if they would put their ideas on paper, agreeably to the wishes of the town, he would send the communication by a despatch vessel, which was to sail the following day, adding, that he believed an arrangement could be made to meet their views. Notwithstanding this favorable opportunity to pursue a very desirable object, prudence prevented the acceptance of his generous offer : and the committee replied, that, however desirous they were to avail themselves of it, yet they had no authority to request any privilege, which it was beyond his power to grant.

The committee then treated with him on the subject of Nantucket prisoners, and set forth the difference between such as belonged to the island and sailed in the fisheries, and those of the United States in general. He readily acceded to their views; and, as a plan for exchange could not be adopted in case of the island's becoming neutral, he gave them authority to call for such prisoners, belonging to Nantucket, as they should find on board of his majesty's vessels, which they might fall in with on their passage home. And he promised to write to his government concerning Nantucket prisoners in general. They had a full opportunity with him, and opened to him every circumstance relating to their mission; to all of which he appeared very attentive, and finally said, that he would do everything for the relief of the people of Nantucket, consistent with his duty to his government; and stated that his secretary was then about finishing a despatch to that his secretary was then about finishing a despatch to Commodore Hotham, which would be a confirmation of what he had heretofore granted. The despatch being finished, they were about to proceed with it to Commodore Hotham, when they were astonished with the information, that a postscript had been added to it, of the following import: "That if Nantucket paid the direct tax, or internal duties, the stipulations entered into for their relief, &c., should become void." There had never been any conversation between Admiral Cochrane and the commissioners on this subject; but however much the latter were astonished at this new condition, they had no opportunity for further negotiation, as the admiral appeared to have done with them, and to have turned his attention to other business.

The postscript, above-mentioned, seemed to threaten a total defeat to all the plans of the town, to save themselves from famine. There appeared to be no probability of being able to evade or elude it. The committee, therefore, left the Chesapeake in dismay; though conscious of having discharged their duties faithfully, and as far as in their power, consistently with the best interests of the town.

A copy of the despatch, which the commissioners took with them, is here inserted.

"SURPRISE, in the Patuxent River, 30th of August, 1814.

"Sir,—A deputation from the island of Nantucket having waited on me in this river, under a flag of truce, to solicit permission to obtain supplies of food and fuel from the continent of the United States, I have referred them to you, and you will be pleased to grant them such indulgences as you may deem proper, consistently with what is prescribed in my letter No. 6, of 26th July, 1814, respecting the inhabitants of that island.

"I have the honor to be, sir,
your most obedient humble servant,
"ALEXANDER COCHRANE,
"Vice Admiral and Commander-in-Chief, &c. &c.
"Rear Admiral the Hon. Henry Hotham, &c. &c. &c.

"P. S. You will be pleased to signify to the inhabitants of the island of Nantucket, that, if it be found they pay any direct taxes, or internal duties, for the support of the government of the United States, I will withdraw this indulgence forthwith, and will call upon them to pay double the amount to his majesty's government.
"ALEXANDER COCHRANE."

The commissioners, having arrived at Gardner's Bay, delivered the despatch to Commodore Hotham, who ordered his secretary to write to the committee which heretofore waited on him from Nantucket, informing them of this new arrangement. The letter was sent by the commissioners, and was as follows :

"His Majesty's Ship Superb, }
off New London, 8th September, 1814. }

" Gentlemen,—I have received instructions from Vice Admiral the Honorable Alexander Cochrane, K. B., Commander-in-Chief, &c. &c. &c., which will require that the inhabitants of the island of Nantucket should distinctly understand that the terms, on which they have stipulated for the neutrality of that island, will not permit them to pay any direct taxes, or internal duties, for the support of the government of the United States of America; and that I should receive an assurance from you, that they conceive a strict neutrality will preclude them rendering any support of that nature to that government; in failure of the execution of which, I am instructed forthwith to withdraw the passports I have granted to their vessels, and to call upon them to pay double the amount of the taxes to his British majesty's government they pay to that of the United States of America.

" I have the honor to be, &c.

" Henry Hotham, Commodore.

" Directed to the town's committee."

" P. S.   A Nantucket vessel having been found whaling with a counterfeit protection, orders will be given to his majesty's ships to capture or destroy all vessels belonging to that island, which shall be found with any other than the original protection granted to them."

The inhabitants of the town immediately convened on the subject of the foregoing communication. The business claimed the serious attention of the people; and, after some debate, it was voted to send the following petition to congress, requesting a suspension of the collection of the direct tax and internal duties, during the existence of the present war :

" *To the Senate and House of Representatives in Congress assembled :*

" The inhabitants of the town of Nantucket are compelled, by calamities beyond their control, once more to petition the constituted authorities of the nation to contribute at least so far to the relief of their sufferings, as to suspend the collection of the direct taxes and internal duties which, by law, are, or may be, liable to be exacted of them. They are convinced that a reiteration of the peculiar, multiplied, and overwhelming evils which assail them, is not essential to procuring the relief for which they are now constrained to petition. Exposed to the free and undisturbed access of the declared enemies of the government of the United States, it is indispensable to their existence, as a component part of that government, that they should not, during the existence of the war, contribute to the means by which it is carried on. Indisposed as your petitioners sincerely are to injure their own country, or to contravene its wholesome laws, they cannot be less anxious to avoid affixing their own seal to their own immediate misery and destruction. It is evidently certain, that while they continue without the protection of the government of the United States, and exposed to all the depredations that may be committed upon them, they cannot justly be reduced to misery and starvation, for pecuniary contribution, so inconsiderable to the government, as that which is required of them. This consideration alone is not only sufficient to justify the respectful application, but it ought, they believe, to claim for it that attention, which will lead to a complete attainment of its object.

"Signed in behalf, and by direction of the town of Nantucket, in a legal town meeting assembled on the 15th day of September, 1814.

"Attest: JAMES COFFIN, *Town Clerk.*"

The same meeting agreed on sending the following letter to Commodore Hotham :

"NANTUCKET, 15th September, 1814.
"The Honorable HENRY HOTHAM, Esquire, commanding his majesty's ships and vessels employed on the coast of North America from Nantucket to the Delaware.

"SIR, — We have the honor to acknowledge the receipt of your communication, dated on the 8th instant, and we now beg leave to reply to the subject of it. The inhabitants of the island are under a full conviction of the heavy pressure, the payment of the direct and other taxes would have upon them at this time of increased and increasing distress, but they have had to act on this subject with much obvious embarrassment, reflecting on the effect that a refusal of the payment would have on the one hand, while they contemplated on the other, with no less anxiety the intimations that the payment should cause the generous privileges granted them to be withdrawn. In this extreme, critical, and perplexing condition, they assembled in town-meeting, and resolved to petition the congress of the United States, if not to remit, at least to suspend the collection of the taxes during the existence of the present unhappy conflict. But to remove all doubt of the intention of the inhabitants fully to comply, as far as practicable, with the requisitions of the Honorable Sir Alexander Cochrane, the officer, deputed to collect the taxes upon the island was prevailed upon immediately to resign his commission.

" We feel confident, that no inhabitant of the island will accept the appointment as collector, and that no stranger will expose himself so much, as he necessarily must, to hold this undesirable office. Under these circumstances, we are persuaded no taxes will be paid; but we think ourselves justified in believing, that a public and direct refusal will not be required of us; for the peculiar favors already granted to this place evince, in his Britannic Majesty's government and in his naval commanders a determination not to embarrass and distress, but to aid and relieve the unoffending inhabitants.

" Respecting the counterfeit protection referred to in your honor's communication, we have made strict inquiry, which has produced in our minds a conviction that the supposed counterfeit papers were merely an attested copy of the votes of the town, and a copy of the protection granted the town, attested by a notary public. These copies were procured to show the neutrality of the island, in the event of the vessel's capture and destruction, to induce the discharge of the men, if such discharge should be consistent with the instructions given to his British majesty's commanders. We do not discover that any injury can result from these copies; but if this use of them, thus explained, does not comport with your honor's views, no pains shall be spared on our part to suppress the use of them.

" In order that you may be better able to judge of the tenor of these instruments granted, we here inclose you a true copy of all the papers which have been given to those vessels who have no protection.

> " We have the honor to be, &c.
>
> " [Signed by the committee.]"

A letter was soon after received by the committee from Commodore Hotham in reply to the preceding, the substance of which was, to require a direct answer, " whether the town is determined to refuse the payment of the direct taxes and internal duties, which are, or shall be required by the government of the United States?"

The committee having no authority to answer this demand, laid the subject before a meeting of the town, warned for the purpose. Many of the inhabitants, believing that the business was about to be conducted in a way that might bring the censure of their government, if nothing more, upon them, concluded that it would be safest for them not to attend the meeting. The meeting was, therefore, but thinly attended.

The following votes were taken on the occasion, with little or no opposition, viz :

" That this town will not pay any direct tax, or internal duties, during the present war between the United States of America and the government of Great Britain."

" That there be a committee appointed to carry into effect the neutrality, which is agreed on with Admiral Henry Hotham."

" That the committee so chosen be a committee to treat with the commanders of all public and private British armed vessels, that are or shall be visiting our shores."

" That this town do now discontinue all other committees that have been heretofore appointed by said town to treat with any of his Britannic majesty's ships or vessels, in behalf of the town."

" That this town will prevent the carrying off any provisions from this island more than shall be permitted by Admiral Henry Hotham."

" Nantucket, Sept. 28, 1814."

A deputation from the committee was sent with the aforesaid reply, who reported, on their return, that no additional extension of the privileges, heretofore granted, could be obtained from Admiral Hotham.

The protections, granted by the British, to bring provisions, fuel, &c., from the continent, were at first of material benefit, and were duly appreciated by the people generally. But the limited conditions specified in them, and the jealousies they created, both amongst the Americans and the English, soon lessened their value; so that some who possessed them, hardly dared to leave port and trust to them.

On the 10th of the 10th month, a remarkable occurrence took place, a description of which, although it does not come within the limits of this work, according to the intention of the writer, seems to be demanded, since the affair happened very near to the island. The American privateer schooner Neufchatel, of New York, and a ship from Jamaica, her prize, loaded with sugar, coffee, &c., were at anchor at the south side of the island, with a small breeze at the northward. There was a ship wide in the offing at the same time, supposed to be a British man-of-war. At two o'clock P. M. the captain of the privateer discovered boats from the ship headed in toward the shore. Being fully convinced that they were British, he made every preparation to give them a warm reception. At sunset five barges were plainly discovered, which appeared to be full of men. At nine in the evening they came within musket shot of the privateer, when the action commenced, and continued about thirty-five minutes. After the firing ceased, it was found that two of the barges had surrendered; one was missing, supposed to have sunk. The other two returned with sixteen men, out of one hundred and forty-six that left the ship, which proved to be the Endymion frigate. From the best information that could be obtained, it was found that about one hundred of the ship's crew were killed, among whom was the first lieutenant, who headed the expedition. Of the privateer's crew five were killed, including the pilot, who belonged to Nantucket. We forbear to state the particulars of this sanguinary engagement, believing that it would neither please nor edify a large part of our readers. what we have related is sufficient both as a record of the fact and as an example of the horrors of war. The action took place within about five miles of the town, and whilst the work of death was going on, the reports of the cannon and muskets were distinctly heard by the inhabitants. Such a scene, almost under the eye of a large community, one of whose most distinguishing, and, as we think, noblest traits, is a strong aversion to war, could not fail to bring a solemn gloom over their minds.

CHAPTER X.

During, and a little previous to the 10th month, 1814, there had been some talk of peace. Ministers of the United States and Great Britain were negotiating a treaty, but there were so many interests involved, that the prospect of an immediate, amicable settlement, was by no means flattering. The winter therefore commenced attended with much of the gloom and despondency which had before prevailed. The market was, however, well supplied with flour and corn. On the 16th of the second month, the glad tidings of a treaty of PEACE were proclaimed. The joy of the inhabitants, on this occasion, we shall not attempt to describe. It was felt, and is still remembered by hundreds, whose connections were then immured in prisons abroad, or whose means of subsistence had been snatched from them by the ruthless hand of war ; by parents whose children, and by children whose parents were asking bread.

The terms of the treaty were represented to be so honorable to this nation, that no doubts of its ratification were entertained. The attention of merchants was immediately turned to their wonted business. The season was yet inclement, and the harbor blocked up with ice ; so that vessels could not go to any port on the continent to procure materials for the outfits of the few ships remaining in port. Mechanics immediately commenced work with what little coopers' stuff, iron, hemp, &c., was on hand. In the mean time all anxiously looked for news from government.

At length, on the 28th of the same month, the conditions of the treaty arrived, ratified by the president. This confirmation of their expectations was hailed with inexpressible joy. The streets were thronged with people congratulating each other on the occasion. Gratitude and thanksgiving to the Author of all good seemed to pervade the community.

The war being closed, all began to turn their attention to business. Some left the island to seek employment in other ports, but the greater part commenced making arrangements for the prosecution of the whaling business.

At the close of the war, it was found that about one half of the ships was left, several of which were not at sea during the war, some had been sent off to neighboring ports on the continent for safety, others were hauled up. In all, including those which arrived in time of war, there remained twenty-three. Twenty-two had been taken and condemned, one was lost at sea. Fifteen returned home in safety, five were not at sea during the war, three were brought to the island after the close of the war. Thus of the whole number belonging to the port at the commencement of hostilities, there remained exactly one half. Of those remaining, many needed extensive repairs.

Business was commenced with alacrity. In a very short time several ships were sent to sea. Small companies were formed by new adventurers, who made considerable additions to the fleet. Believing that the first oil imported would command a high price, many were stimulated to embark in the business, beyond the extent of their funds. Thus a system, if it may be so called, of long credits was introduced, which, though it promised some advantage to the community by bringing more ships into the service, and employing a greater number of men, was nevertheless pregnant with evils. Mechanics were under the necessity of trusting out their wares, for an unusual length of time, and were subjected to the necessity of hiring money to purchase their stock, a practice which proved very injurious to them. And some owners, who did not meet with success, found themselves much embarrassed by thus transacting business.

From the time of which we have just spoken, to the present date, 6th month, 1835, our history must necessarily assume the form of a diary. No events have occurred which admit of a connected narrative. During the long continuance of peace, the whale fishery, like all other business, has had its fluctuations; at times prosperous and encouraging, at other times dull and unprofitable.

Hitherto we have purposely avoided touching on some subjects of general interest, deeming it more expedient to devote a portion of our limits purposely to them, than to interweave them among the other incidents of our narration. Among these are some notices of religious societies, education, shipwrecks, &c., which will be found in our Second Part.

On the first of the second month, 1815, the weather was remarkably cold. The thermometer was eleven. degrees below zero; lower by several degrees than had ever before been known.

Although peace was now concluded between the two governments, the evils occasioned by the war were not entirely done away. The taxes for the support of the poor department, on account of the great increase of the poor, had increased nearly one hundred per cent. The town was called upon to pay large amounts to the government, as a direct tax, which was a heavy burden on a great number of the inhabitants, many of whom were possessed of nothing more than a small estate in land, or, perhaps, an old house. Some of these were aged people, or widows, whose scanty means should have rendered them rather objects of charity, than contributors to the expenses of government; while seafaring men and merchants were very generally exempted. These considerations caused many to pay with reluctance. Some were even obliged to sell a part of their interest, to meet the demand, their taxes amounting to more than their whole cash receipts for the year.

In the 7th month many of the ships, left at the close of the war, had proceeded to sea; some to the coast of Brazil, but the greater part to the Pacific Ocean. Ten ships were, this month, at one time lying at the bar, all waiting to complete their outfits in order to commence their voyages.

In the 5th month, 1816, a newspaper was issued by Tannatt and Tupper, entitled the Nantucket Gazette. This was the first paper published on the island. It did not receive the expected patronage, and after a short time it was discontinued.

In the 11th month, the lighthouse on Great Point was destroyed by fire. The year following, a new one of stone was erected by the goverment.

In 1817, two years after the war, its effects in some respects were more severely felt than during its existence. The people generally, and particularly the poorer classes, were more distressed for want of the necessaries and comforts of life, than when we were surrounded by the enemy. This may, at first view, seem paradoxical, but it can be explained as follows: At the close of the war, merchants and mechanics, in their avidity to extend their business to the farthest limits of their means, dispossessed themselves of nearly all their trading capital. Long voyages, and long credits put their property far beyond their immediate control. The excitement, produced by the return of peace, was succeeded by a season of languor. Want of employment compelled great numbers of the laboring poor to call for assistance. In the early part of the winter the weather was extremely cold, which obstructed a great part of the supplies intended for the consumption of the inhabitants. The price of flour presently rose to seventeen dollars per barrel, that of corn to two dollars per bushel, and there was very little of either article to be bought at even those prices. Beggars were now as numerous in the streets, as at any time during the revolution. Here was a scene which called forth the spirit of true benevolence; a field for all to labor in, whose hearts were not like adamant. With many, doubtless, the precept of Jesus was carefully observed, "when thou doest thine alms, do not sound a trumpet before thee." The charitable hands of females, never closed and never idle when the sick and the naked call for help, were now busily employed in administering to the necessitous. The refuse of the rich was by their ingenious needles converted into comforts for the poor. The first ray of the lamp of life, and its last expiring glimmer, shone upon their ministrations. Infancy, and disease, and age, were their peculiar care. Still neither private beneficence nor female associations were sufficient to satisfy the cravings of hunger, and additional means were resorted to for affording sustenance to the poor. Soup being considered a cheap and nutritious food, an establishment was fixed upon where it was daily made, and where the necessitous were supplied free of expense, and others, if they chose, might buy. This establishment was kept open till spring, at which time business of various kinds presented, and the poor were enabled to contribute to their own wants.

The whale ships now began to arrive with good voyages and new life was given to every branch of business. The merchant, the mechanic, and the day-laborer, all felt the change. Ship-owners began to make further advances, by which the fleet was likely to be considerably increased. Candle-factories and many dwelling-houses were erected· How different was the situation of the people, now, from what it was only a few months before! Then the greater part of the people were without employment, and hundreds were dependent on charity for their daily bread; now all were busy, and friends and connections were daily returning home, laden with "rich experience" of the blessings of peace.

Although the principal articles required in the outfits of ships were held at exorbitant prices, yet the price of oil and candles was proportionately high, so that the whaling business was on the whole profitable.

A good market for considerable quantities of oil opened in London, and some other ports in Europe, which had an immediate effect on the prices in this country. The reason of this unexpected demand in England was the failure of their northern whale fishery during two successive years.

The value of houses and settlements, which had depreciated during the war by removals and other causes, now began to rise. Another species of real estate, called cows' commons or cow rights, which in the first year of the war were sold for sixty or seventy dollars each, was now reduced to about one third of that value.

In the year 1819 the number of ships and vessels belonging to the island had increased to

57 ships, } in the whale fishery;
 4 brigs, }

 4 brigs,
15 schooners, } principally in the coasting business.
62 sloops,

The amount of tonnage of the whole was 23,565 tons.

The success of the whale fishery at Nantucket did not pass unnoticed at the different seaports throughout the United States. The depression of commerce generally induced many to embark in this business. Whale ships were sent from New York, Long Island, New London, New Bedford, Cape Cod and Boston, the effect of which was, in a short time, to introduce into the country a greater quantity of oil than was demanded by the common consumption. The same depression of commerce was felt in France and England, and led new adventurers to engage in the whale fishery in those countries. In England, particularly, the business increased to a great extent. In consequence of this, shipments abroad could no longer be made profitable.

By the enumeration of the inhabitants, taken in the year 1820, it will appear by the following table that there were

	Males.	Females.	Total.
Under 10 years of age,	875	861	1736
Over 10 and under 16,	515	490	1005
Over 16 and under 26,	709	710	1419
Over 26 and under 45,	763	828	1591
Over 45,	484	757	1241
	3346	3646	6992
Persons of color,			274
			7266
Number of inhabitants in 1810,			6807
Increase in 10 years,			459

We need not attempt to account for so small an increase in ten years, in any other way than by reminding our readers of the many removals which took place during the war.

The following is a statement of the number of vessels and tonnage belonging to Nantucket on the first of the 9th month, 1821.

No of Vessels.	Description.	Employed in whale fishery.		Employed in coasting trade.		Employed in cod fishery.		Total.	
		Tons.	95ths	Tons.	95ths	Tons.	95 hs	Tons.	95ths.
78	Ships,	22,648	52					22,648	52
6	Brigs,	339	21					690	93
16	Schooners,			871	73	46	87	918	65
59	Sloops,	225	14	3,012	57			3,237	71
3 Brigs in foreign trade.								27,495	91

We have now completed, according to our design, that part of the work which may properly be denominated historical. Some subjects have been slightly touched upon, some wholly omitted, which might, with propriety, have been introduced. These, together with others of merely local interest, we have reserved for our Second Part. Our reasons for this arrangement are as follows: Whilst preparing our book for the press, facts have been presented to us, that could not be noticed at the time without much interruption to our labor; and subjects of merely local interest seemed to demand, for convenience of reference, a separate place.

It is said with some truth, that the history of our island presents little that is novel or interesting. The ground is not consecrated by deeds of chivalry: no ruined towers, no warlike mounds, no mouldering abbeys, nor any other objects meet the eye, over which the genius of romance will deign to preside, or to which popular superstition can appeal for confirmation of the strange and wonderful. No spot is memorable for martial acts. The soil is unstained with blood; its history is that of peace. Notwithstanding this total want of every thing grand or terrible in the annals of the past, we trust that many events herein re-

corded will be found worthy of remembrance, and we
believe that many equally interesting are now lost forever, merely because they were not recorded. Tradition,
it is true, has not been idle. Indeed we are indebted to
her for much that we know of the settlement of our beloved island, and of the character, manners and occupations of our fathers. But our tradition, for the most part
deals in generals. It contains little to diversify the dull
monotony of the peaceable settlement of a few enterprising families, and their slow progress in wealth and numbers, from the commencement down to the present
moment. We look, almost in vain, for those apostrophes
which enliven history, those little events which have their
beginning, their middle, and end, within the narrow
compass of a few years or months, without being attended
with any consequences that can influence succeeding time.
Yet we know that such an event must have taken place.
The nature of man has ever been the same in all ages and
countries. Hopes deferred, disappointed loves, and
ambitious schemes defeated, expectations lively and cheering met by some melancholy or fatal reality,—these make
the scene and drapery of the stage of life. They are
mingled with our blessings, they are the dates from which
we mark the lapse of our individual lives.

PART SECOND.

CHAPTER I.

To give our readers, who may not be familar with a seaman's life, some ideas of its vicissitudes, we insert the following sketches of the adventures of two of our whalemen. The whaling business is peculiarly an ocean life. The sea, to mariners generally, is but a highway over which they travel to foreign markets; but to the whaler it is his field of labor, it is the home of his business. The Nantucket whaleman, when with his family, is but a visitor there. He touches at foreign ports merely to procure recruits to enable him to prosecute his voyage; he touches at home merely long enough to prepare for a new voyage. He is in the bosom of his family weeks, on the bosom of the ocean years. His youth, and strength, and best manhood, are all devoted to a life of tedious labor and great peril. His boyhood anticipates such a life, and aspires after its highest responsibilities; his age delights in recounting its incidents. We read, and sometimes, perhaps, dwell with delight on the daring exploits of those whom the world calls heroes; and in proportion to the victims sacrificed on the altar of ambition, we attribute glory and honor to the victor. Alas! what is bloodshed but murder; what are the pretences of war but words;

what its dire effects but cold-blooded, purchased butchery. For deeds of true valor, done without brutal excitement, but in the honest and lawful pursuit of the means of livelihood, we may safely point to the life of a whaleman, and dare the whole world to produce a parallel. The widow and orphan mourn not over his success, oppression and tyranny follow not in his paths. No; his wife and his children reap the reward of his toils and dangers, society is enriched by them, and his prosperity is his country's honor.

Captain Benjamin Worth has given us, by our request, the following statement of his adventures :

" I began to follow the sea in 1783, being then 15 years of age, and continued until 1824. During this period of 41 years, I was a shipmaster 29 years. From the time when I commenced going to sea till I quitted the business, I was at home only seven years. At the rate of 4 miles an hour whilst at sea, I have sailed more than 1,191,000 miles; I have visited more than 40 islands in the Atlantic and Pacific Oceans, some of them many times; and traversed the west coasts of North and South America from Baldivia, lat. 40 ° S. to 59 ° N. on the N. W. coast, and up Christian Sound to Lynn Canal. I have assisted in obtaining 20,000 barrels of oil. During the last war I was taken by the English, in the ship George, and lost all I had on board. Whilst I commanded a vessel, not one of my crew was killed, or even had a limb broken by a whale, nor have any died of the scurvy."

Statement by Capt. George W. Gardner.

" I began to follow the sea at 13 years of age, and continued in that service 37 years. I was a shipmaster 21 years. I performed 3 voyages to the coast of Brazil, 12 to the Pacific Ocean, 3 to Europe, and 3 to the West Indies. During 37 years I was at home but 4 years and 8 months. There were 23,000 barrels of oil obtained by vessels which I sailed in. During my following the sea, from the best estimate I can make, I have travelled more than 1,000,000 miles.

"I was taken by the English in the late war, and lost all the property I had with me."

DESCRIPTION OF THE OUTFITS AND CRUISE OF A SPERM WHALE SHIP.

We are indebted to an experienced and very intelligent whaleman for the following description of the outfits and cruise of a sperm whale ship.

The class of ships built immediately after the last war were about 300 tons burthen; there has, however, been a steady advance, our ships are now larger, better constructed, and built of the best materials. The live oak and yellow pine, being found most durable for marine architecture, is brought from the southern states, and no expense is spared to make the ships what they ought to be, fit for the arduous and protracted voyages they are destined to perform. A fair average price of a ship, ready for the reception of her appropriate stores for a three years' voyage, is about $22,000, and the outfits about $18,000 more. Some have sailed at a much higher price, near $60,000. Many are got to sea, fitted in the same efficient manner for the same period of time, for about $34,000, but they are of a smaller size. The necessary articles put on board a ship for a sperm whale voyage are too numerous to mention; it will suffice to name a few of the principal ones. Beef and pork, 100 bbls. each; 11 tons of bread, baked from superfine flour; 80 bbls. of flour packed, for puddings, &c.; 1400 gallons of molasses; peas, beans, corn, dried apples, coffee, tea, chocolate, butter, in ample quantities, and of good quality. About 4000 barrels of new casks are made for each ship, from the best white oak stuff, each cask containing from three to six barrels, at the cost of about $1.50 per barrel. These article, together with spare duck, cordage,

&c., make the ship quite full when she sails on her voyage. A ship which mans four boats, six persons to a boat, requires, including the number necessary to take care of the ship, when the boats are in pursuit of whales, 30 or 32 men. It may be interesting, to those who are not acquainted with this business, to give a brief account of a whale voyage, and the several duties, together with the pay of the persons composing a ship's crew.

The substance of the contract between the owners on the one part, and the captain, officers, and crew, on the other, is, for the former to furnish a ship and all the necessary outlay for the voyage, and the latter to perform the several duties assigned them, and to have, as a compensation, such part of oil or whatever else may be obtained as may be agreed upon. And in case of death or accident, by which any of the crew shall not be able to perform the whole voyage, they or their representatives shall draw of the proceeds in the proportion which the time served bears to the whole time of the voyage; thus, a voyage is performed in 30 months, a man died five months after the ship sailed, and before one drop of oil was obtained, he is entitled to one sixth part of the whole he would have drawn, had he continued in the ship to the termination of her cruise. The captain's and officers' lays or shares differ on account of more or less experience, those of the men depend somewhat on the wages given in the merchant service. When wages are high in New York and Boston, it is more difficult to procure men for our business. The captain's lay is generally one seventeenth part of all obtained; the first officer's, one twenty-eighth part; the second officer's, one forty-fifth; the third officer's, one sixtieth; a boatsteerer's, from an eightieth to a hundred and twentieth; and a foremast hand's from a hundred and twentieth to a hundred and eighty-fifth each.

The ship being at sea, the company is divided into two watches, as in the merchant service. On the outward passage, all hands are, in good weather, actively, engaged in making the necessary preparations for taking whales. Two men, generally accompanied by an officer, are stationed at the mast heads to look out for whales. They are relieved every two hours from sunrise to sunset. This is when the weather is suitable for taking whales; for it is to be understood, that, even on whaling ground, there are many days in succession, when the weather prevents the pursuit of whales, if they are seen near by.

The first ships that went into the Pacific Ocean after sperm whales, found them in sufficient numbers on the coast of Chili; but subsequent voyagers kept advancing northward until they got quite to the equator. There, from the time of our ships first going to the Pacific, till the war of 1812 put a temporary stop to the business, they continued taking cargoes; and the cruising ground was confined to the coasts of Chili and Peru, at unequal distances from the land, from four leagues to a hundred. When the business recommenced after the late war, the fleet constantly increasing, and the whales becoming more scarce, it was necessary to explore new regions. Captain George W. Gardner, in the ship Globe, was the first that steered off to the west. When he arrived in long. 105° to 115° west, and lat. 5° south, he found sperm whales plenty, and obtained considerable oil. He had what has since been termed the off-shore ground quite to himself; in two years after that time, more than fifty ships were cruising in the same regions; and immense quantities of oil have been taken in that neighborhood. But even that extensive ground failed in a measure, and other places were sought. In 1820, Captain Joseph Allen, in the ship Maro, of Nantucket, sailed for the Japan coast, where he found sperm whales plenty. In 1821 six or seven ships, and in 1822 more than thirty were cruising there. Some seasons since that period, there have been cruising in the North Pacific, between the coasts of New Albion on the east and the Japan Islands on the west, near a hundred ships, one third English, and the others American; and now no part of the navigable ocean has been left unexplored; every sea has been visited and revisited, and the most remote parts have become familiar to our navigators.

Most of our whale ships go into the Pacific by the way of Cape Horn: some by the eastern route south of New Holland and Van Dieman's Land; others, after cruising awhile in the Indian Ocean, in the neighborhood of Madagascar and the mouth of the Red Sea, pursue their way into the Pacific through the Straits of Timor, between New Guinea on the south, and the Pelew Islands on the north, touching at the Ladrone Islands, and then onward to the Japan coast. They there meet ships, which sailed from home about the same time with themselves, and came by the way of Cape Horn. Others to meet at the same place, that came by the route south of New Holland. It must appear obvious, that our whale ships are exploring, in a more effectual manner than twenty national ships could, every part of the vast Pacific. They have discovered many islands, reefs and shoals, which navigators, sent out expressly for exploring purposes, had passed unseen. The captains and officers are lunarians, and the ships are generally furnished with chronometers.

It is rather difficult to give a very correct idea of the method of taking a whale, to persons entirely unacquainted with the business. As soon as a whale is discovered by the men at mast head, the first inquiry from deck is, "in what direction?" That answered, the sails are trimmed according to distance, and the ship made to head as directly for the object as possible. It is not desirable to approach the whale nearer than within about one mile. When at about that distance, the ship is stopped, and the boats are lowered into the water. If the whale is down, each boat takes the station where the officer commanding her believes the whale will come up. A large sperm whale remains under water from forty-five minutes to an hour and fifteen minutes. Their usual rate of going, when undisturbed, is about two and a half miles an hour. Being satisfied which way the whale was headed, when it went down, each one exercises his judgment as to where he thinks it will come up. There they anxiously wait; when it does appear, the nearest boat pulls on (the other boats take a position near by) and strikes as soon as possible, which is done by the officer in the head of the boat, who darts two harpoons into the whale. These harpoons, or, as we term them, whale irons, are attached to a line of 280 or 300 fathoms, coiled in a tub. The effect produced by the harpoons is various. Sometimes it penetrates a vital part and kills the whale in a few minutes. This, however, is not often the case. The irons are not so much intended to kill the whale as to fasten to her. A more proper instrument, called a lance, is used to despatch the whale; its head is much like the centre-piece in an eel spear, the shank is about three feet long with a socket, in which is fixed a pole of about eight feet. It is easily darted six or eight fathoms. It has a line or warp attached to it, by which it can be drawn back after being thrown.   But it is better not to use the warp, but to go to the whale's side, and with your hand set the lance to the whale's life, and the work is done.   Sometimes, immediately after the whale is struck, it stops, being severely hurt, and rolls, threshes, and tumbles about at a grea rate, making the water fly in all directions.   It is best to keep close to the suds, but not quite in it, and when she straightens out on the water after her paroxysm, it is a good time to pull up and throw in a lance.   Sometimes, on being struck, they descend with great rapidity, taking three, or four, or even five hundred fathoms of line.   If another boat is near by, and the line is likely to be run from the first boat, it is knotted to a second, and sometimes to a third, making in all eight hundred fathoms in one continued string.   We do not think that whales descend to that depth; considerable line is taken out when they are coming up.   When the whale is dead, it is taken to the ship, which keeps at a proper distance during the action.   The work of taking off the blubber, that part from which the oil is extracted, then commences.   This is done by putting heavy tackles at the mainmast head. An aperture near the fin is made in the blubber, sufficiently large to admit a strong hook, which is attached to the winding tackles before mentioned, and the purchase is brought to a windlass.   This is what is called raising a piece.   After cutting what is necessary upon the head, as the men heave, the blubber is peeled or separated from the body or carcass by a sharp instrument made for the purpose, called a spade.   When the blanket-piece as it is called, is hove up to the masthead, another hole is made, and the strap of the other tackle is put through, toggilled and hove tight, and the piece above cut off and lowered into the ship's hold between decks. The second tackle, now having its piece, is hove till that is at mast-head and is relieved. Thus the whale is kept rolling until it is rolled out of its jacket, just as a person would haul a piece of tape from a cane, if it were wound around it spirally from end to end. After the whale is once turned around, the head is separated from the body and taken on board according to convenience; it generally produces about one-third of the oil taken from the whale, which is much more valuable than that taken from the blubber of the body, as most of the spermaceti used in making candles comes from it.

Sperm whales vary much in size. The *cows* and *calves* are generally found in shoals. Ten, twenty, and sometimes hundreds, constitute a school; and, when discovered, some of them are constantly on the surface of the water, spouting, jumping, playing, &c. The cows make from eight to forty barrels of oil. The male grows much larger; and what is termed a large whale will yield from sixty to a hundred barrels. It is thought by some, that the males, or at least the most of them, about the third year of their age leave the cows and calves and gang together; and it is not uncommon to see a school of forty barrel whales, and so on to sixties. Sometimes single whales are seen of a large size. To what depth a sperm whale descends in search of food, (which is always squid) no person, whatever his experience may have been, can tell. One thing is certain, that the larger the whale, the longer it stops under water.

After the blubber is hoisted on board, the ship's company immediately proceed to boil it out, while it is sweet. Before sailing, there is built on deck a solid, substantial brick work, called a caboose, with a watercourse beneath it, in which are set two, and sometimes three pots, holding from 140 to 200 gallons each, for the purpose of trying out the oil. The blubber, now in the ship's hold, called blanket-pieces, is cut into smaller parts, about five inches wide, and from twelve to eighteen long, called *horse-pieces*, from a piece of plank bearing that name. It is then *minced* by a tool shaped something like a scythe, with a handle on each end, and is now prepared for the pot. After the oil is tried from the blubber, it is put into a large copper cooler, and thence into casks. When the oil is as cool as the climate will make it, the casks, having shrunk considerably, are coopered again, and put away in the hold, not to be moved again, unless they should leak, until the termination of the voyage.

THE RIGHT-WHALE.

This species of whale differs materially from the spermaceti. The whales obtained in the Gulf of St. Lawrence, about the year 1761, produced from 100 to 230 barrels of oil each. The vessels engaged in the right-whale fishery, at that time, were from 45 to 60 tons burthen, so that one which took a whale of the largest size would make a profitable voyage. The bone from one of these whales weighed from 2500 to 3200 pounds, and sold at $1 or $1.25 per pound; the slabs were 10 feet in length. A stranger to the business may ask, what these monsters of the deep live upon to grow to such an enormous size? Their principal food is an animal of the fish kind, not bigger than a spider, which it resembles somewhat in shape: the color is of a reddish cast. It is called bret, and is frequently seen on the surface of the water in such quantities as to make a reddish appearance of several acres. These the whales take into their mouths in large quantities, and the

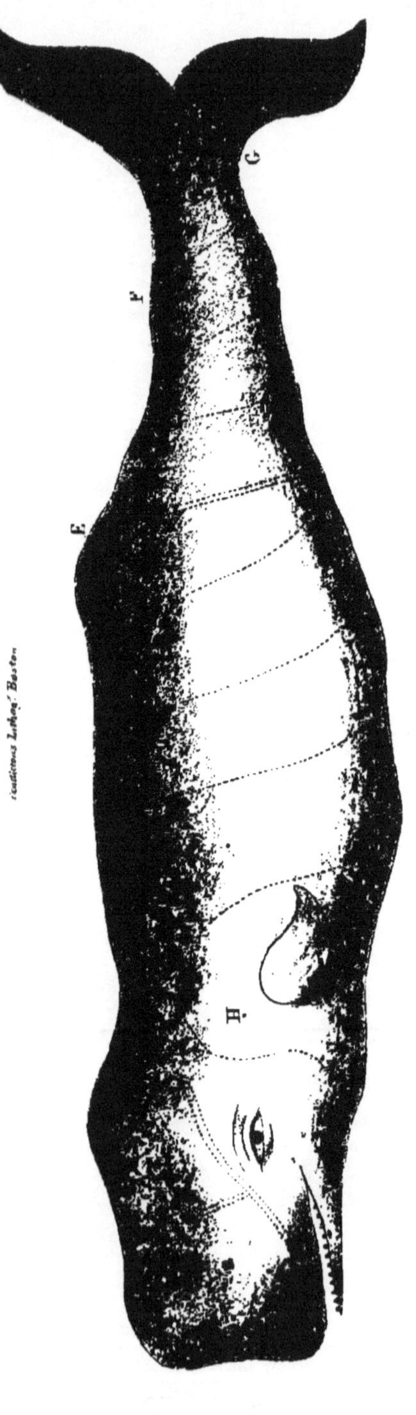

PHYSETER OR SPERMACETI WHALE.
Pendleton's Litho'y Boston

slabs of bone serve as strainers to discharge the water and retain the food.

DESCRIPTION OF A SIXTY BARREL SPERM WHALE.

Length, 60 feet. Circumference of the largest part of the body, 24 feet. Distance from one point of the fluke, or tail, to the other, 7 feet. Length of each fin, 3½ feet. Length of the jaw bones, 14 feet. Number of teeth 46. From the spout holes or nostrils from the end of the nose, 10 inches. From the end of the nose to the eyes, 14 feet. The color of the skin, similar to that of a common felt hat. Thickness of the skin, 1 inch. Thickness of the blubber, or fat on the ribs, 5 inches; on the breast, 9 inches. The proportion of blubber is about ⅙ of the whole animal.

The accompanying figure of a sperm whale is copied from Captain James Colnett's Voyage to the South Atlantic and Pacific Ocean.

A. Part of the head containing liquid oil, or head matter. B. The spout-hole, A.B. The part of the head of a large whale which is too bulky and ponderous to be hoisted on board, it is suspended on tackles, and the front part being cut off, the oil is bailed out with buckets : but the head of a small whale is divided at the double line below C.C. and hoisted on deck. ■ ■Where the tackles are fastened. D. where the tackles are first hooked, which is called raising a piece ; being thus steadied in the tackles, the head is divided at the lowest double line. E. A large hump of fat. F. A smaller hump of fat. When the whale is flinched, or peeled to E., it will no longer cant or turn in the tackles, it is therefore cut through at the first double line and also at G., the tail being of no value. H. The ear, which is remarkably small, as is also the eye from which a hollow or concave line runs to the fore part of the head. The eyes being prominent, the whale is enabled to pursue his prey in a direct line, and by inclining his head a little to the right or left, he can see his enemy astern. There is one row of teeth, in the lower jaw, and sockets in the upper, to receive them. The number of teeth depends on the age of of the animal. When the sperm whale spouts, he throws the water forward and not upward, like other whales, except when he is enraged.

The tail is horizontal; with it he does much mischief in defending himself. The ambergris is generally discovered by probing the intestines with a long pole, when the fish is cut in two at E.

The different species of whales nurse their young as cows do their calves. The age, at which the young are weaned, is probably 12 months. Whales have no means of carrying their young, to preserve them from danger. When attacked by a school of killers, a species of whale not larger than a sperm whale 2 months old, they stop entirely, and lay like logs on the water; then the calves collect between the cows and run their heads as far out of water as they can. When whales are frightened, they go as fast as their calves can swim, and no faster. Cows and calves associate very freely together. There is a marked difference in the spoutings of different species of whales. A sperm whale has but one spout hole, and throws the spout forward at an elevation of about 45 degrees. It is much thicker, and does not go as high as that of most other whales. A right-whale has 2 spout holes about 18 feet from the nose, and consequently much nearer the lungs : the spout is thrown nearly perpendicularly, widening as it rises. The fin-back has 2 spout holes ; yet the spout often rises in one jet, so as to cause it to be sometimes mistaken for the spout of a spermaceti : and the same may be observed of the humpbacks. Some whales appear more vicious than others. It rarely occurs, that they show a disposition to act on the defensive. No rules can be given for the management of a whale which shows a disposition to attack a boat. All must be left to the judgment and courage of the officer.

The sagacity of sperm whales is in no way so remarkably manifested, as in the instantaneous knowledge they possess when one of their number is struck and wounded, at a distance of two, three and even four miles apart. Whether they receive this knowledge by sight or sound, we shall not pretend to say. When a whale is struck, those around, and feeding undisturbed, sometimes instantly, as with one accord, make the best of their way towards the wounded whale which gives the boats that are disengaged a fine opportunity to fasten. At other times, they will collect in a body, and go in a contrary direction, as fast as possible, to all appearance much frightened. Sperm whales migrate far and wide. Ships cruise on the coasts of Peru and Chili from ten to one hundred leagues from land. It has often been observed, that both the in and off-shore vessels are sometimes doing nothing, and at other times are all engaged. Where the whales are in the interim, none can tell.

Instances can be cited of whales having been struck, and making their escape in the Atlantic Ocean, being afterwards taken in the Pacific, with the heads of harpoons in them bearing the marks of ships known to have been cruising to the East of Cape Horn. Whales are not easily driven away from their feeding-ground by ships. Ships passing the Cape of Good Hope, Vandieman's Land, and Cape Horn, frequently see whales making their passages.

PROGRESS OF THE WHALE FISHERY AT NANTUCKET.

[From the Historical Society's Collection.]

Whale fishery originated at Nantucket in the year 1690, in boats from the shore.

1715.	6 sloops, 38 tons burthen, obtained about 600 barrels of oil, and 11,000 pounds of bone. Value,	1,100
1730.	25 sail, from 38 to 50 tons, obtained annually about 3,700 barrels, at £7 per ton,	3,200
1748.	60 sail, from 50 to 75 tons, obtained 11,250 barrels, at £14,	19,648
1756.	80 sail, 75 tons, obtained 12,000 barrels at £18,	27,600
1768.	70 sail, 75 tons, obtained 10,500 barrels, at £18,	23,600
	N. B. Lost ten sail, taken by the French, and foundered,	
1770.	120 sail, from 75 to 110 tons, obtained 18,000 barrels, at £40,	100,000

From 1772 *to* 1775. 150 sail, from 90 to 180 tons, upon the coast of Guinea, Brazil, and the West Indies, obtained annually 30,000 barrels, which sold in the London market at £44 to £45 sterling, — 167,000

N. B. 2,200 seamen employed in the fishery, and 220 in the London trade,

1783.	7 sail to Brazil, from 100 to 150 tons, obtained	2,100	
	5 to the coast of Guinea	600	
	7 to the West Indies	500	
	At £40 per ton	2,200	16,280

N. B. No duty exacted in London.

1784.	12 to Brazil, obtained	4,000	
	5 to the coast of Guinea	400	
	11 to the West Indies	1,000	
	At £23 to £24	5,400	14,500

N. B.   The price fell by the exaction of a
duty in London to £18 3s. sterling per
ton.

1785.   Now at sea,
8 to Brazil.
2 to the coast of Guinea.
5 to the West Indies.

Before the war, there were annually manufactured in Nantucket, 380 tons spermaceti candles.*

---

* This state of the whale fishery in Nantucket was written in the year 1785.

PRODUCE OF THE WHALE FISHERY

Carried on at Nantucket, between the years 1804 and 1834 inclusive.

Year.	OIL.		Whale.	Whalebone.
	Spermaceti.			
	Body.	Head.		
	Barrels.	Barrels.	Barrels.	
1804	4,730	2,665	6,718	46,690
1805	5,459	2,034	4,507	13,131
1806	7,701	3,084	15,954	86,544
1807	7,914	3,235	13,959	72,784
1808	5,602	2,105	10,503	49,970
1809	6,641	2,695	7,256	17,092
1810	5,117	2,130	7,929	41,437
1811	15,355	6,745	6,377	43,200
1812	5,116	2,475	2,230	6,266
1813	774	359	2,567	9,901
1814	1,146	498	83	
1815	636	284	138	
1816	1,550	682	2,700	796
1817	15,401	6,813	5,771	19,444
1818	10.496	4,378	13,426	65,446
1819	12,901	5,621	11,511	62,403
1820	11,884	5,027	11,736	59,794
1821	16,196	6,719	8,632	38.092
1822	19,392	8,009	5,407	3,197
1823	25,260	10,803	3,808	20,243
1824	29,355	11,875	4,322	22,063
1825	22,795	8,985	7,191	39,596
1826	11,373	4,951	2,402	16,002
1827	19,529	8,441	583	5,152
1828	30,130	13,044	1,033	8,662
1829	23,334	10,159	8,576	76,808
1830	24,509	11,504	7,758	67,508
1831	27,954	13,335	8,568	83,206
1832	21,193	9,695	16,364	155,379
1833	19,965	9,546	5,422	49,429
1834	14,170	6,347	4,747	37,137

LOSS OF A SCHOONER AND SLOOP, THE FORMER COMMANDED BY PELEG SWAIN THE LATTER BY DAVIE SQUIRES.

These two vessels left Nantucket in company, in 1774, bound on a whaling voyage to the coast of Africa. Having taken their departure from Sancota Head, the weather being pleasant, the men were mostly below, when the cry of breakers alarmed both crews. A boat's crew from the sloop attempted to carry out an anchor, with a faint hope that they might get the vessel off the shoal, but the sea ran so high as to compel them to drop the anchor under the bows. The boat was carried over the shoal, and, not being able to regain the sloop, the crew made the best of their way for the shore, but, as the weather was pleasant, they came round the point and landed in the harbor. A vessel was immediately sent to the relief of those in peril, which returned the next day, without making any discoveries. The shoal, called the Great Rip, where the vessels were stranded, is about 15 miles from the east end of the island. There was some hope that the remaining crews might be saved; and accordingly a large number of the inhabitants traversed the shore, and kept a constant lookout.

The quarter-deck of the sloop departed from the body of the vessel nearly whole. The crew, 13 in number got upon it, and exerted themselves to gain the shore. Their only provisions consisted of a jug of rum and about three quarters of a barrel of flour. At dawn of day they reached the S. E. part of the island, whence they travelled to Siasconset. The crew of the schooner did not fare so well. Their boats being dashed to pieces, they made a raft of spars, and, without provisions of any kind, with paddles and pieces of board, attempted to gain the shore. With unremitted labor, they got within a short distance of Siasconset in the evening of the same day, on which the other crew landed. The tide was sweeping them by undiscovered by the people of the village. They then hallooed with their united voices many times, at length they were heard and responded to. A boat was immediately sent off, which took them from their perilous situation and brought them on shore, exhausted with fatigue and hunger. But for the fine weather they must have inevitably perished. This occurrence is remembered by many aged people of the island, and it has been the theme of more than one poet, yet the name of neither of the vessels is recorded in memory or verse.

NARRATIVE OF THE LOSS OF THE SHIP UNION.

The ship Union, of Nantucket, Edmund Gardner, master, took her departure from Nantucket Point on the 19th of the 9th month, 1807, bound on a whaling voyage to the coast of Brazil. Nothing material occurred until the 1st of the 10th month. At 10 o'clock, P. M., of that day, they had a brisk breeze from the N. W. with a high swell, and were sailing at the rate of seven miles an hour, when the ship struck on a whale. The shock was tremendous. The blow was on the starboard bow, ten or twelve feet from the stem, and seven below the wale. Their astonishment, at this sudden accident, cannot be described. But a moment before, they were pursuing their course with cheerful hearts and a prospect of a fine run. Now they found themselves in a sinking condition, with a long and darksome night before them.

From the tafferel the captain saw the whale spout, whereby he ascertained that it was a spermaceti. The whole crew were immediately summoned on deck. Some were directed to take in sails, others to work at the pumps; but it was soon discovered that the ship was in danger of sinking. She was then hove to, in a situation that she would lay in with the least motion, and the pumps continually kept going. In order to examine the ship, and, if possible, to find the extent of the injury, they hoisted their casks out of the hold, and cast them overboard.

The captain then went into the hold, with a lantern and axe, and, with such assistance as was needed, succeeded, after much difficulty, in finding a part of the wound; which appeared to be one streak of the ceiling and two timbers broken. It was evident that nothing could be done to save the ship; for it was reasonable to conclude that the worst part of the injury was not in sight. Although both pumps were kept going, the water increased in the hold, and very soon got above the wound.

Being now convinced that his whole attention should be directed to the safety of the crew, the captain gave orders to prepare to leave the ship; and with this view the boats were got in readiness. The people willingly subjected themselves to the directions of the captain and officers, and with alacrity obeyed their commands as before the disaster. The boats were lowered into the water, and every article likely to be needed, such as bread, water, fireworks, books and nautical instruments, was put on board. At midnight the water had got up between decks, and it was necessary to leave the ship immediately. This was effected with great difficulty and hazard. In an hour after leaving the ship they saw her upset. They left the ship in three boats, but finding it difficult to keep together, which was considered most advisable, they thought it best, for the safety of the whole, to discharge one boat, and for the crew, sixteen in number, to divide themselves, and man but two boats. This was done, and eventually proved advantageous. The captain was a young man, and this was the first voyage under his command : yet his prudence, courage, and fortitude, and the co-operation of his officers, were effectual in preserving good order, and in encouraging the crew to use their best exertions for the common safety.

The weather being very rough, they kept before the wind until morning, when it became more moderate. They concluded to keep an easterly course, and endeavor to reach one of the Azores, or western islands. The prevailing N. W. winds were favorable to this determination. The island of Newfoundland was probably the nearest land, at the time of leaving the wreck, but the season of the year and the prevailing winds, as before stated, rendered it plainly imprudent to attempt to reach that island. The following morning they made a sail for each boat, with which they were enabled to pursue their course with greater speed and less fatigue than by rowing. The same day at 10 A. M. they discovered a schooner to the northward of them, which for a moment cheered their despondency, but they soon found that they could not reach her, as the wind blew strong from the N. W. They were not in lat. 38 ° 40′ N. long. 41 ° 52′ W.

On the day following they had a brisk breeze, with the help of which they pursued their course with cheerfulness ; but at 8 P. M. the wind increased, so that they could not run. The weather became squally, with frequent and heavy peals of thunder. The wind soon increased to a gale. They could do nothing but lay to. Their only hope for safety rested on that Power who

commands the waves and holds the winds in his hands.
Their situation was critical, and they were not without
strong apprehensions that they should not survive the
night. In this condition they were dismayed by the
breaking of a sea into the captain's boat. With some
difficulty the boat was cleared. To prevent, if possible,
the like recurrence, they were driven to the necessity of
discharging a great part of their fresh water, and all their
clothing, except what they wore, to lighten the boat. In
order to keep the boats as near together as was prudent,
a line thirty fathoms in length was attached to the head
of one and the stern of the other. In this situation they
lay till morning, which was more than they expected,
viewing their situation, in the open sea, during a heavy
gale, depending on boats made of cedar boards not exceeding half an inch in thickness. But through the favor
of God they were rescued from a watery grave. In the
morning the wind abated and the sea became smooth.
The wind shifted from S. W. to N. N. W. the weather
became pleasant, and they had an opportunity to dry
their clothes. They had been drenched with rain almost
the whole time since they left the wreck, which kept
them very uncomfortable and cold. At meridian lat.
39 ° 4′ N. long. 40 ° W. Their enjoyment of pleasant
weather was of short duration. The following night the
wind increased until it became a dangerous gale, which
prevented their pursuing their course, and rendered it
necessary to lash their boats together and let them drift.
Their water was now so nearly exhausted, that they were
obliged to submit to the close allowance of three quarts
to be divided between sixteen men for twenty four hours.
Their bread was also nearly spent, so that one cake was

the portion of each man for the same length of time. Lat.
39 ° 19′ N. long. 39 ° 5′ W.

The succeeding twenty-four hours they had a strong
breeze from N. N. W. and squally weather. At 3 o'clock
A. M. they lay to until 6 A. M., then set their sails and
steered east. Lat. at noon, 39 ° 40′ N. long 36 ° 35′ W.
During three succeeding days they had moderate breezes
from the north, and continued their course east without
meeting any thing remarkable. At the end of that time
they found their lat. 39 ° 40′ N. long. 31 ° 35′ W.

On the 8th, at 4 P. M., to their unspeakable joy they
saw the island of Flores, one of the Azores, bearing from
E. by S. to S. E. At 8 P. M. they got under the lee
of the land. The wind was now N. E. and the weather
very squally. At 9 A. M. they landed at St. Cruz, the
principal town on the island of Flores. Their water was
now wholly exhausted. They had been at sea seven days
and eight nights, and had rowed or sailed nearly six hundred miles.

The people of the island received the sufferers with
hospitality and kindness. The governor of the island and
the vice consul of the United States provided houses for
them, and every thing necessary for their comfort, free of
expense. As the captain had several times before been
there, the governor immediately knew him on seeing him,
and took him by the hand with that cordiality which
characterizes the gentleman. They left the island for the
United States on the 27th of 1st month, 1808. The crew
were Edmund Gardner, Captain, Barnabas Russell, David
Bunker, Roland Hussey, Charles Folger, Linzee Coffin,
David Cleveland, William Morris, Samuel Peters, and
seven others, strangers to Nantucket.

LOSS OF THE SHIP ESSEX.

A very interesting narrative of the loss of this ship, and the consequent sufferings of the crew, was published a few years since, which we recommend to the perusal of our readers. In the following account we shall confine ourselves to only a few of the events consequent to the singular accident, which occasioned the loss of the Essex.

The ship Essex, Captain George Pollard, sailed from Nantucket, 12th of 8th month, 1819, on a whaling voyage to the Pacific Ocean. Her crew consisted of 21 men, 14 of whom were whites, mostly belonging to Nantucket, the remainder were blacks. On the 20th of the 11th month, 1820, in lat. 0 ° 40′ S. lon. 119 ° W. a school of whales was discovered, and in pursuing them the mate's boat was stove, which obliged him to return to the ship, when they commenced repairing the damage. The captain and 2d mate were left with their boats pursuing the whales. During this interval the mate discovered a large spermaceti whale near the ship, but, not suspecting the approach of any danger, it gave them no alarm, until they saw the whale coming with full speed towards them. In a moment they were astonished by a tremendous crash. The whale had struck the ship a little forward of the fore chains. It was some minutes before the crew could recover from their astonishment, so far as to examine whether any damage had been sustained. They then tried their pumps, and found that the ship was sinking. A signal was immediately sent for the boats. The whale now appeared again making for the ship, and, coming with great velocity, with the water foaming around him, he struck the ship a second blow, which nearly stove in her bows. There was now no hope of saving the ship, and the only course to be pursued was, to prepare to leave her with all possible haste. They collected a few things, hove them into the boat and shoved off. The ship immediately fell upon one side and sunk to the water's edge. When the captain's and 2d mate's boats arrived, such was the consternation, that for some time not a word was spoken. The danger of their situation at length aroused them, as from a terrific dream, to a no less terrific reality. They remained by the wreck two or three days, in which time they cut away the masts, which caused her to right a little. Holes were then cut in the deck, by which means they obtained about 600 pounds of bread, and as much water as they could take, besides other articles likely to be of use to them. On the 22d of 11th month, they left the ship, with as gloomy a prospect before them as can well be imagined. The nearest land was about 1,000 miles to the windward of them; they were in open boats, weak and leaky, with a very small pittance of bread and water for the support of so many men, during the time they must necessarily be at sea. Sails had been prepared for the boats, before leaving the ship, which proved of material benefit. They steered southerly by the wind, hoping to fall in with some ship, but in this they were disappointed. After being in their boats 28 days, experiencing many sufferings by gales of wind, want of water, and scanty provisions, they arrived at Ducie's Island, in lat. 24 ° 40′ S. lon. 124 ° 40′ W. where they were disappointed in not finding a sufficiency of any kind of food for so large a company to subsist on. Their boats being very weak and leaky, they were hauled on shore and repaired. They found a gentle spring of fresh water, flowing out of a rock at about half ebb of the tide, from which they filled their kegs. Three of the men chose to stay on the island, and take their chance for some vessel to take them off.

On the 27th of the 12th month, they left this island, and steered for Easter Island; but passed it far to the leeward. They then directed their course for Juan Fernandez, which was about twenty-five hundred miles E. S. E. from them. On the 10th of 1st month, 1821, Matthew P. Joy, the 2d mate, died, and his body was launched into the deep. His constitution was slender, and it was supposed that his sufferings, though great, were not the immediate cause of his death. On the 12th, the mate's boat separated from the other two, and did not fall in with them afterwards. The situation of the mate and his crew, became daily more and more distressing. The weather was mostly calm, the sun hot and scorching. They were growing weaker and weaker by want of food, and yet, such was their distance from land, they were obliged to lessen their allowance nearly one half. On the 20th, a black man died. On the 28th, they found, on calculation, that their allowance only one and a half ounces of bread per day to a man, would be exhausted in fourteen days; and that this allowance was not sufficient to sustain life. They therefore determined to extend the indulgence, and take the consequence, whether to live or die. On the 8th of the 2d month, another of the crew died. From this time to the 17th, their sufferings were extreme. At 7 o'clock A. M. of that day, they were aroused from a lethargy by the cheering cry of the steersman, "there's a sail." The boat was soon descried by the vessel, the brig Indian, Captain Grozier, of London, which shortened sail and took them on board, lat. 33 ° 45′ S. long. 81 ° 3′ W. They were treated by Captain

Grozier with all the care and tenderness, which their weak condition required. On the same day they made Massafuero, and on the 25th arrived at Valparaiso.

Captain Pollard and Charles Ramsdell, the only survivors in the captain's boat, were taken up on the 23d of the 2d month, 1821, by the ship Dauphin, of Nantucket, Captain Zimri Coffin, in lat. 37 ° S. off St. Mary's. The captain relates, that, after the mate's boat was separated from the others, they made what progress their weak condition would permit, towards the island of Juan Fernandez; but contrary winds and calm weather, together with the extreme debility of the crew, prevented their making much progress. On the 29th of the 1st month the 2d mate's boat separated from the captain's in the night, at which time their provisions were wholly exhausted, since which they have not been heard from.

We shall not attempt a sketch of the sufferings of the crews of these boats. Imagination may picture the horrors of their situation, and the extremes to which they were driven to sustain life, but no power of the imagination can heighten the dreadful reality.

The following is an account of the whole crew:

In the captain's boat two survived, viz: Captain Pollard and Charles Ramsdell. In the mate's boat three survived, viz: Owen Chase, the mate, Benjamin Lawrence and Thomas Nickerson. Left on Ducie's Island and afterwards taken off, Seth Weeks, William Wright and Thomas Chapple. One left the ship before the accident. In the second mate's boat, when separated from the captain's, three. Dead nine, which added to the second mate's crew, doubtless lost, makes total deaths twelve.

LOSS OF THE SHIP HENRY.

The ship Henry, Isaac Gardner, master, on the 27th 7th month, 1813, being on her return from the Pacific Ocean with a cargo of oil, when within a few day's sail of the island of Nantucket, in lat. 38 ° N. lon. 69 ° W., experienced a terrible gale of wind. While lying to, the wind struck her so forcibly, that all three of her masts were carried away together. The upper deck was torn up, and every man swept overboard except the two mates, who were at the time in the run of the ship, where they were both drowned. Of those who were swept overboard all succeeded in getting back to the ship, except one black man.

The ship immediately sunk to the water's edge, having no part clear of the water except the bowsprit, on which the crew were obliged to take refuge. The next day the captain was swept off and lost. Nine were now left, with very little prospect of continuing long. The sea frequently washed over them, rendering their situation uncomfortable as well as dangerous. They could get but little provision or water out of the ship. Their sufferings were extreme, they were exposed at times to the scorching rays of the sun, and at times to cold. They died one after another till only five remained, who, after the expiration of forty days, were taken off the wreck by a cartel ship from England.

LOSS OF THE SHIP COMMERCE.

Very little can be said of the loss of this ship, as the crew all perished with her.

In the 6th month of 1806, the ship Commerce, Jesse

Bunker, master, was spoken on her homeward bound passage, near the line, with a cargo of oil. Soon afterwards there was a heavy gale of wind, in which it was supposed the ship was lost. About the same time a number of casks of oil and some other articles were seen floating on the water, which were thought to have come out of her.

LOSS OF A BOAT'S CREW ON NANTUCKET BAR.

This melancholy event happened on the 1st of the 1st month, 1782. Captain Robert Barker, commander of a brig lying without the bar of the harbor, bound to Virginia, on the morning of the above-mentioned day, invited a number of his intimate friends to spend a day on board with him. Seven in number, accepting his invitation, left the wharf with him in a whale boat. The weather was cold, and the wind blowing strong from the N. W., caused a heavy sea on the bar. These circumstances occasioned some anxiety for their safety. Every movement of the boat was carefully watched by the friends of those on board of her. The company pursued their course with safety, until they attempted to cross the bar; then the boat was seen to upset. The distance from the shore being about two miles, every motion was observed. Some of the company were not seen after the accident, others clung to the boat awhile, but were soon, one by one washed off into a watery grave. As soon as it was discovered that the boat had upset, two boats went to their relief. It was hoped that those in peril would be able to cling to their boat, until they had drifted across the bar. But this hope was fallacious.

The bodies of most of those who perished were found in the following spring. We shall introduce, hereafter among some specimens of our island poetry, an elegy written on this mournful occasion.

LOSS OF THE SHIP GENERAL LINCOLN.

The ship General Lincoln, Shubael Chase, master, sailed from Nantucket on the 21st 9th month, 1818, on a whaling voyage to the coast of Brazil. Six days after sailing, being in lat. 39 ° 30′ N., lon. 45 ° W., a heavy gale was experienced from S. S. E. to E. S. E., and continued through the night. At 8 o'clock in the morning the gale abated, and a calm very soon ensued, but a heavy and dangerous swell continued. The calm continued but about 15 minutes, when the wind sprung up from the westward, and very soon became a perfect hurricane. The swell was of mountain height. The ship was soon thrown on her beam ends. Her total loss seemed inevitable. Although it was day, the vapor and spray made it almost as dark as night. The roaring of the wind, not unlike that of heavy thunder, rendered it almost impossible to understand language. In this desperate situation, attempts were made to clear the ship of some of her spars, which were finally successful, and she righted. They soon afterwards shipped a sea, by which six men were washed overboard, three of whom were saved, the others lost. The decks were swept of nearly every valuable article. After the gale had abated, they set the pumps to work and cleared the ship of water. Although a mere wreck, they concluded to stay by her, and attempt to get her into some port. But they could make but little sail, and the weather proved very unfavorable. Falling in with the brig Telegraph, Captain Hill, of Providence, they took a few things from the ship and put them on board that vessel, and themselves took passage with him.

LOSS OF THE SHIP TWO BROTHERS.

The ship Two Brothers, George Pollard, Jr.,* master, sailed from Nantucket 26th 11th month, 1821, on a whaling voyage to the Pacific Ocean. Nothing took place worthy of remark on the passage round Cape Horn, nor in the subsequent part of their voyage, till the night of 11th of 2d month, 1823, when cruising near lat. 24° 9′ N. long. 167° 30′ W., the ship struck on a reef of rocks. It was presently found, that the ship leaked badly, and was beating to pieces. The water flowed in so fast, as to render the pumps entirely useless. Notwithstanding the darkness of the night, it was necessary to leave the ship immediately, which they did in two boats, only fifteen minutes after she struck. Half an hour after the ship was left, not a vestige of her was visible. The crew, twenty-one in number, now found themselves confined in two boats, with very little to subsist on. In this forlorn situation, surrounded by rocks and shoals, they passed the night, during which the boats unintentionally separated. At daylight the next morning, their eyes were met with breakers as far as any thing could be discerned. At sunrise they were cheered by the sight of a ship to the southward of them, towards which they steered their course. At 11 o'clock, A. M., to their great joy, they got on board the ship, which proved to be the

---

* Captain Pollard, on his voyage immediately preceding this, was master of the ship Essex, of the loss of which we have already given an account. Though singularly unfortunate as a sailor, he enjoys that which is more valuable than any other wordly consideration, a good name, and the esteem of his fellow-citizens.

Martha, Captain John H. Pease, of Nantucket. About noon the other boat was in sight, and soon came along side. The crew of this boat stated, that they had landed on one of the islands in the vicinity of the reefs, where they found sea elephants and one green turtle. They were treated with great kindness by Captain Pease. The Martha, after this, made the best of her way to the Sandwich Islands, and anchored at Woahee on the 29th, and on the 21st of the month following, left that port for America.

LOSS OF THE SHIP LADY ADAMS.

This ship sailed from Nantucket, 3d month, 1822, on a whaling voyage to the Pacific Ocean. By the last accounts from her, dated 7th month, 1823, she was on the coast of Japan with 800 barrels of oil. She is supposed to have taken fire and burnt. A great light was seen by an English ship, soon after the date above-mentioned, in the latitude and longitude where the Lady Adams probably was at the time. The following are the names of the Nantucket persons on board. Charles B. Toby, master, Fordom Pease, mate, Robert G. Coleman, 2d mate, Frederick A. Riddell, cooper, Peter Morse, boy.

LOSS OF SHIP LYDIA.

The ship Lydia, Edward Joy, master, sailed on the 18th 11th month, 1833, on a whaling voyage in the Pacific Ocean. Nothing remarkable occurred before the 31st of 1st month, 1835, when in lat. 11 ° 15′ S. lon. 84 ° 80′ W., the ship was discovered to be on fire. The fire increased so rapidly, that all attempts to extinguish it were unavailing. The crew left the ship in three boats

about one and a half hours after the alarm, having saved
but very few things; and in about one and a half hours
got on board the bark Washington, of Hudson, William
Clark, master, and went into Payta.

The fire was first discovered issuing out of the steerage
hatchway, about six feet from the main hatchway, between decks. The ship had on board 400 barrels of oil.

LOSS OF THE SHIP FRANKLIN.

This ship, George Prince, master, sailed from Nantucket, on a whaling voyage in the Pacific Ocean, 6th
month, 27th, 1831. Her cruise, up to the time of her final
loss, was an almost unbroken series of misfortunes. Soon
after leaving, one of the crew, William L. Bunker, fell
from the loft and was laid up two months. 11th month,
15th, 1831, another hand, Frederick C. Whippy, fell from
mizzen-top-gallant-head and broke both legs. He was
left on board the sloop of war Falmouth at Callao. At the
same time a black man was landed, sick with consumption; he died soon afterwards. About the middle of 2d
month succeeding, a boat, fast to a whale, was carried
down, and two men, probably entangled with the line,
were drowned. In 2d month, 1833, a native of the Sandwich Islands fell from the loft and was killed. In 5th
month of the same year, the ship went into Callao, where
a man, John Robson, a native of Massachusetts, was
shipped : he had the fever-and-ague at the time. He died
of the scurvy about four months afterwards. While the
Franklin was at Callao, a man was shipped as boatsteerer;
on the 12th of 8th month he was carried out of the boat by
a line and lost. At Hood's Island the mate strained himself while getting terrapins. He never was well after-

wards, and finally died 3rd of 6th month, in 1834, off Cape Horn, on the homeward bound passage. About five days afterwards, the captain and the steward died both on the same day. The steward's name was Eben Kelton. About four days after this William L. Bunker died, and in a few days from that time, Michael Norman, an Irishman; and on the 30th of 6th month, Charles Thompson, a colored man, also died, all of the scurvy. On the 3d of 7th month the ship came to anchor in Maldonado harbor, mouth of the river La Plata. On the same day another of the crew, Christian Wing, died of the scurvy. On coming to anchor the crew that remained were so worn with sickness and fatigue, that they were not able to furl their sails, which was done by the assistance of the crew of a French ship, who also generously assisted to get the ship up to Monte Video. A new mate and some hands were shipped there, and the Franklin sailed thence on the 12th of 8th month. After much bad weather, on the night of the 5th of 10th month, she ran ashore on the reef Diego Roderiquez, on the coast of Brazil, about 45 miles from the harbor of Macceio. All hands and about one third of her cargo were saved. The ship immediately bilged and went to pieces in about ten days.

VESSELS LOST SINCE THE SETTLEMENT OF THE ISLAND.

The whole number of vessels lost, exclusive of captures, since the settlement of the island, is 168. Of these 78 were sloops, 31 schooners, 18 brigs, and 41 ships. Loss of lives four hundred and fourteen. Among this great number of shipwrecks, there are some cases as remarkable, perhaps, as any above narrated. Our limits will not allow us to dwell longer on this interesting though melancholy subject.

The following proposal to transfer the whaling business of Nantucket to France, will, we think, be read with interest. The time has long gone by, when the publication would excite any political feelings hostile to the French government; and we insert it without comment, as it contains within itself almost all that is known respecting the transaction.

"DUNKERQUE, 10th March, 1786.

"CAPTAIN SHUBAEL GARDNER.

"The present distressed situation of your worthy brethren, the inhabitants of the Island of Nantucket, occasioned not only by their unmerited suffering during the late war, and by the late act of the British government, which imposes a duty on all foreign oil equivalent to a prohibition, obliging a great many of the sufferers to quit their natif-spot and remove to some other country, where their industry may meet its due reward, has created in me the idea to procure them an azilum in my own country, where they may not only find an alleviation of their misfortunes and recuperate their losses, but also where they may expect that comfort and protection due to their honest principles. Anxious to accomplish an object, in which I am moved by no other motif than that of humanity, and a desire of offering a friendly hand to a set of people who in my opinion greatly deserve the assistance of all men who can be, instrumental in contributing to the welfare of their fellow-creatures, has induced me, after a mature conversation with you on so laudable an object, to make an application to this government in their behalf, and to make use of all the interest with the king's ministers I was capable off, to make such proposals as were penned by our friend William Rotch, and which you delivered me in his name on your arrival from London in November last. I think it needless to repeat here the exertions I have made, as well by my correspondence as by word of mouth, during the time we were together at Paris, as you was personally present, and of which you shall be able to give an exact account. Through the assistance of Providence, my exertions have met with a success far exceeding my sanguine expectations. Every article which I thought capable of contributing to the welfare and happiness of those inhabitants, who would choose to remove to the town of Dunkerque, has been granted. I here join a faithful translation of the articles, which I request, on your arrival at Nantucket, you will communicate, with all the prudence you are capable of, to the selectmen of the island, and acquaint them with all the real advantages the town, port and country offers for their establishment. The unlimited freedom it enjoys, the abundance and cheapness of all sorts of provisions, no custom-house nor custom officers to embarrass a free trade, the small taxes, the regularity of the town, the manners and industry of the inhabitants, and its situation, render it the most eligible place in the universe for the people of Nantucket to remove to. To particularize all the advantages Dunkerque offers, would be too long a task for a letter; but as you are well acquainted with them, you may verbally add those which are not here related. You may also communicate to the selectmen the negotiation commenced with our friend William Rotch, and inform them of the predicament he finds himself under at present by the inattention of the British government to the business he is intrusted with. The knowledge of all these circumstances appears to me necessary, in order to enable the people to judge what plan will be most advantangeous to follow. Unless they should be blinded to their own interest, there is no doubt but they will prefer that which is here proposed. Therefore, as I have reason to hope that they will be sensible of the advantages offered them, your first care must be to engage them to name and impower a committee to correspond with me on this subject, and you may assure them of my friendship and ready interference and exertions in the obtention of any other matter, which has not been foreseen by the annexed articles. You may assure the proprietors of the ships, that are now on their fishery, that, if they choose to send them with their cargoes and family on board with an intention to settle, their oil shall be admitted in the country duty free, and that they will enjoy all the advantages and privileges of the natif subjects. On their arrival, they shall be put in possession of the ground allotted to them, and in every respect experience the reality of what I advance. As your stay at Nantucket will be short, on account of the advancement of the season, which will barely leave you time to proceed on the fishery, it is absolutely necessary that the committee of such trustworthy men be appointed to correspond with me by every conveyance to Europe, and if you find the people disposed to remove, you may transfer to such committee the power, that is herewith intrusted to you, of chartering one or two ships, at the most reasonable freight that can be obtained, to transfer a number of tradesmen that are not able to transport themselves at their own expense, proportionable to the number of ships that will stand in need of their assistance when arrived, provided that the expense of freight and provisions for the passage does not exceed at first fifteen or eighteen hundred pounds sterling. The committee, after a knowledge of the disposition of the people, may appreciate and inform me, as near as possible, what the whole expense of transporting may amount to, in order to obtain authorization to pay it. The committee may likewise send one of the members, by the first ship that will come here, with full powers and instructions to conclude in due form all articles and conditions which may appear necessary to the acoomplishment of such a desirable object. But it is absolutely necessary that the greatest secrecy and prudence be observed by all parties in the whole course of the negotiation, in order to avoid creating jealousy between two nations, on whom the tranquility of the world depends, and save mankind from a repetition of the horrors of war, which have brought on the people of Nantucket their present distresses. I am sensible that leaving one's natif spot and separating from some of the nearest connexions is an unpleasing step, but of two evils the least must be preferred; and the people, in their present situation, must, in my opinion, offer their thanks to Divine Providence, that a mild, humane and a generous government offers them a safe azilum, and a friendly hand to alleviate their distress and make them and their posterity happy. I rely on your best exertions to carry on this business to a favorable issue. It will not only tend towards many personal advantages towards yourself, but it will reconcile you the gratitude of the people on both sides. You may assure the inhabitants of my constant protection and friendship, and that in all occasions I shall be their zéalous advocate, and as I am no ways induced by view of personal interest, I shall recommend them to such trustworthy merchants here, to whom they may at first consign their ships and cargoes till they will be able to manage their own business themselves, and in every other respect give them the best advice in my power. I shall be anxious to hear from you, therefore I request you will neglect no opportunity to write to me, interim I wish you a safe and speedy voyage, and remain with lasting regard,

"Dear friend, your truly affectionate friend,

L. COFFIN."

"*Copy of the advantages, granted to the people of the Island of Nan-tucket, who may wish to settle at Dunkirk, and establish the whale fishery.*

"1st.   An entire free exercise of their religion or worship within themselves.

"2d.   The concession of a tract of ground to build their houses and stores.

"3d.   All the privileges, exemptions and advantages promised by the king's declaration in 1662, confirmed by letters patent of 1784, to all strangers who come to establish there, which are the same as those enjoyed by the natif subjects of his majesty.

"4th.   The importation into the kingdom, free from all duties whatever, of the oil proceeding from their fishery, and the same premiums and encouragement granted for the cod and other fisher-ies to natif subjects.

"5th.   A premium per ton on the burthen of the vessels that will carry on the whale fishery, which shall be determined in the course of the negotiation either with Mr. Rotch or with the select-men of the island.

"6th.   All objects of provisions and victuals for their ships shall be exempted from all duties whatever.

"7th.   An additional and heavier duty shall be laid on all foreign oil, as a further encouragement to them, in order to facilitate the sale of their own.

"8th.   The expenses of removing those of the inhabitants, who are not capable of defraying themselves, shall be paid by the gov-ernment.

"9th.   A convenient dock shall be built to repair their ships.

"10th.   All trades-people, such as smiths, boat builders, coopers and others, shall be admitted to the free exercise of their trade without being liable to the forms and expense usually practiced and paid by the natif subjects for their admittance to mastership.

"11th. They shall have liberty to command their own vesssels, and have the choice of their own people to navigate them.

"12th. They shall be free from all military and naval service, as well in war as in peace, in the same manner and extent as expressed by the king's ordinance of the 16th of February, 1759."

"NANTUCKET, June the 15, 1786.

"I, Abner Coffin, notary and tabellion public, by legal authority duly constituted, dwelling in Sherborn, in the county of Nantucket, in the commonwealth of Massachusetts, do hereby certify and attest, that the letter of instructions and twelve articles preceding this certificate are genuine copies of the original, to me the said notary from Shubael Gardner produced.

"In witness whereof I have hereunto affixed my notarial seal and signature.

"In testimonium veritatis,

[Seal.]   ABNER COFFIN, *Not. Pub.*"

FISHING STAGES.

During many years after the settlement of the island, fishing near the shores was one of the principal occupations of the people. Cod fishing was found very productive, and received particular attention. For the accommodation of the fishermen, small houses, adapted to the accommodation of five men each, that being the number of a boat's crew, were erected on the margin of the shore on the south and east sides of the island. Those on the south were at a place called Weweeders. At the east was the village of Siasconset. One mile and a half northward from Siasconset were a few houses at Pedee. A considerable number were built still further northward at Sesacacha; and in the same direction onward, near the head of the harbor, at a place called Quidnet, there was a small number. These clusters of houses were called *fishing stages*.   No uunecessary expense was bestowed on the buildings; they were of wood, the roofs only were shingled.   The place for fire was at one end of the house, a fire-place of brick or stone was raised at some distance above the hearth, thence the chimney of one or the other of those materials was continued to the ridge and finished above the house, with wood.   At the opposite end of the house were two convenient bed-rooms, containing two berths each, and above them was a cockloft where the boys usually lodged.   The principal article of furniture was an ample table of common boards, fastened to the partition by hinges, so as to allow of its being turned up against the side of the room, when not in use, and then fastened with a button.   There are still a few of these houses remaining at the village of Siasconset, but none at the other fishing stages.

SIASCONSET.

This village is situated at the south-east extremity of the island, and contains about 70 houses.   The cod fishery, which was carried on there a few years since pretty extensively, has recently dwindled, so that it can hardly be said to be the business of the place.   The houses, with few exceptions, are occupied only in the warm season. As a summer resort, no place in the United States presents greater attractions for the invalid than Siasconset. It is not, indeed, the focus of fashionable life; but the fine bracing air, the excellent water, and the unique customs and "laws" of the place, are admirably adapted to refresh and invigorate both mind and body.   At Siasconset, all are on a level, or rather on an equal elevation.   Useless forms and ceremonies are laid aside, and the little community, for the time being, indulge in a reciprocity of good feeling and interchange of civilities, which can be found in no place but one situated precisely like Siasconset, and no other such place exists in the known world.

The village is compactly built on a level grass plat, near the edge of a steep cliff; the land rises in the rear, so as to cut off a view of the town of Nantucket, and serve as a barrier to the cares and bustle of a turbulent world. In front, the eye rests on a broad expanse of the Atlantic, and below, the surf rolling and breaking, gives animation to the scenes by day, and lulls to repose by night. Fleets of fishing smacks are frequently anchored or sailing near the shore, catering for distant markets; and larger vessels on longer voyages are continually passing. The sea-bird is ever skimming over the ocean, now eyeing the waters beneath, and now darting headlong at his prey. Shoals of small fishes may be seen blackening the surface, sometimes floating leasurely with the tide, at others fleeing from the pursuit of the shark: and occasionally the majestic whale comes so near that one may see his breath and hear him breathe.

In the vicinity, on the margins of some small swamps, there are berries in sufficient abundance to tempt the resident to a healthful walk; and within the distance of two miles is a sheet of fresh water, spreading over several hundred acres, a visit to which will be repaid by a pleasant ride and a good fare of perch.

From a neighboring eminence, called Sancoty Head, the eye commands almost the entire horizon. In the distant west is seen the town and shipping, and beyond, the sound, often decked with numerous sails; nearer, and on the right, are rich pastures and neat farm-houses, and, further on, stretches out the long Sandy Point, the extremity of which is marked by a light house. On the

left is a broad valley, diversified by swamp and plain, and
bounded by an elevation which extends to the ocean, and
terminates in a high cliff, called Tom Never's Head, between which and the position we are supposed to occupy,
is the village of Siasconset with its diminutive houses
huddled together, resembling a patch of salt-works. A
view from Sancoty Head, at a clear sunset, can hardly be
surpassed in beauty and grandeur. The rich coloring of
the sky, reflected by the distant waters, the distinct out-
lines of the town, with its steeples and busy windmills,
the repose of the surrounding plains, contrasted with the
gloom which broods over the rolling and roaring ocean in
the rear, give rise to sensations which can be felt, indeed,
but not described.

*A letter from Zaccheus Macy, forwarding to the Historical Society
an account of the former Indian divisions of the island, &c.*

NANTUCKET, ye 2d ye 10mo 1792.

" *My Friend and Kinsman:*—Agreeable to the request of the
Massachusetts Historical Society, I have wrote and explained many
words and names of certain parts and places of or on the island of
Nantucket, both in English and Indian, as well as I could: but
there is not one person now left that I can get any help from in
these matters. So I have wrote as well as I can on the affairs or
matters, but I sometimes almost fear, whether it may not seem flat
and old to them, but I have not wrote any thing but what I am
very sure is true, according to the best account I could get.

" Further please to inform our said society, that I received a
small letter from them, expressing their thanks for my little book
I sent them before, which I kindly received and here return the
same to them for their notice on such an old flat piece, and I have
sent them an old stone pipe, such as our old native Indians made
and smoked in, before the English came amongst them. They had
a sort of weed or herb they called *poke*, which they used instead of
tobacco, which weed resembled tobacco, but I do not know of any
now growing on said island.

"The said pipe is something marred and broke, but still shows some considerable curiosity,—but I only suppose it was made out of blue clay and muscle shells, pounded, and mixed, and then burnt, but it is commonly called a *stone* pipe. I once had a complete one, but it is lost. And I have sent them a shell taken out of my well thirty-nine feet below the face of the earth: and I have taken many sorts of shells out of wells near forty feet down. And one time when the old men were digging a well at the stage called Siasconset, it is said, they found a whale's bone near thirty feet below the face of the earth, which things are past our accounting for.

" So I must break short, and only have to send you all my love and respect, which comes from your old and ready friend to serve·

ZACCHEUS MACY.

" To Peleg Coffin, Esquire, of Nantucket,
    now resident in Boston.

" P. S. Please to take a copy of my last work or Journal by reason I have not got it on my book all, for I have enlarged on many things and names, which we may want for our own curiosity."

Account of the names of the old Sachems and some of the most respectable Indians, and their habitations, taken from the best authors that could be had ye 15 ye 3mo., 1763. At that time there were living near about 370 of the natives on the island of Nantucket—p^r me the subscriber.

" Wannochmamock was the first Sachem at the southeast part of the island, when the English first came to Nantucket. Next to him was his son, called Sousoauco, and next to him were his two sons called Cain and Abel. These two agreed to divide the sachemright, two third parts to Cain and one third part to Abel. The said Cain had one daughter, whose name was Jemima, married to James Shaa. From Abel sprang Eben Abel, and from him sprang Benjamin Abel, the last sachem, from whom I bought all his right, title and property that he had on said island, for and in behalf of the whole English proprietors. All the said Jemima's right was bought by our old proprietors many years before, as may fully appear on our records. Their lands or bounds began at a place on the south side of the island, called Touphchue Pond ; and ran across to the northward to a brown rock marked on the west side, that lies to the northward of our washing pond, called Gibb's

Pond, on the west side of Saul's hills and so over towards Podpis swamp, and then to the eastward to a place, Sesacacha Pond by the east sea. At the south-east part of said tract is a high bluff head of land, called Tom Never's Head ; and about two miles to the northward stands our famous fishing stage houses, where our sick people go for their health, called Siasconset; and about a mile still to the northward is a very high cliff of land called Sancota Head, then about a mile still to the northward stands another fishing stage called Sesacacha.

" Next begins the old sachem called Wauwinet; his bounds begin adjoining to the northward of the said Wannochmamock's land and run still along to the northward and take in all Squam, and run on to our long sandy point, called Coetue or Nauma, which in the English is Long Point where our Massachusetts light house now stands, and then to the westward to New Town, then to the southward to a place called Weweder Ponds, which in English signifies a pair of horns, by reason there are two ponds that run to a point next to the sea, and spread apart so as to leave a neck of land, called Long Joseph's Point; which two ponds spread apart so as to resemble a pair of horns. And the said Wauwinet had two sons, the oldest son was named Isaac, but was mostly called Nicornoose, which signifies, in English, to suck the fore teat; and his second son was named Wawpordonggo, which in English is white face, for his face was one side white, and the other side brown or Indian color. And the said Nicornoose married; and had one son named Isaac, and one daughter; and then he turned away his proper wife, and took another woman, and had two sons, named Wat and Paul Noose; and when his true son Isaac grew up to be a man, he resented his father's behavior so much, that he went off and left them for the space of near fifty years, it was not known where. And in that time his true sister married to one Daniel Spotsor, and he reigned sachem, by his wife near about forty years: and we made large purchases of the said Spotsors. And then about sixty years past or more, there came an Indian man from Nauset, called Great Jethro, and he brought Judah Paddack and one Hause with him, and he challenged the sachem-right by being son to the said true son of Nicornoose; and when they first opened the matter to our old proprietors, they contrived to keep the said Jethro close, until they could send some good committee to find out by our old Indians, whether they ever knew or heard of the said Nicornoose having such a son gone, and they soon found out by the old Indians, that he had, but they had not heard what was become of him. So they soon found, they should loose all they had bought of the said Spotsors, then they held a parley with him said Jethro, and agreed to buy all his right, title and property that he owned on said island, as appears on our records. And the said Nicornoose gave deeds to his two bastard sons, Paul and Wat Noose, forty acres each, a little to the eastward of Podpis village.

"The first sachem at the south-west part of said island. His bounds were at the said Weweder Ponds, and from thence to the northward to a place called Gunsue meadow at Monemoy, where we now call New Town, and from thence westward along to the southward of the hills called Popsquatchet Hills, where our three mills now stand, and so to the west sea, called Tawtemeo, which we call the Hummock pond. And his name was Autapeeot. Next to him was his son called Harry Poritain. Next to him was Peter Mausauquit. Next to him was Isaac Peter. Next to him was lame Isaac, of whom we bought the last and all that sachem-right: and their habitation was Moyaucomet, which signifies a meeting-place, and their meeting-house they call Moyaucomor. And the said Autapeeot was called a great warrior, and got his land by his bow.

"The fourth sachem was at the north-west part, called Potconet, and owned all the little island called Tuckernuck, which signifies, in English, a loaf of bread, and his bounds extended from Madaket down eastward to Wesko, which in English is the white stone, and so on to the north side of Autapscot land, all bought of him at the coming of the English, saving some particular tracts that belonged to the Jafets and the Hoights and some others.

"Now I shall give some of the most respectable Indians in Wannochmamock's bounds. There was James Mamack, a minister of the gospel, and justice of the peace, and behaved well in his station. Old Aesop, the weaver, was a schoolmaster; old Saul, a very stern looking old man. Joshua Mamack succeeded in his father James Mamack's place. Richard Nominash and his brother Sampson and little Jethro were all very substantial, and a number more very trusty men.

"The most noted Indians in Autapscot's bounds were Benjamin Tashama, a minister of the gospel, and a schoolmaster to teach the children to read and write. He was grandson to the old sachem. But there was an old Indian, named Zacchary Hoite, a minister before the said Tashama, but he did not behave so well. He told his hearers they must do as he said, but not as he did.

"And there was one Indian man, his name was James Skouel, but was mostly called Corduda. He was justice of the peace, and very sharp with them if they did not behave well. He would fetch them up, when they did not tend their corn well, and order them to have ten stripes on their backs, and for any rogue tricks and getting drunk. And if his own children played any rogue tricks, he would serve them the same sauce. There happened some Englishmen at his court, when a man was brought up for some rogue tricks, and one of these men was named Nathan Coleman, a pretty crank sort of man, and the Indian man pleaded for an appeal to Esquire Bunker, and the old judge turned round to said Nathan and spoke in the Indian language thus, ' chaquor keador taddator witche conichau mussoy chaquor,' then said Nathan answered thus, ' martau couetchawidde neconne sassamyste nehotie moche Squire Bunker;' which in the English tongue is thus, ' what do you think about this great business?' then Nathan answered, ' may be you had better whip him first, then let him go to Squire Bunker;' and the old judge took Nathan's advice. And so Nathan answered two purposes, the one was to see the Indian whipped, the other was, he was sure the Indian would not want to go to Esquire Bunker for fear of another whipping.

"I will say something more in recommendation of some of our old Indian natives. They were very solid and sober at their meetings of worship, and carried on in the form of Presbyterians, but in one thing imitated the Friends or Quakers, so called: which was to hold meetings on the first day of the week and on the fifth day of the week, and attended their meetings very precisely. I have been at their meetings many times and seen their devotion; and it was remarkably solid; and I could understand the most of what was said; and they always placed us in a suitable seat to sit; and they were not put by, by our coming in, but rather appeared glad to see us come in. And a minister is called cooutaumuchary. And when the meeting was done, they would take their tinder-box and strike fire and light their pipes, and, may be, would draw three or four whifs and swallow the smoke, and then blow it out of their noses, and so hand their pipes to their next neighbor. And one pipe of tobacco would serve ten or a dozen of them.

And they would say ' tawpoot,' which is, ' I thank ye.' It seemed
to be done in a way of kindness to each other.

"And as I said before, they had justices, constables, grand-
jurymen, and carried on for a great many years, many of them
very well and precisely, and lived in very good fashion. Some of
them were weavers, some good carpenters.

   *   *   *   *   *   *   *

" Now I will begin at the west end of the island, which we call
Smith's Point, but the Indians call Nopque, which was called a
landing place, when they came from the Vineyard, but they call it
Noapx; then eastward about three miles comes the Hummock
Pond, where we once had a great number of whale houses with a
mast raised for a look-out, with holes bored through and sticks put
in like a ladder, to go up; then about three miles eastward to the
said Weweder ponds, stood another parcel of whale houses; then
about three miles eastward to Nobedeer Pond was where Benjamin
Gardner lived formerly; then about three and one half miles
eastward is the aforesaid Tom Never's Head; then two miles to
the northward is the famous town or fishing stage called Siasconset; then about one mile northward is the high head of land called
Sancoty Head, and the Indians called Naphchecoy, which signifies
round the head; then about one mile northward is the aforesaid
Sesacacha pond, where our other fishing stage stands. Then
begins the said Squam, and runs northward two miles to the
beginning of our said long sandy point called Naauma; and the
first is one mile to a place called Causkata pond, where are some
woods and meadow; and four miles northward is where the said
Massachusetts lighthouse is, on the north end of said point. Then
about one mile to the northward of the entering on of the above
said long point, begins another neck or beach, called little Coetue
and runs about five miles on about a west by south course till it
comes within about one mile of our town called Wesko, which
makes the east side of the entering-in of our harbor. Then next
to the said Squam, westward, is the village called Podpis Neck,
where our fulling-mill stands; then next westward is the famous
neck of land called Quaise or Maisquatuck Neck, which in the
English signifies the reed land, which was a tract of land given to
Thomas Mayhew from one of the old sachems, and was reserved
by the said Mayhew to himself when he sold his patent-right to
the proprietors; which neck makes the west side of the said Podpis

Harbor, now owned by Josiah Barker, Esquire, and Captain Shubael Coffin and Captain Thomas Delano. The next westward is the Josiah Barker's lot or field, called Show Aucamor, which in English signifies the middle field of land. Then about four miles westward is the town called Wesco; then next westward is a place called Watercomet, which signifies a pond field, which formerly was owned by the old natives called the Hoites. Then next westward is the great pond called Cuppame, where old Tristram Coffin lived, the old grandfather to almost all of us, which was owned by the old families of the natives called the Jafets; then next westward about four miles is called Eel Point and Madaket Harbor, which is the north-west part of the said island; and then about two miles westward is the said little island, called Tuckernuck, which signifies, in English, a loaf of bread, for it appears round, and in the middle pretty high: which was bought by the said old Tristram Coffin from the old sachem Potconet, in the year 1659, by virtue of a patent he had from New York.

"Excuse me for errors and poor writing and spelling, and consider me in station of life worn out.

"Nantucket, ye 2d 10th month, 1792.

By ZACCHEUS MACY.

"To Peleg Coffin, Esquire, now resident in Boston. For the perusal of our Historical Society for the Massachusetts, in Boston.

EDUCATION.

Previous to the year 1827 very little was done, for the support of schools, by the town in its corporate capacity. The youth, indeed, had ever had an opportunity of acquiring the rudiments of an English education in private schools, and some appropriations had been made to instruct the poor. In 1827 the town appropriated a sufficient sum to maintain two large schools on the monitorial plan, which went into operation immediately. Since that period some changes have taken place, both in the number of public schools and in the system of teaching. There are at present two large grammar and four primary schools, at which there are taught about 800 scholars. There are also, besides the Coffin school, which will be subsequently noticed, some excellent private schools. The young possess advantages for common education not exceeded by those of any other place in the Union : whether these advantages are duly appreciated by the community, we shall not pretend to decide ; but if the rising generation do not carry into the world a sufficient stock of knowledge for all the best purposes of life, the fault must rest elsewhere than on the town or on the teachers of schools.

THE COFFIN SCHOOL.

In the year 1826, Admiral Sir Isaac Coffin, of the British navy, visited the island. He found that a large part of the inhabitants were more or less remotely akin to him. Possessing a mind trained to active benevolence, he expressed a disposition to confer on his kindred some mark of his attachment to them, and of his regard for his ancestry. The establishment of a school was suggested to him, as a means of permanent good to his relatives, and immediately met his approbation. He accordingly authorized the late WILLIAM COFFIN, Esq., to purchase a building then vacant, which had been used for a Lancasterian school, and shortly afterwards funded, for the support of the proposed institution, *two thousand five hundred pounds sterling.* An act of incorporation was passed at the succeeding session of the legislature, and the school was opened in the spring of 1827. The selection of the first board of trustees was confided to William Coffin, Esq.

The school was first taught on the monitorial plan, which was laid aside about four years since. The pupils are now arranged in four classes, denominated first, second, third and fourth. The fourth, or primary class, is preparatory to the third, and studies are laid out for the three higher classes, calculated to occupy each class one year. Class succeeds class precisely on the college plan. Those who have attended the school three whole years, and completed the studies of the first class, are entitled to one year's tuition gratis, with liberty to review past studies or commence such new ones as can be conveniently attended to.

The income from the fund is not sufficient for the support of the school, as it is at present arranged, so that there is a necessity of charging each pupil $2.50 per quarter. The two departments, male and female, occupy separate rooms, but corresponding classes in each pursue the same studies and recite together. There is a principal and assistant in each department. The examinations of the school are quarterly, on the last fifth day or Thursday of each season; and the succeeding quarter commences on the following second day, or Monday, unless a vacation intervenes. The vacations are not at present fixed to any times, but are adapted to the convenience of the teachers; except one of a week at the season of sheep-shearing.

" *Copy of the Act of Incorporation of the Coffin School.*

" COMMONWEALTH OF MASSACHUSETTS.

" In the year of our Lord 1827.

"An Act to incorporate a school at Nantucket by the name of Admiral Sir ISAAC COFFIN's Lancasterian School.

" *Sec. 1st.* Be it enacted by the senate and house of representatives in general court assembled, and by the authority of the same, That there be and hereby is established in the town of Nantucket, in the county of Nantucket, a school by the name of *Admiral Sir Isaac Coffin's Lancasterian School,* for the purpose of promoting decency, good order and morality, and for giving a good English education to youth who are descendants of the late Tristram Coffin (who emigrated from England about the year 1641, first settled at Salisbury, in Massachusetts Bay, now state of Massachusetts, and from thence removed to the town of Sherburne, now Nantucket,) as the trustees for the time being shall direct, and that William Coffin, Ariel Coffin, Gorham Coffin, Jared Coffin, Thaddeus Coffin and Charles G. Coffin, with such others as they may add to their numbers, be nominated and appointed trustees, and they are hereby incorporated into a body politic by the name of the Trustees of Admiral Sir Isaac Coffin's Lancasterian School, and that they and their successors shall be and continue a body politic for ever.

"*Sec. 2d.*   Be it further enacted, that all lands, buildings, moneys, or other property heretofore given or subscribed for the purpose of establishing the aforesaid school, or which shall be hereafter given, granted, or assigned to the said trustees, shall be confirmed to the said trustees and their successors in that trust for ever, for the uses for which said school is established, and the said trustees shall be capable of having, holding and taking in fee simple, by gift, grant, devise or otherwise, any lands, tenements, or other estate real or personal, *provided* that the annual income of the same shall not exceed the sum of three thousand dollars, and shall apply the interest, rents and profits thereof so as most to promote the design of the institution.

"*Sec. 3d.*   Be it further enacted, that the said trustees, for the time being, shall be the visitors and governors of said institution, and shall have full power, from time to time, to elect such officers thereof as they shall judge necessary and convenient, and fix the tenor of their respective offices, and to fill up all vacancies that may happen in the board of trustees, by death, resignation or removal from the town of Nantucket. *Provided always*, that the trustees shall all be the descendants of the above-mentioned Tristram Coffin in the male or female line,—to determine the times and places for holding their meetings—the manner of notifying the trustees—to ascertain the powers and duties of their several officers—to elect instructors and prescribe their duties—to make and ordain reasonable rules, orders and by-laws for the government of the institution, provided the same be not repugnant to the laws of the commonwealth.

"*Sec. 4th.* Be it further enacted, that the trustees of said school may have a common seal, which they may change at pleasure, and all deeds sealed with the said seal, and delivered and acknowledged by the secretary of said trustees by their order, shall be valid and binding in law—and said trustees may sue and be sued in all actions, and prosecute and defend the same to final judgment and execution by the name of the trustees of Admiral Sir Isaac Coffin's Lancasterian School.

"*Sec. 5th.* Be it further enacted, that the number of trustees shall never exceed nine nor be less than six, one of whom shall be appointed as president, three of whom with the president, or five without the president, shall be necessary to constitute a quorum for doing business, but a less number may adjourn from time to time,—and a majority of those present shall decide all questions that may properly come before said trustees.

"*Sec. 6th.* Be it further enacted, that William Coffin, Esq., be and he is hereby authorized and empowered to fix the time and place of holding the first meeting of the trustees and to notify them thereof.

"*Sec. 7th.* Be it further enacted, that this act may at any time be modified or repealed by the legislature of this commonwealth.

"*Sec. 8th.* Be it further enacted, that an act passed in the year of our Lord one thousand eight hundred and twenty-seven, entitled 'An Act to Incorporate a School at Nantucket, by the name of *Admiral Isaac Coffin's Lancasterian School,*' be and the same hereby is repealed.

"Passed June 8, 1827."

NANTUCKET ATHENÆUM.

This institution was incorporated in 1834. It took its origin from two societies, one the Mechanics' Association, formed in 1820, the other the Columbian Library Association, formed in 1823. These were united in 1827, under the name of the United Library Association. In 1833, two of the members, Charles G. Coffin and David Joy, offered the society a valuable tract of land, in the central part of the town, on the condition of there being erected

on it a substantial building for the uses of the Association.
A subscription was immediately opened and in a short
time a greater amount was obtained than that required by
the conditions of the donation. Thus encouraged, the
Association, with the consent of the donors of the land,
purchased the house and land then recently occupied by
the Universalist Society, and made such alterations in the
building as were required for their accommodation. The
addition of a portico, which is about to be annexed to the
building, will make it one of the handsomest edifices in
the town. The apartments of the building are a convenient lecture room sufficiently large to accommodate an
audience of about four hundred and fifty persons, a library
room, a spacious room for curiosities, and a committee
room. The library consists of more than two thousand
volumes, and is rapidly increasing. The museum contains a large number of curiosities, consisting chiefly of
weapons, dresses and utensils of the natives of the Pacific
Ocean Islanders. It is a valuable collection, becoming
daily more valuable; for the character of those people is
constantly changing, and if they should survive a contact
with civilized nations, their habits, customs and mode of
warfare will be learned, a few generations hence, only
from these relics of their former simplicity.

SLAVERY.

The Society of Friends, in New England, were probably the *first* associated body that bore testimony against
slavery. About the year 1717, as we have been informed
by William Rotch, Jun., of New Bedford, a friend of the
highest respectability, clerk a number of years of the
Nantucket monthly meeting of the Society of Friends,
they expressed their views on the subject on their records

in the following language, according to his best recollection :—" That they considered it inconsistent with truth to purchase mankind as slaves, and hold them term of life."

We regret that we have not been able to obtain more information respecting the early proceedings of the Friends, in relation to slavery. The inhabitants of the island may well be proud of the decided stand, which their ancestors took against the odious traffic in human flesh. We felt it due to our native place, and it would have been peculiarly grateful to our personal feelings, to present the public with authentic documents connected with this subject; but the ancient records in possession of that part of the society, called orthodox, have not been made accessible to us, though we have sought, through the recorder, either to examine them ourselves, or be furnished with a copy of the minute, on record, at that early period.

It is enough to say, that we have not been able to obtain them, and that we feel a reluctance, from the very high respect we entertain towards the greater part of the members constituting that body, for their candor and courtesy, to enter at all into an explanation of the irreconcilable procedure connected with this application.

We are willing thus, to suffer, in silence, the seeming reproach, which such a refusal casts upon us; for we cannot be insensible to the surprise, which it must produce in the minds of those, unacquainted with the causes, which have probably operated to produce it. It would be more gratifying to us to apply, without any reserve whatever, the acknowledgment which Clarkson, the author of the " Portraiture of Quakerism," did to the society of Friends in England, while in the prosecution of his writings; but the pleasure is denied to us.

We have been obliged to give the above explanation; for we had no other means to account for the non-appearance of the record, and self-respect alone demands of us to say, that in the compilation of this history, we have received the most prompt and kind attention from every other source, to which we have applied, for records or information, in the prosecution of our labors.

"One of the first public advocates for the cause of the oppressed Africans in New England," was Elihu Coleman, of Nantucket. "He was a minister of the society of Friends. We have before us, a work written in 1729 –30, and published in 1733, entitled '*A Testimony against that anti-Christian Practice of* MAKING SLAVES OF MEN.'" In a preliminary address to his readers, he uses these words, " And now, though some may think it hard to have this practice spoken against, that has been carried on so long pretty much in silence, I may let such know, that I have found it hard to write against it ; yet nevertheless believing it my duty so to do, I have written according to my understanding thereof.   And although I have written but little, and in a very plain way, yet I hope that those remarks I have made thereon, may serve as a text for some to preach to themselves upon.   I am not unthoughtful of the ferment or stir that such discourse as this may make among some, who (like Demetrius of old) may say, by this craft we have our wealth, which caused the people to cry out with one voice, great is Diana of the Ephesians, whom all Asia and the world worship." In the course of his work the author says : "I have often considered how earnestly some men will search into the etymology or original of some things that may be but small, and in the mean time omit the greater.   Now in my judgment every thing out to be looked upon according to the importance, weight, or value of the thing; for to be very zealous in a small thing, and to pass lightly over a greater, that zeal may be more properly called superstition, than good zeal, which should be grounded on knowledge. Now I would have all to consider of this practice of making slaves of negroes, or others that we can get the mastery over, to see upon what foundation it stands, or to see what the original of it was, whether or no pride and idleness was not the first rise of it, that they might go with white hands, and that their wives might (Jezebel like) paint and adorn themselves, and their sons and daughters be brought up in idleness, which may be very well termed the mother of all vice; for it is generally the richest sort of people that have them, for the poor are not so able to get them."—" But some may object, as I myself have heard them, that there was a mark set upon Cain, and they do believe, that these negroes are the posterity of Cain;" " but if we do but observe, and read in the genealogy of Cain, we may find that they were all drowned in the old world, and that Canaan was of the line of Seth.' " Christ forbids his followers to meddle with the tares, lest they hurt the wheat, therefore none can have any plea for making them slaves; for their being ignorant or wicked; for if that plea would do, I do believe they need not go so far for slaves as now they do."

" Now although the Turks make slaves of those they catch that are not of their religion, yet (as history relates) as soon as any embraces the Mahometan religion, they are no longer kept slaves, but are quickly set free, and for the most part put to some place of preferment; so zealous are they for proselytes and their own religion. Now if many among those called Christians would but consider, how far they fall short of the Turks in this particular, it would be well; for they tell the negroes, that they must believe in Christ, and receive the Christian faith, and that they must receive the sacrament, and be baptized, and so they do; but still they keep them slaves for all this."

N. B. Since noticing the proceedings of Friends in regard to slavery, a very obliging friend, Thomas A. Greene of New Bedford, has furnished us with extracts, made by him in 1820, from the records of the Nantucket monthly meeting. We feel too proud of this testimony of our fathers against slavery, to withold the record in its original form, from the world, though we have already given it in substance.

26th day of ye 9th mo., 1716.

"An epistle from the last Quarterly Meeting was read in this, and ye matter referred to this meeting, viz: whether it is agreeable to truth for friends to purchase slaves and keep them term of liffe, was considered, and ye sense and judgment of this meeting is, that it is not agreeable to truth for friends to purchase slaves and hold them term of liffe.

"Nathaniel Starbuck, jun^r is to draw out this meeting's judgment concerning friends not buying slaves and keeping them term of liffe, and send it to the next Quarterly Meeting, and to sign it in ye meeting's behalf."

RELIGIOUS SOCIETIES.

In the town of Nantucket there are eight religious societies or congregations, viz: one Unitarian Congregationalist, one Orthodox Society, two meetings of Friends, one attached to the New York yearly meeting, the other to that of New England; one Methodist Episcopal, one Reformed Methodist; and two for colored persons, one of them Baptist, the other denominated Zion's Church.

SUMMARY of the number of DEATHS of persons belonging to Nantucket, in each year from 1820 to 1834 inclusive.

1820		65
1821		—
1822		160
1823		167
1824		133
1825 under 10 years	114	
" over 10, under 70	92	
" over 70	35	
		241
1826 under 10 years	73	
" over 10, under 70	67	
" over 70	19	
		159
1827 under 10 years	34	
" over 10, under 70	63	
" over 70	20	
		117
1828 under 10 years	56	
" over 10, under 70	70	
" over 70	31	
		157
1829 under 10 years	59	
" over 10, under 70	63	
" over 70	19	
		141
1830 under 10 years	41	
" over 10, under 70	49	
" over 70	28	
		118
1831 under 10 years	47	
" over 10, under 70	81	
" over 70 .	25	
		153
1832 under 10 years	47	
" over 10, under 70	74	
" over 70	17	
		138

<pre>
1833 under 10 years   145
  "   over 10, under 45   .   49
  "   over 45, under 70   20
  "   over 70   22
                                          ----   236
1834 under 10 years   76
  "   over 10, under 45   55
  "   over 45, under 70   23
  "   over 70   23
                                          ----   177
</pre>

FIRES.

We subjoin an account of fires, which have occurred
within the town of Nantucket. There may be some
omissions, and the estimate of losses may in some
instances be incorrect, but we believe that the error, if
there be any, will consist in overating the property
destroyed. That there should be so few losses in a town
compactly built of wood, is to be attributed, perhaps
equally, to the steady habits of the inhabitants, and the
promptness, energy, and activity of the young men of the
island. The means for extinguishing fires consist of a
sufficient number of engines, good apparatus, a bountiful
supply of water from the harbor, public cisterns and
private wells.

Buildings destroyed by Fire.

<pre>
In 1736 Friends meeting house, estimated loss, $400
   1762 Peter Barnard's house,   400
   1765 Mill,   500
   1769 Several buildings on South Wharf,   11,000
     "   "   "   at Brant Point,   1,000
   1774 Enoch Gardner's barn,   100
   1782 Light-house at Brant Point,   1,000
   1786   "   " Great Point,   1,000
     "   Nicholas Meader's house at Sesacacha,   100
</pre>

1797 Two barns,	$300
1799 Isaac Folger's shop,	1,500
1802 Nathan Bebe's bake-house,	2,000
1810 George Russell's shop,	350
1811 Matthew Myrick's rope-walk,	3,000
1812 Samuel Swain's house at Phillips' Run,	200
" Several buildings at South Wharf,	6,000
1814 George Myrick's farm house,	300
1816 Light-house at Great Point,	500
1820 Jethro Dunham's house at Tuckernuck,	400
1823 T. & H. Starbuck's shop,	100
1832 Isaac Coffin's barn,	900

Buildings injured.

Thomas Smith's shop,	1,000
John R. Macy's shop,	600
Elizabeth Chase's shop,	1,000
Adding to these losses $3,000, for slight injuries sustained at different times,	3,000

It is believed that the total value of property destroyed by fires, since the settlement of the island, has not exceeded $36,000

POETRY.

We insert the following specimens of our island poesy, not because we consider them the best collection that can be made, nor because we suppose them, taken collectively, to possess very extraordinary merit. Some of the pieces have been deemed worthy of being handed down from a considerably remote period. Our fathers wielded the harpoon, and our mothers the distaff, with better effect, and certainly with more profit, than they did the pen; yet they were not all insensible to the smiles of the muses, nor were the muses always averse to their devotions. It seems necessary to possess some familiarity with an art in order to judge of others' skill therein; we deem it prudent, therefore, to withhold our opinion in the premises, and leave it for others to decide, whether we have added to the value of our work by our selections. And yet we are willing to take our part in the censures which may befall these productions, so far as taste and poetic feeling are at stake; and, if these qualities are not found to have been possessed by some of the writers, we shall plead guilty of the like deficiency ourselves. It is said that, when one chord of the stringed instrument is touched, all the kindred chords are made to vibrate; so, whether from local partialities or not we cannot determine, the sentiments of our own poets have awakened sympathetic emotions in our breasts.

(272)

The following is extracted from a work written by Peter Folger, of whom some mention is made in the second chapter of this history. The title is as follows:

A LOOKING-GLASS FOR THE TIMES, OR THE FORMER SPIRIT OF NEW ENGLAND REVIVED IN THIS GENERATION.

By Peter Folger.

Let all that read these verses know,
That I intend something to show
About our war, how it hath been
And also what is the chief sin,
That God doth so with us cont end
And when these wars are like to end.
Read then in love ; do not despise
What here is set before thine eyes.

New England for these many years
  hath had both rest and peace,
But now the case is otherwise:
  our troubles doth increase.
The plague of war is now beg un
  in some great colonies,
And many, towns are desolate
  we may see with our eyes.
The loss of many goodly men
  We may lament also,
Who in the war have lost their lives,
  and fallen by our foe.
Our women also they have took
  and children very small,
Great cruelty they have used
  to some, though not to all.

    * * * * *

Let us then search, what is the sin
  that God doth punish for;
And, when found out, cast it away
  and ever it abhor.

Sure 'tis not chiefly for those sins
  that magistrates do name,
And make good laws for to suppress,
  and execute the same.

But 'tis for that same crying sin,
  that rulers will not own,
And that whereby much cruelty
  to brethren hath been shown;

The sin of persecution
  such laws established,

By which laws they have gone so far,
  as blood hath touched blood.

It is now forty years ago,
  since some of them were made,
Which was the ground and rise of all
  the persecuting trade.

Then many worthy persons were
  banished to the woods,
Where they among the natives did
  lose their most precious bloods.

And since that, many goodly men
  have been to prison sent;
They have been fined, and whipped also,
  and suffered banishment.

The cause of this their suffering
  was not for any sin,
But for the witness that they bare
  against babes sprinkling.
          *   *   *   *   *
And though that these were harmless men,
  and did no hurt to any,
But lived well like honest men,
  as testified by many;

Yet did these laws entrap them so,
  that they were put to death,
And could not have the liberty
  to speak near their last breath.

But these men were, as I have heard,
  against our college men;
And this was, out of doubt to me,
  that which was most their sin.
          *   *   *   *   *   *
Now to the sufferings of these men
  I have but gave a hint;
Because that in *George Bishop's* book
  you may see all in print.
          *   *   *   *   *
Now, loving friends and countrymen,
  I wish we may be wise,
'Tis now a time for every man
  to see with his own eyes.

'Tis easy to provoke the Lord
  to send among us war,
'Tis easy to do violence,
  to envy and to jar;

To show a spirit that is high,
  to scorn and domineer;

To pride it out; as if there were
  no God to make us fear;

To covet what is not our own,
  to cheat and to oppress,
To live a life that might free us
  from acts of Righteousness;

To swear and lie, and to be drunk,
  to backbite one another;
To carry tales that may do hurt
  and mischief to our brother!

To live in such hypocrisy,
  as men may think us good,
Although our hearts within are full
  of evil and of blood.

All these and many evils more
  are easy for to do;
But to repent, and to reform,
  we have no strength unto.

Let us then seek for help from God,
  and turn to him that smite;
Let us take heed, that at no time
  we sin against our light.

    *   *   *   *   *

I would not have you for to think,
  tho' I have wrote so much,
That I hereby do throw a stone
  at magistrates *as such*.

The rulers in the country I
  do own them in the Lord:
And such as are for government,
  with them I do accord.

But that which I intend hereby,
  is that they would keep bounds,
And meddle not with God's worship,
  for which they have no ground.

And I am not alone herein,
  there's many hundreds more,
That have for many years ago
  spake much upon that score.

Indeed I really believe,
  it's not your business
To meddle with the Church of Christ
  in matters more or less.

There's work enough to do besides,
  to judge in *mine* and *thine*,

To succor poor and fatherless,
  that is the work in fine.
        *   *   *   *   *
The Church may now go stay at home,
  there's nothing for to do;
Their work is all cut out by law,
  and almost made up too.
        *   *   *   *   *
If we do love our brethren,
  and do to them, I say,
As we would they should do to us,
  we should be quiet straightway.

But if we a smiting go
  of fellow-servants so,
No marvel if our wars increase
  and things so heavy go.

'Tis like that some may think and say,
  our war would not remain,
If so be that a thousand more
  of natives were but slain.

Alas! these are but foolish thoughts;
  God can make more arise,
And if that there were none at all,
  He can make war with flies.
        *   *   *   *   *
Let's have our faith and hope in God,
  and trust in Him alone, ,
And then no doubt this storm of war
  it quickly will be gone.

Thus, reader, I, in love to all,
  leave these few lines with thee,
Hoping that in the substance we
  shall very well agree.

If that you do mistake the verse
  for its uncomely dress,
I tell thee true, I never thought
  that it would pass the press.

If any at the matter kick,
  it's like he's galled at heart,
And that's the reason why he kicks,
  because he finds it smart.

I am for peace, and not for war,
  and that's the reason why
I write more plain than some men do,
  that use to daub and lie.

But I shall cease, and set my name
  to what I here insert,

> Because to be a libeller,
>   I hate it with my heart.
>
> From *Sherbon** town, where now I dwell,
>   my name I do put here,
> Without offence your real friend,
>   it is PETER FOLGER.   *April* 23, 1676.

We insert the following, not for its intrinsic merit, but as a specimen of much of a similar character, which has fallen into our hands, and also as an apology for not publishing more.

AN ELEGY ON THE SUDDEN AND AWFUL DEATH OF SEVEN MEN, WHO WERE DROWNED ON NANTUCKET BAR, 1ST OF 1ST MONTH, 1782.

> Kind heaven assist my feeble muse,
>   And help me to relate
> Unto my friends the dismal news
>   Of my poor townsmen's fate.
>
> O, what a sad and awful time,
>   Which caused our eyes to weep,
> For seven men, all in their prime,
>   All drowned in the deep.
>
> In seventeen hundred eighty-two,
>   The first of new year's day,
> This poor unhappy crew of men
>   Were sadly swept away.
>
> They from Nantucket shore put off,
>   And for the bar did try,
> In hopes to get on board a brig;
>   But could not her come nigh.
>
> The wind did blow, the sea run high,
>   They strove the brig to gain,
> But all endeavors fruitless were—
>   Their striving proved in vain.
>
> Their boat upon the ocean fill'd,
>   And two were then swept out,

---

* Nantucket.

And five, remaining in her still,
  Some time were toss'd about.

Their friends on shore saw their distress,
  And for their help did try;
But nothing could in time be done ;
  It was their lot to die.

Four mournful widows, left that day,
  And eleven children small,
And two besides that were unborn,
  Which makes thirteen in all.

Their sorrows surely must be great,
  Which I full well do know,
Having once shared the same fate,
  And tasted the same woe.

Now in the scriptures we may find
  These words recorded be :
The fatherless leave to my care,
  Their widows trust in me.

The following piece is from the pen of Peleg Folger, a member and an elder of the Society of Friends. He died in the year 1789, aged 55 years. In early life he exhibited traits of character, which gave him a great superiority over others of his age. His literary acquirements were the result of his own unaided industry, for his school education was very limited, his youth being principally employed in the farming business. At about the age of 21 he began the business of a seaman, which he followed many years, both in whaling and cod fishing. On examining the journal which he kept during this period, we find it couched in the language rather of a scholar than of a farmer or sailor. In addition to keeping the run of the vessel, like an experienced navigator, he frequently introduced, in his journals, pieces of poetry, and compositions in prose, and occasionally sentences in Latin, besides arithmetical and algebraical problems. His general deportment was serious and contemplative. It was rare that he indulged in levity, but he was free and sociable in conversation on useful subjects, whether moral or religious. He was considered as a monitor in all his conduct through life; beloved by all good people, he commanded the respect and obedience of those who looked to him for support and protection, among whom were several fatherless children.

His knowledge of mathematics, and of the natural sciences generally, was considered by judges to be far superior to that of many who had had the advantages of a classical education. His character as a Christian, from his youth to the time of his decease, was almost without blemish. For several days previous to his departure, he appeared to have a satisfactory presentiment of his approaching end, and that the sting of death was entirely removed. He had much to say by way of advice to his friends and neighbors, who visited him in his last moments.

DOMINUM COLLAUDAMUS. [LET US PRAISE THE LORD.]

Praise ye the Lord! O celebrate his fame;
   Praise the eternal God that dwells above:
His power will for ever be the same,
   The same for ever his eternal love.

Long as that glittering lamp of heaven, the sun,
   Long as the moon or twinkling stars appear,
Long as they all their annual courses run,
   And make the circle of the sliding year;

So long our gracious God will have the care
   To save his tender children from all harms;
Wherever danger is he will be near,
   And underneath, his everlasting arms.

O Lord, I pray, my feeble muse inspire,
   That, while I touch upon a tender string,
I may be filled as with celestial fire,
   And of thy great deliverances sing.

My soul is lost, as in a wondrous maze,
  When I contemplate thine omnipotence,
That did the hills create and mountains raise,
  And spread the stars over the wide expanse.

Almighty God, thou didst create the light
  That swiftly through th' ethereal regions flies;
The sun to rule the day, the moon the night,
  With stars adorning all the spangled skies.

Thou mad'st the world and all that is therein—
  Men, beasts and birds, and fishes of the sea.
Men still against thy holy law do sin,
  Whilst all the rest thy holy voice obey.

Monsters that in the briny ocean dwell,
  And winged troops that every way disperse,
They all thy wonders speak, thy praises tell,
  O thou great ruler of the universe.

Ye sailors, speak, that plough the wat'ry main,
  Where raging seas and foaming billows roar,
Praise ye the Lord, and in a lofty strain
  Sing of his wonder-working love and power.

Thou didst, O Lord, create the mighty whale,
  That wondrous monster of a mighty length;
Vast is his head and body, vast his tail,
  Beyond conception his unmeasured strength.

When he the surface of the sea hath broke,
  Arising from the dark abyss below,
His breath appears a lofty stream of smoke,
  The circling waves like glitt'ring banks of snow.

But, everlasting God, thou dost ordain
  That we, poor feeble mortals should engage
(Ourselves, our wives and children to maintain,)
  This dreadful monster with a martial rage.

And though he furiously doth us assail,
  Thou dost preserve us from all dangers free;
He cuts our boat in pieces with his tail,
  And spills us all at once into the sea.

 o o o o o o

I twice into the dark abyss was cast,
  Straining and struggling to retain my breath;
Thy waves and billows over me were past;
  Thou didst, O Lord, deliver me from death.

Expecting every moment still to die,
  Methought I nevermore should see the light;
Well nigh the gates of vast eternity
  Environed me with everlasting night.

Great was my anguish, earnest were my cries—
  Above the power of human tongue to tell;
Thou heardst, O Lord, my groans and bitter sighs
  Whilst I was lab'ring in the womb of hell.

Thou savedst me from the dangers of the sea,
  That I might bless thy name for ever more.
Thy love and power the same will ever be;
  Thy mercy is an inexhausted store.

O may I in thy boundless power confide,
  And in thy glorious love for ever trust,
Whilst I in thy inferior world reside,
  Till earth return to earth and dust to dust.

And when I am unbound from earthly clay,
  Oh, may my soul then take her joyful flight
Into the realms of everlasting day,
  To dwell in endless pleasure and delight,

At God's right hand, in undiminished joy,
  In the blest tabernacles made above,
Glory and peace without the least alloy,
  Uninterrupted, never dying love.

There angels and archangels still remain,
  The saints in their superior regions dwell,
They praise their God and in a heavenly strain,,
  The wondrous works of great Jehovah tell.

And when I shall this earthly ball forsake,
  And leave behind me frail mortality,
Then may my soul her nimble journey take
  Into the regions of eternity.

Then may my blessed soul ascend above,
  To dwell with that angelic, heavenly choir,
And in eternal songs of praise and love
  Bless thee, my God, my King, for evermore.

FAREWELL TO RACHAEL WILSON* OF ENGLAND,—1769.

[Author unknown.]

Happy the humbled soul that lives to God,
  Refined from sensual dross, pursues the way,
The only blessed way, true pleasure's road,
  Leading through time's thick night to endless day.

In humble hope let honest hearts unite,
  That the great harvest's Lord may yet endow

-----

*A minister of the Society of Friends then on a visit to Nantucket.

More faithful laborers with immortal might,
　And willing minds the Master's work to do.

Wilson, the field is wide, the harvest great,
　Noble the purpose of thine embassy,
Stupid the mind unfeeling of the weight
　Of potent love that operates in thee.

Weaned from the love of life and earthly things,
　Obedient to the soul-redeeming power,
Borne o'er the deep on evangelic wings,
　A welcome envoy to this western shore:

The straying mind descends from barren heights,
　Soft melody vibrating in her ear,
And in the lowly, verdant vale delights
　The gospel music of thy song to hear.

Thus the good shepard tunes his rural reed,
　The stragglers of his flock are gathered near,
Charmed by his voice, they in his presence feed,
　Safe from the beasts of prey, and void of fear.

Clothed with His love who made the lily white,
　Thy fervent labor, Wilson, has been blest;
Or this my verse had never seen the light,
　Nor thus a fellow worm had been addressed.

And is thy task fulfill'd?　Must thou depart?
　Go, then, and may angelic peace be thine;
Absence cannot erase thee from my heart
　In years to come, if years to come be mine.

Divinely fitted for a sacred use,
　As such, 'tis sure no flattery to commend;
A vessel honored in thy master's house,
　As such I but salute thee as a friend.

Favored of God, farewell! and to thy shore,
　Bless'd with celestial calm, though billows foam,
May gales propitious waft thee safely o'er,
　Endeared Rachael, to thy native home.

MY NATIVE ISLE.

Is there within wide nature's bound,
In realms above, or depths profound,
　Or on this terrene globe,
A goddess shrewd, as Pallas wise,
Or spirit of infernal guise,
　Or aught of mortal made;

Is there no sylph of wood or mead ·
No sea-nymph in her watery bed,
　No genius of the Nile,

No one in mountain, grot or dell,
Invested with the power to tell
   Whence sprung my Native Isle?

Was it from ocean's coral caves,
Toss'd by old Neptune to the waves,
   A gift in merry glee?
And will he not some future day,
In wonder at its lengthened stay,
   Back hurl it to the sea?

Or was it severed from the shore
Of neighboring lands, in days of yore,
   By strong volcanic shock—
Hurled into the Atlantic main,
A barren, sandy, dreary plain,
   A bit without a rock?

Perchance it floated from the north,
Issued from Zembla's regions forth,
   To find a kinder sky.
Perchance it may again set sail,
Propelled by Boreas' fav'ring gale,
   The torrid zone to try.

Undecked, unlovely as thou art,
A speck upon the world's great chart:
   Thou art our native spot;
And true to nature, still we love,
And by affection still we prove
   Thy faults can be forgot.

We know the grandest, loftiest pines
Have left to grace more genial climes;
   Yet lovely plants here thrive,—
The violet bland, and violet blue,
And violet of cerulian hue,
   Betokens spring's alive.

Thy fatal shores, and sandy shoals,
Round which the foaming white cap rolls, .
   All hopes of safety blast;
The pale affrighted sailor eyes
The dangers that around him rise,
   .,And turns away aghast!

Hence! all ye light, fantastic schemes,
Teeming with fancy's flimsy dreams,
   No more my thoughts beguile;
It is not in your power to tell
Who toss'd it up on ocean's swell,
From what empyrean realms it fell,
   Or whence my Native Isle.

PART THIRD.

Shortly after the History of Nantucket was published, occurred one of those financial revulsions, which, in addition to immediate disaster to many of our merchants, entailed upon the town and its people, a series of misfortunes, consequent upon this panic, and which continued their havoc through many years thereafter. There are many now living who recall with painful sensations the panic of 1837, the suspension of specie payment by the banks, and the long tedious train of evils which followed. In 1838, the High School was opened, with Cyrus Pierce as principal. The teachers' names who have succeeded him will be found elsewhere. In the same year a large fire destroyed a rope walk, candle works, houses, oil sheds, oil, &c., on the south beach.

In 1841, there were 29 ships fitted for sea, and a better feeling seemed to prevail in regard to whaling than for many years. The great difficulty existing of being obliged to load the ships either at Edgartown or back of the bar, had long been felt, both as regarded the inconvenience of it and the expense. About this time Peter F. Ewer, Esq., conceived the idea that the difficulty of the bar might be overcome by the use of what were in reality a species of dry docks, denominated camels, whereby vessels loaded and ready for sea could be taken over the bar, and could proceed directly to sea. After a season of annoyances in creating any interest in anything partaking of the nature of an innovation on old customs to such an extent as these did, the project was, by herculean efforts, carried through, the huge camels built and successfully launched, and in September, 1842, the first ship, the Constitution, Capt. Obed R. Bunker was carried over the bar, loaded, by these floating docks or camels.

The only description I can give of these camels, which is from memory, will necessarily be crude as regards technical terms, but the idea of the manner of operating them may be obtained in this way.

They resembled two immense blocks of wood, each half as large as a ship, with no top rigging, each block with a concave side the shape of a ship. They were 135 feet long, 19 feet deep, and 29 feet bottom, 20 feet wide on deck, drawing 2 feet 10 inches, connected at the bottom by 15 chains, capable of bearing 800 tons. Each camel was divided into two parts, the lower hold and between decks. The lower hold contained 12 apartments, six on each side. The between decks 10 apartments each. These huge arrangements were easily filled with water and sunk to any required depth. The ship then sailed between the two and (I can think of no other expression) was clasped in the embrace of the camels whose concave sides just fitted the shape of the ship. Of course these fifteen chains were under her bottom, and when she was securely in the embrace of the camels, they being drawn together and secured tightly, the pumping out of the 12,000 barrels of water each held, commenced. The race-way running through each camel from stem to stern, and through which they were filled with water, was closed, and by the use of a double acting force pump of 6-horse power, in a comparatively short time the water was pumped or forced out, and as the water left, the ship and camels rose together,

the whole drawing so little water that, as was the
case with the Constitution, a ship could be taken over the
bar fully loaded. These cumbrous arrangements were
but little used, however, and were in time abandoned entirely, and finally sold for comparatively nothing. The
idea was a good one, but the circumstances were not
favorable for a full and complete trial of the same principle but not so expensively illustrated. There was nothing of special note in the history of the town from 1842
until 1846. In 1842, there were 14 ships fitted for sea,
in 1843, 16; in 1844, 15; in 1845, 29; in 1846, 14.

In July of the latter year occurred one of those sweeping disasters which are enough of themselves to paralyze
the efforts of any community, but when coupled with the
discouraging aspect which the principal business of the
place, whaling, had already assumed, and the effects of
the panic of ten years preceding, with all that followed,
down almost to this date, surely was sufficient to make
the stoutest heart quail and tremble. The season had
been unusually dry, and a more unfortunate occasion
could not have been selected for such a conflagration.
Perhaps a few personal reminiscences of this most fearful
night will more fully describe the scene, than to simply
relate the facts and figures. It was not far from 11
o'clock at night, when the writer, standing on the street
in conversation with a gentleman, heard the cry of " fire,"
a dismal sound for that hot, dry, July night. Losing no
time, we repaired to the spot where the fire originated, on
Main street. We were among the first to arrive, and at
that time the flames had not burst through the roof of
the hat store where it originated, occupied by Wm. H.
Geary, the block of which his store was one, standing on
the site of the brick block belonging to T. W. Calder,

Esq., and now occupied by Mr. Barreau and others. A good smart stream of water at this juncture would have quenched the flames, which were in a few moments bursting from the roof. Once upon the dry roof, the adjoining buildings were an easy prey for the fiery fiend. One engine arrives. The flames mount higher! Washington Hall is on fire; and now the crackling sound of dry burning wood tells the people the awful story. Another engine arrives; one, two, three streams are sent into the flames, but on, on rushes the terrible blaze, relentlessly pursuing its course. And now the roar of the great conflagration is heard, and the hoarse cry of firewards, as they almost in vain give their orders. Then above the whole came the sound of falling buildings as gunpowder did its work; across the street swept the flames, and seized upon vast piles of this scattered wood, and with the rapidity of lightning the huge volume of flame enveloped at once whole buildings. It turns the corner, rushes north, rushes south in another direction, east in another! What earthly power can prevail against it? The writer witnessed what seems almost incredible, but which can be vouched for by many. A fire brand was hurled through the air by the current which had now been created, and starting from a burning building very near what is now the corner of Main and Federal streets, landed on the roof a building standing on North Water street, and while the occupants were standing in the doorway looking at the conflagration, their dwelling was all on fire, and in a short time was a heap of ruins. Standing on the steps of the Pacific Bank and looking east and north on Centre street, east side as far as the Ocean House, every building was at one time on fire save the old insurance office building on the lower square. It was a sight never to be forgotten;

depressing, depressing indeed. The fire department of course at this time had become utterly powerless, and as the sun rose the next morning the slowly burning turrets of the beautiful Trinity Church, then standing on the lot east of the Ocean House, and now occupied by dwelling of Mrs. E. W. Albee, seemed to announce from their eminence that the work of destruction was nearly ended, and then the flames slowly descending to the body of the church consumed that portion of it not yet fully destroyed. The loss by this fire was upward of one million dollars. The insurance obtained amounted to $300,000, and there were received from different sources beside some seventy thousand dollars.

Notwithstanding the various ways the people of the island were now called upon to suffer, and extend aid and sympathy, one loss seemed to appeal to all classes, and one common grief and regret was manifest. The Atheneum was an institution all took pride in, and a feeling as of common ownership seemed to pervade the community. Many were the sighs and heavy hearts, as we gazed on the ruins of that favorite institution, as in the general distress, what was there to hope for in the future, as far as the rebuilding of any such building was concerned? and yet, on the first of February, 1847, by the aid, and generous aid, too, of noble persons everywhere, together with funds obtained from insurance, the present building was opened for the delivery of books, and on the evening of March 29th, the first lecture was delivered in the building, by Rev. Mr. Osgood, who made appropriate remarks preceding the lecture in reference to the new building. He then delivered to an audience of 300 his lecture on "The New England Home." The institution started on its new career with somewhat of a depleted library, but at present it contains upward of 5000 volumes.

The evening of March 24th, 1847, was made rather a gala occasion, being the first evening the stores on Main street had been lighted since the fire. The reader can judge from this as to whether all the ambition and old time energy of Nantucket had departed. May 14, 1847, the Ocean House was opened to the public by Mr. and Mrs. Robert F. Parker. August, 1847, the subject of the Cape Cod railroad was discussed freely. In 1848, quite a movement was made in reference to a railroad to Siasconset. The sum appropriated for schools that year was $11,188-.59. March 14th, same year, the Atlantic House was opened at 'Sconset, by H. S. Crocker. September 29th, same year, the straw business was suggested for the town ; in fact it was apparent that new branches of business must be introduced, as the whaling interest was anything but encouraging, and ships were being sold as they arrived from sea. This feeling of anxiety was apparent with all classes, the capitalist whose means were invested in the business, which now was dying beyond the hope of resuscitation, and the mechanic who had for years relied for occupation on the same. Previous to this period there had been seasons of depression in the whaling business, but there were causes operating in those seasons which there was a possibility of removing. This was not the case now, as in addition to substitutes coming into the market, rapidly taking the place of oil, many other obstacles had arisen for a thoroughly successful whaling voyage. Many were the projects suggested for new branches of business, and with every issue of the papers appeared editorials, and communications from private sources suggesting cotton mills, straw works and many others. A branch of the straw works at Foxboro was finally established, and for some time furnished employment for many females of the town, at remunerative prices. With the introduction of the sewing machine came the competitor which robbed the island of this business, and the sewing of the braid, which here had been performed by hand, was concentrated in the main works at Foxboro, and accomplished by sewing machines.

In 1849, the California fever, so called, having spread to our shores, there was a still greater feeling of interest among the people, and the fitting of ships was of secondary importance, save with a few who had favorite vessels lying at the wharves, and the owners of these found it no easy matter to find suitable officers and men for the voyage. There were only seven ships fitted that year, three of the number only making successful voyages. Nine vessels sailed that year for San Francisco from this port; three fitted from Boston and two from New York, also owned or officered by Nantucket men. The Aurora was the first ship which sailed for that port, clearing January 9th, under command of Capt. Seth M. Swain. The ship was owned by C. G. & H. Coffin and others, and was loaded with building frames, lumber, naval stores, candles, &c. The crew were to receive one dollar per month and rations, with liberty to leave the ship on arriving at San Francisco. As this was the pioneer ship in this venture, the names of the officers, crew and passengers are appended: Captain, Seth M. Swain; Mate, Alexander Paddack; 2d Mate, Benjamin Winslow; Seamen, James A. Law, Roland Folger, Jr., Thos. F. Swain, Geo. H. Depress, Augustus Ellis, Chas. F. Alley, Thos. Allen, Geo. Randall, Thos. M. Folger; Stewards, Wm. H. Harper, and Arthur Cooper, Jr.; Passengers, Dr. J. B. King, Benjamin F. Folger, James H. Gibbs, James M. Bunker, 2d, Thos. F. Mitchell, Chas. Wood, Albert Macy, Wm. C. Pease, Wm. Summerhays, John H. Russell, Edwin Hiller. The ship arrived at San Francisco July 1st.

The ships previously mentioned as having also sailed from this port for California, sailed as follows: Henry Astor, Capt. Geo. F. Joy, March 12; Montana, Capt. Edw. C. Austin, May 31; Edward, Capt. Shubael Clark, June 5; Brig Joseph Butler, Capt. Francis F. Gardner, July 1st: Sarah Parker, Capt. James Codd, July 7th; Fanny, Capt. Uriah Russell, Aug. 22d; Martha, Capt. Eben M. Hinckley, Oct. 16th; Citizen, Capt. Oliver C. Coffin, Dec. 17th. The George and Martha, Capt. Richard Gardner; Japan, Capt. Henry Bigelow, and Scotland, Capt. Barzillai T. Folger, sailed from Boston. The Manchester, Capt. Job Coleman and schooner Two Brothers, Capt. Edwin Baldwin, sailed from New York.

In 1850, the first excitement of the California fever having somewhat subsided, whaling was again of some little interest, with, however, the same difficulties in regard to officers and men. During the year there were fourteen ships fitted for whaling voyages and three for California. The price of every article entering into the outfit of a whale ship was advancing, on account of the promising market opening in California, but with the advance of these articles came an advance of sperm oil, giving hope that the returns from ships fitted this year, would make a profitable business. And so it proved, as for instance the oil of ship Mohawk, which sailed May 29, 1850, and arrived April 20, 1854, sold for $1.50 per gallon. The population of the town at this time was 7779, a decrease of about 1000 since last census in 1840. In 1851, still encouraged by the continued high price of oil, the business was still pursued with a semblance of old time activity; but the catches of the vessels were now becoming less and less, which was a discouraging feature in the business. This year 18 vessels were fitted, a few as sperm whalers and others for the North Pacific, which ground now seemed to be yielding rich returns for ventures in this direction by vessels fitted from Sag Harbor, New London and New Bedford. It was difficult however for the people of the island to relinquish their old hunting ground, and as it proved, too many held to their faith in that, to the neglect, or ignoring entirely of other fields, which for a time at least gave great profits to those of other places who had more faith in the locality spoken of. From this time down to the year 1869 the business of the whale fishery went steadily down, although in 1852, '53, '54 and '55 some of the best ships owned were fitted, with, however, on the whole, rather unremunerative returns. During these years there would be spasmodic movements in the business, occasioned either by the price of oil, or some solitary instance of a great catch. Even as late as 1856, the new ship Islander was fitted and sailed Aug. 19th, of that year, returning June 9th, with 800 barrels sperm oil, which, however (and it is mentioned to show the uncertainty and many vicissitudes of the business), was compensated for by the voyage made in the same ship, which sailed in 1862, June 13, under command of Capt. Wm. Cash, and arrived July 13, 1865, with 2400 barrels of sperm and 560 of whale oil. In 1863, no ship was fitted, and from that period down to the period of which I have spoken, the attempts at whaling were mostly with small vessels. The business finally became extinct with the sale at Panama of the ship Oak, which sailed for the Pacific Ocean, November 16, 1869. The facts in relation to ships and business herein mentioned I have culled from various sources—some from files of Nantucket *Inquirer* and *Inquirer and Mirror*, some from Hussey & Robinson's "Catalogue of Nantucket Whalers," and from my own memory.

At a town meeting February 13th, 1852, it was voted to petition the legislature to pass a special act, to enable the town to subscribe for $50,000 worth of stock in the extension of the Cape Cod railroad to Hyannis. Earnest speeches were made on this occasion, and urgent appeals made for this action, as it seemed to promise a more ready communication with the main-land. The final result of the matter was, the town did take stock in the road, and communication was opened between the island and the main-land via Hyannis. The steamer Massachusetts, Capt. Brown, commenced her trips on that route October 9, 1854. This year gas was introduced, and the use of it quite generally adopted.

September 6, 1855, the steamer Island Home, arrived here, having been built for Nantucket waters. She was built in New York under the supervision of Edward Field, Esq., one of the board of directors of the company. Mr. Field was a practical mechanic, and was a competent judge of every inch of material which entered into her construction, and it may be safely stated that not a bolt, spike or stick of timber was used which was in the least grain doubtful. The company, and the travelling public since her construction, have cause for thankfulness that the services of a gentleman of Mr. Field's judgment and capacity could be secured and retained from the moment her keel was laid till the final blow was struck. She is to-day, although twenty-five years old, regarded by competent judges to be the best sea boat, and in every way

the most reliable of any one of her size running on a
similar route. During the many years she has been running no accident of a serious nature has occurred, or that
could have been avoided by careful management, which
reflects great credit on those who have been in command,
and the company under whose auspices she has been run.

In 1857, occurred another panic, which again swept
through the land with its disastrous effects, not however
with the severe blows to the island as that of 1837, as the
business of the town had become curtailed to such an
extent that comparatively few felt it. Still it was not
without its effect on some, and did its work in depleting
the town of some of its most active citizens. From that
period until the year 1860, when the census was taken, a
continued exodus of the inhabitants went on, and the
result of the enumerators' work of that year showed
6094, a falling off of 2685 since 1850. In the year 1857,
the work of establishing communication between the
island and the main-land by sub-marine cable, was commenced by Mr. S. C. Bishop, gutta percha and cable
manufacturer, of New York. The first cable was laid
from Great Point to Monomoy in 1855, and did not prove
successful; subsequently was taken up, and laid from
Maddaket to Tuckernuck, and across to Martha's Vineyard. In October, 1857, for a few days dispatches were
received from abroad, but they were considered of doubtful authenticity. In February, 1860, this dispatch was
received: "Forney was elected Clerk of the House, and
Hoffman Sergeant-at-Arms." In March, May and June
dispatches were received, most of which were considered
doubtful. In January, 1861, news was telegraphed from
Boston to Wood's Hole, taken from thence to Holmes'
Hole, and from thence to Edgartown on horseback, and

cabled to Nantucket. For some time this was successfully carried on, even into the time of the breaking out of the rebellion, but finally, after repeated breaks in the cable, the line was abandoned, and since 1861, no attempt has been made to replace it.

A period of inactivity in business from 1857 to 1861, followed, creating no events of special importance, save those mentioned. The population was rapidly decreasing, buildings were being taken down and removed to other places, and a feeling that the island was to become simply a fishing village, pervaded a large portion of the community. Some, however, clung resolutely to the belief that Nantucket would yet assert herself, and made every effort to keep alive that feeling, exhibiting it not only by speech but by action, continuing to fit their ships as we have stated, in many cases with no prospect of remuneration. In addition to this continued attempt to keep whaling alive, some branches of business were started, as for instance, the manufacturing of shoes, established in 1859, and continuing with varied fortune until 1862, when the building was burned and the business discontinued.

In the spring of 1861, the war of the rebellion broke out, and with the firing at Fort Sumpter, commenced the firing of every manly heart of Nantucket, and before any order came from headquarters, the cry of "To Arms!" was raised throughout the island.

May 1st, of this year, a mass meeting was called, and a committee appointed to devise means for affording aid to the soldiers in the field and plans suggested for fortifying the island from depredations at the hands of the ruthless invaders. Flag raising was now the order of the day, and many were raised with patriotic speeches as an accompaniment.

May 21st, a home guard was organized.   July 12th, a reception and entertainment were given to the Marine Coast Guard.   About this date a company of volunteers was organized under the command of Wm. Summerhays, in obedience to the call for 75,000 men.   Geo. N. Macy, in July, received his appointment as 1st Lieutenant of Co. I, 20th Regiment, under Col. Lee.   July 17th, Lieut. Macy left with 21 men for his regiment.   A war meeting was held in July, 1862, and one hundred dollars bounty offered for each volunteer under the call of the President for three hundred thousand men for three years, these volunteers to be credited to the quota of the town. Another meeting was held September first, when it was voted to pay a bounty of one hundred and fifty dollars to each volunteer, for nine months' service, when mustered in, and credited to the quota of the town.   On the 3d of the same month, 27 enlisted men left for camp.

In December, at a special town meeting, it was voted to authorize the Selectmen, to advance money to volunteers enlisting to the credit of Nantucket, not to exceed three hundred dollars to any one person, provided the money so advanced can be deducted from the town bounty, which will be due to the soldier, when he shall have been properly mustered into the United States Military service, and credited as part of the quota of the town.

Nantucket filled its quota, on every call of the President, and at the end of the war, had a surplus of fifty-six, over and above all demands.   Between four and five hundred men, good and true, responded to the call of their country, and reflected credit on the town, in their various capacities.

Those who so nobly distinguished themselves in that

struggle, and will carry the evidence of their courage and bravery to their dying day, are so well known, and their deeds of valor have been so often recounted, that perhaps it would be superfluous for me to attempt any further eulogy. General Macy, by his heroism, and cool judgment in the field, secured promotions which were well deserved, and which gave him such prominence, and reputation, through the country, as any man might justly be proud of. But, while joining in the general admiration for the military ability he displayed, and feeling a portion of the pride in his career his towns-people all entertained, we yet feel like paying full homage to the other commissioned officers, as well as the humblest soldier, who endured the dangers and hardships of war that the nation might live. The feeling of gratitude we could not resist, in the trying days and years of the rebellion, that others took our places on the field of battle, should never be suffered to fade away, and be forgotten. As Memorial Day approaches, not only the few companions left, of those who laid down their lives in the great contest for the preservation of the Union, should do honor to the heroic dead, but, that general feeling of respect and gratitude, which, as I have remarked, should not be suffered to gradually die out, as the years roll away, should inspire us all to participate in the beautiful custom of strewing flowers at the graves of the departed, and in recalling their noble, unselfish deeds. While our country is of value to us, and the freedom gained for all, a subject we delight to boast of, let us also delight to do honor to the memory of those who fought to secure it. The roll of honor numbers 67 ; 12 died in the navy, and 55 in the army.

The whole amount of money raised and expended by

Nantucket for State aid to soldiers' families during the years of the war, and which was repaid by the Commonwealth, was as follows: In 1861, $591.58; 1862, $5,-338.45; 1863, $9,362.17; 1864, $8,700.00; 1865, $3,-500.00. Total amount, $27,492.20. The ladies of the town began early in the war to furnish money and various articles for the soldiers. In 1861, they held a soldiers' fair, from which they realized $2,038.12, of which, $1,000 was given to the Sanitary Commission, and the balance among the soldiers and their families. The Ladies' Soldiers' Relief Society raised during the war $2,579.46; all of which was for the soldiers and their families.

During the war there was a little impetus given to the local business of the town by the circulation of money, in hands heretofore (in many cases) empty, but it was painfully apparent that something must be done, and that right early, for the future support of even the small population which the census of 1865 revealed, which now had decreased to 4830.

In January, 1855, a citizen's meeting was called, to make vigorous efforts to bring Nantucket to the notice of those who visit watering places during the summer. Mark Salom, of Boston, who had purchased quite a number of pieces of property in real estate on the island, made vigorous speeches, and he, together with some of our spirited citizens, were empowered to use every effort in their power to bring about the result of placing the island in a proper light before the country, as a desirable place for a summer resort. It may be well to mention that at this time the summer vacation mania was rapidly spreading among all classes, and some places in our immediate vicinity were reaping a harvest from this increase of travel.

On January 22d, 1865, the Nantucket *Inquirer* and *Mirror* became consolidated and the name changed to *Inquirer and Mirror*, and has continued to be published under that title since. In August of the same year the first meeting of the High School Alumni Association took place, the oration being delivered by Rev. F. C. Ewer. This brought together in the most happy manner many who had been separated for many years, and the varied experiences in life were related, and comparisons made of the rough and smooth periods along life's pathway, by many a former smart or " stupid " pupil. The entertainment given under the tent, and the ball, were two most delightful occasions. At the former, Rev. F. C. Ewer was the toast master, and in the happiest manner called out the wit and humor of the company. It was a sparkling assemblage, and the (now) veteran teacher, Augustus Morse, who was present, must have been gratified that so many of his " stupid fellows " had acquitted themselves so well thus far in life, of the charge, and had disproved his oft repeated assertion to that effect. The ball was a great success, and on that occasion the teacher turned his attention from the west windows, overlooking the play-yard on Academy Hill, and beheld, not the boys and girls of the past, but fathers and mothers, some adorned with silver threads upon the head (even as he was), dancing together, in joyous remembrance of the past, and utter forgetfulness of the cares and anxieties of the present.

The second reunion took place August 25, 1866, at which time Wm. B. Drake, of Meadville, Pa., delivered the oration. The third reunion occurred August 21, 1869, when Charles H. Glover, Esq., of New York, delivered the oration. There has been no gathering of this nature since.

In 1865 and '66, the attempt was made to establish the fishing business, and several vessels were purchased and fitted for the purpose, but meeting with little success, in a few years it was abandoned.

In 1870, Nantucket had not a ship, bark, brig, or vessel of any kind, suggestive of the vast amount of business done in the past. In place of the busy click of the caulker's hammer, as it sent its echo from one wharf to another, naught could be heard but the lick of the wave as it washed, and washed again, the ruins of piers which once groaned beneath the weight of millions of wealth.

We have thus, in a condensed manner, followed the steady decline in business of the once enterprising and prosperous Island of Nantucket.

At this point of her history the bottom line had been reached. What was there in store for a place crowded and crushed by oft repeated misfortunes, struggling and hoping against hope for years, and finally, yielding to the inevitable? This was the question asked repeatedly and every day, and every year was being answered. The efforts which had been put forth in times past to bring the island to the notice of the entire country was beginning to be felt, and these efforts, seconded and aided by the Old Colony railroad, which had an interest in making Nantucket a desirable point, gave the island a prominent position on the list of watering places. In July, of 1872, the Hyannis route was abandoned, and the boats connected with the trains at Wood's Holl instead. This proved more popular with the travelling public, and travel in this direction increased rapidly.

During the years of continued business depression, and when it became an established fact that the great business of the place was gone, many turned their attention to the land, and the result of that is some fine, profitable farms, and many practical farmers. Without questioning the wisdom of the early settlers of the island, or those of half a century later, or even a century, we are of the opinion that if the acres of idle, useless land, which gave a miserable support to large numbers of sheep, could have been brought under cultivation, it would have resulted in far greater pecuniary advantages, and developed the full resources of the land, as it would the energy of the people, and in place of the barren waste bequeathed to us, hundreds of well-tilled farms would to-day adorn the outlying country. In our youthful days, even, when the happy period of shearing time would come, we remember of thinking what a range of territory it took to accommodate the eight or nine thousand sheep, at that time kept on the island, and the idea occurred then and there that a better use could be found for it. The objection is raised that the land was always poor, very poor, and is poor, very poor, now. It seems it was considered good enough for sheep by the thousands to live on, and land that will produce something, can in these days of fertilizers, adapted in their chemical properties to all kinds and nature of soil, be made to produce a good deal more. We grant it is hard work; everything is hard work which amounts to anything; but the farming already done on the island proves that productive farms can be created, and with the increasing interest in the subject by practical men, it is by no means impossible that in ten years there will be on the island a dozen good paying farms, where now there is one. This, then, is one business as a nucleus, and the nucleus already grown to a very commanding size.

In addition to this, thousands of visitors are landed on our shores every year, and besides the profit accruing from their visits, in the actual amount of money they expend, the relations being established, and year by year extended between these yearly visitors and the resident population, is doing much to awaken a most genuine feeling of attachment for this most delightful retreat. It is to the credit of the people of the Island, that, since efforts have been made to bring Nantucket more fully to the notice of the. outer world, the same hospitality, for which this people were always credited, continues unabated, and it is rarely the case, that a visitor leaves with aught save the most pleasant impressions of this summer resort.

The reputation Nantucket has obtained for quaintness, arises more from the appearance of certain localities in the town, than from any habits or customs of the people. Whatever may have been the case, fifty years since, the customs of the place at present are not unlike those of any town in the Commonwealth; in fact, it may be said to be remarkably free from any distinguishing feature in this way. It may be truthfully stated, that any peculiarities existing, are very limited in extent, and confined to very few persons, and anything like provincialism is less apparent here than in many places of greater renown.

There is a quality, rather than peculiarity, pertaining both to the island and the people, which attracts the better class of summer tourists to its shores; and by better class we mean not those who are usually styled thus, by reason of wealth, but by every consideration of means, intelligence and culture. It is here that the body and mind can be recuperated in the most natural and effective manner, as there are less of the modern appliances for ordinary watering places than elsewhere, while there are sufficient natural advantages, combined with the cultured character of the people, to attract and hold those to whom the characteristics of many summer resorts are tedious and common place, and lacking this element of a resident population of recognized intelligence and refinement. This latter consideration enters largely into the enjoyment of a few weeks' sojoun at Nantucket, and visitors to the island, whom one meets in his travels, will as frequently speak of the people they met, as the day at 'Sconset, the trip to Wauwinet, or the great catch of blue-fish.

This then is, as I believe, a true sketch of Nantucket in the light of a watering place. But is this all that remains for this island to hope for? its few farms, its limited fishing resources, its summer visitors? These comparatively small branches of business appeared in answer to this question ten years ago, but how shall the question be answered in 1880? There are events in a town's history, as with a nation's, unlooked for, not always unaccountable, but often puzzling to comprehend the results to follow.

In a day, comparatively, there have arisen schemes for the people of Nantucket to consider, which in their magnitude, might temporarily, at least, cause a people of more scheming natures than those of this island, to look aghast, and for a time to doubt their feasibility, and even create a doubt as to the sincerity of the projectors of the enterprises, so huge do these schemes seem in their proportions, and so little in keeping with the absence of activity in business for the past ten or fifteen years. What wonder then, that in view of the utter failure of the principal business of the place, and a similar fate attending other enterprises which had been conceived and established by men of energy and brains, that the young man of comparatively few years, but of large and mature ideas, should have been ridiculed and derided, to a degree sufficient, with some natures, to have crushed not only the ideas but the individual man himself, when he broached the subject of introducing pure water into the town. The idea was so preposterous, yea, foolish to many, that it seemed utterly out of all reason to think of its ever being accomplished, or even undertaken. "What do we want more water for?" "I've got a good well, that's all I want." "Who'll take it when it's brought in?" "It never'll pay in the world." "Who'll drink that pond water?" These and a thousand more daily ejaculations were about all the prime mover in this enterprise had for a capital to enter into the work. His, fortunately, was not a nature to be discouraged by these obstacles, but on the contrary they were the very incentives to renewed activity in the work. A few sympathizers in the movement were finally called together, and the matter laid before them in the most practical manner. It was evident that a careful estimate had been made of the cost, and the difficulties to be overcome. Several gentlemen becoming interested, pledged their names for an amount sufficient to inspire a belief that this was a nucleus around which more capital would gather, if sufficient energy and perseverence were put into the work. The burden of the project was on young shoulders, and with this comparatively small encouragement the work was commenced, and without the exact figures, dates, and names before us (which we endeavored to obtain, but failed to do so in time for this history), we simply record the actual results of this well directed energy.

While the labor of laying the pipes was progressing, requiring constant attention on the part of the gentleman who had assumed this undertaking, the more important work of creating an interest in the work in others, looking to the formation of the very company now existing, was also in progress, quietly, but as the sequel proves, surely. Thus the mechanical portion of the work was thoroughly performed, while the source from which was to issue the means not only to carry on the work to a successful completion, but to satisfy promptly, and with no delay, all demands for labor already performed, was also secured. Here was a work demanding a versatile brain, which few men possess. A large portion of the ground work in the success of the enterprise was a perfect confidence in its ultimate value, and this conviction, combined with the versatility manifested in the projector, swept away all obstacles, and at the date of this writing the fruits of indefatigable labor are manifest.

If ever a person erected his own monument, while living, a monument more enduring, even, than the granite shaft, it is the young man, of scarcely 27 years of age, Moses Joy, Jr., whose noble work carves the inscription indelibly on the smooth surface of Wannacomet Pond, "He had faith in me, and dared to show it."

The pond from which the water is introduced, is situated at the west of the island, between two and three miles from town, and formerly bore the homely title of the "Washing Pond," but, at present, the more euphonious one of Wannacomet. So quietly and unostentatiously did the work at first proceed, that many were not aware of any actual labor being performed, in this direction, until, suddenly, a strange object loomed up on the western landscape. This was the beginning of the actual, not theoretical, water-works. The reservoir was built, and reared its head above the lonely plains, as much as to say, " In the face of all obstacles, and opposition, I am here, and you shall hear from me." From that time until the present, the work has been going steadily on, until all the prominent streets are piped, and nearly one hundred families are now in the enjoyment of as pure water as ever flowed. There are many orders now on the books, which, with those who will probably apply for it, during the season, will swell the number to two hundred water takers. The doubters are quiet, save when they apply for the water, and the Nantucket Water-works, are pronounced a success.

While this is in progress, "history repeats itself," and the subject of the improvement of the harbor, which our fathers' fathers agitated in their day, again rises to the surface, and an interest manifested which would have done credit to the business men of 1800. To Allen Coffin, Esq., who has been a prominent leader in this movement, I am indebted for the following facts, in relation to the improvement of Nantucket harbor.

It is authentically stated, that, since the occupation of the island by whites, a limited depth of water has existed at the harbor entrance, of about six feet, at mean low water, to the great hindrance of navigation. Various schemes for remedying this obstruction have been projected at different epochs, the earliest, in 1803, being substantially the plan now adopted by the Government engineers, though then rejected by the same authority, as impracticable.

Congress was petitioned, in 1878, for an appropriation

of money, to improve Nantucket Harbor, by what was know as the Haulover project, which proposed the cutting of a channel so as to connect the waters of the upper harbor, with the ocean, through the Haulover beach. This petition was started by Mr. John W. Rand, and secured the signatures of three hundred persons, including the underwriters of New York, and Boston. A survey was thereupon ordered by Congress, and, in October, 1879, Gen. G. K. Warren, of the Engineer Corps, made a survey of the harbor, and its obstructions. Gen. Warren's report, dated Nov. 25, 1879, did not favor the Haulover project as the best plan for improving the harbor, but proposed the construction of jetties at the present harbor entrance, one to be first constructed upon the west side, running from Brant Point, almost due north and south, to deep water, beyond the bar, about where the bell-buoy in now stationed ; the other, if necessity should call for it, to be built from Coatue, to deep water, beyond the bar.

A large meeting of citizens of Nantucket, was held at the Atheneum, on Saturday evening, Jan. 10, 1880, at which Allen Coffin, Esq., presided. The recommendations of Gen. Warren were almost unanimously approved, and a committee, consisting of Messrs. Allen Coffin, George K. Long and Benjamin F. Brown, was chosen to memorialize Congress, for an appropriation of money, for the improvement of Nantucket Harbor, in accordance with the plan proposed by the Government engineer. The committee elicited and embodied in the memorial the following facts : That the number of vessels which annually passed within sight of the Cross Rip light-ship, was upward of 30,000 ; that since the year 1800, 530 vessels had been wrecked around Nantucket Island, the estimated

value of which, including cargoes, was upward of $5,000,-
000; that seventy-three per cent of these disasters occurred on the north side of the island; that sixty per cent
of the number were totally lost, and with them more than
200 lives had been sacrificed.

The memorial was extensively signed by Nantucket
citizens, and by the leading ship-owners and masters of
Boston, New York and Philadelphia, as also by the
underwriters of the same cities. To the efforts of Capt.
Benj. F. Brown and George H. Folger, Esq., in Boston;
Charles B. Swain, Esq., and Capt. George C. Allen, in
New York, and Capt. David Thain, in Philadelphia, the
success in obtaining signatures to the memorial is largely
due. Allen Coffin, Esq., was chosen to proceed to Washington and present the memorial to Congress, and to
urge the granting of the request of the memorialists. The
work of the committee was so well and thoroughly accomplished, and the facts and arguments so concisely stated,
that the jetty now seems to have been an assured fact
from the start. The River and Harbor Bill, which passed
the last session of Congress and was approved by President Hayes, in June, 1880, contained an appropriation of
$50,000 for the improvement of Nantucket harbor, which
is nearly one-half of the estimated cost of its entire construction, and the funds will be available July 1st, 1880.

The jetty is to be rip-rap stone, triangular in section,
with side slopes of 45 degrees—the top to be five feet
above mean low water for a distance of 4,000 feet from
the shore. The outer 2,500 feet being more exposed
to the action of the waves will be four feet wide on top
with the same side slopes and same height. The outer end
or head being in deep water, will have increased dimen-

sions to meet the greater shock of the waves, and the effect of ice in winter.

On the 19th of the 3d month, 1803, Obed Macy wrote in his journal a report of a town meeting held that day, for the purpose of hearing the report of a committee consisting of Messrs. Isaac Coffin and Gideon Gardner, sent by the town to Washington to urge Congress to appropriate money for the improvement of Nantucket harbor. Congress ordered a survey, and the committee's report was satisfactory. To show how near the present plan is to the one then proposed by Nantucket people, the following quotation is made from the journal: "The town appears highly flattered with a prospect of obtaining sufficient aid from Congress at next session to complete the business of not only digging a channel, but of building off piers of stone from Brant Point and from Coatue to the outer bar." In his report of the town meeting held on the 15th of the 1st month, 1803, when the committee was chosen to visit Washington upon this mission, he writes: "It will be a matter of very great advantage to the place if it is ever effected; but the improbability (in my opinion) is so strong, that I believe none of the present generation will have the pleasure of seeing it completed."

The government survey proved adverse to the plan; yet it appears that "the stone which the builders rejected is to become the chief of the corner." Though the prophetic part of Obed Macy's writing in 1803, has been amply verified, the wisdom and judgment of the citizens who early projected the plan of piers, is about to be confirmed; not, however, until the vast maritime interests of the island have dwindled into nothing, and her proud pre-eminence, which had been fairly won as the home of the whale fishery, have become obscured by the dazzling brilliancy of the modern electric light. Not a whaler is owned at the island; but, as a harbor of refuge to passing commerce, Nantucket may again shed lustre upon the world, and again become an important sea-port in the ship-news columns of marine newspapers.

It would seem that, to a people who had somewhat retired from the field of gigantic operations, a remarkable influx of great problems was being presented, as in addition to the water-works, and improvements in the harbor, comes the cry of a railroad. The rumor of this enterprise was greeted with the usual attacks, and the customary number of doubters. This, however, has little to do with the facts in the case, which are simply these: The road bed has been laid for a long distance on the proposed route, starting from the south beach, and turning westward, crosses Orange street, thence past the Fair Grounds and the Hooper farm, and south, by way of Weeweeder, to Surf Side. The road will thence extend easterly, along the southern coast of the island, to Siasconset. The exact route on returning is, at the time of this writing, not ascertained. John W. Cartright, Esq., is President, and Philip H. Folger, Superintendent, who are pushing the road rapidly to completion. The road is being built independent of Nantucket capital, and is an experiment the company feel confident will be a successful one.

Having touched the bottom line, a line from which there was no possibility of a still further receding of the wave of former prosperity, Nantucket seems about to plant upon this low water mark, that its future prosperity may have a distinct starting point, the appliances of business, which may yet place it in the position her patience, her unfaltering courage, and energy, entitle her. In this connection we may be allowed to recapitulate a little in regard to the population, which, while showing the depleted condition of the town in inhabitants, will show the starting point, as is believed, for a prosperous condition in the future, as it will also correct an error in numbers, which, in some way, crept into one of the first pages of this supplementary history. The figures we here subjoin are from State statistics, and, although differing from other statements, are, or should be correct. The population in 1840, was 9712; 1850, 8779; 1860, 6094; 1865, 4830; 1870, 4123; 1875, 3201. In the year last mentioned, or thereabouts, we must find the period of " dead low water " for the island, as the census of this year (1880), shows an increase of population of several hundred.

The increased facilities for travel offered by the Old Colony Railroad, culminating in two boats a day to the island, and a re-opening of the old route to New Bedford, in connection with the Wood's Holl route, have doubtless brought this island to the notice of thousands. Whether this increase of population is due to to this new acquaintance, or not, we cannot tell. It is but reasonable to suppose that, with thousands of strangers visiting the island every year, some of them, clear headed business men, it may be, will see in the low rents, comparatively cheap labor, and healthy climate, combined with the facilities about to be offered in pure water, navigation improvements, &c., an opportunity for manufacturing not to be neglected.

In concluding this enumeration of events of importance which have occurred since 1835, I am reminded of many incidents which though not coming under the head of history, yet would add to the humor, and perhaps interest of the volume. I am obliged, however, to omit them for other reasons than that mentioned. Then too, in connection with the observations herein contained in relation to farming, I fully intended commenting to some extent on the present, and what promises to be the future growth of pine trees, which originally were started by Josiah Sturgis in 1847. I reluctantly omitted this, together with other points in the same category, farming, as being topics of more personal than of general interest to many non-residents. I cannot leave these pages, however, without expressing the hope that whatever may be the nature of the business to be introduced in the future to the island, the farming interests may be still considered of great importance. If the young men of Nantucket, with the assistance of the many modern appliances for farming, would put that energy and determination into this business which formerly were required in the whaling business, in five years the name might appropriately be applied to this island—The Garden of the Sea.

We subjoin the names of the Principals of the High School from 1838 to 1880: Cyrus Peirce, Augustus Morse, Alden B. Whipple, B. F. Morrison, Henry Dame, Galen Allen, Lorin L. Dame, George R. Chase, Charles A. Baker, C. M. Barrows, A. B. Whipple, Wm. H. Spinney, G. P. Hopkins. The names are placed in the order of their teaching, Mr. Whipple being twice called to the position.

THE END.